A Complete Guide to
PivotTables

. . . .

A Visual Approach

A Complete Guide to
PivotTables

A Visual Approach

Paul Cornell

Apress®

A Complete Guide to PivotTables: A Visual Approach
Copyright © 2005 by Paul Cornell

ISBN-13 (pbk): 978-1-59059-432-2
ISBN-13 (electronic): 978-1-4302-0307-0

Printed and bound in the United States of America (POD)

Lead Editor: Dominic Shakeshaft
Technical Reviewer: Andy Pope
Editorial Board: Steve Anglin, Dan Appleman, Ewan Buckingham, Gary Cornell, Tony Davis, Jason Gilmore, Jonathan Hassell, Chris Mills, Dominic Shakeshaft, Jim Sumser
Project Manager: Tracy Brown Collins
Copy Edit Manager: Nicole LeClerc
Copy Editor: Julie McNamee
Production Manager: Kari Brooks-Copony
Production Editor: Kelly Winquist
Compositor: Diana Van Winkle
Proofreader: Linda Seifert
Indexer: Kevin Broccoli
Cover Designer: Kurt Krames
Manufacturing Manager: Tom Debolski

Distributed to the book trade in the United States by Springer-Verlag New York, Inc., 233 Spring Street, 6th Floor, New York, NY 10013, and outside the United States by Springer-Verlag GmbH & Co. KG, Tiergartenstr. 17, 69112 Heidelberg, Germany.

In the United States: phone 1-800-SPRINGER, fax 201-348-4505, e-mail orders@springer-ny.com, or visit http://www.springer-ny.com. Outside the United States: fax +49 6221 345229, e-mail orders@springer.de, or visit http://www.springer.de.

For information on translations e-mail info@apress.com, or visit http://www.apress.com.

The source code for this book is available to readers at http://www.apress.com in the Source Code section.

Contents at a Glance

Contents

Appendix PivotTable Differences Between Excel 2000, 2002, and 2003

About the Author

Paul Cornell has, for the past five years, created documentation for Microsoft Office System business solution developers. Paul has contributed to developer documentation for Microsoft Office VBA Language References, Microsoft Office Primary Interop Assemblies, Microsoft Office Web Services Toolkits, and other Office development technologies. Paul was a past Web site editor and frequent Web columnist for the Office Developer Center on the Microsoft Developer Network (MSDN). He was also one of the founding columnists for Microsoft Office Online. Paul is currently the Documentation Manager for Microsoft Visual Studio Tools for the Microsoft Office System, as well as a contributor to blogs covering Visual Studio Tools for Office. He occasionally helps customers at events such as VSLive! and Microsoft Tech-Ed. Paul lives in the mountains of Washington State with his wife and two daughters.

About the
Technical Reviewer

Andy Pope is a computer programmer based in the United Kingdom. In 2004, Microsoft recognized Andy as an Excel MVP. Andy maintains a Web site focusing on Excel charting at http://www.andypope.info.

Preface

I have been interested in writing a book on PivotTables for several years. Most folks don't know what PivotTables are. Those that do use PivotTables don't always use them to their full potential. When I tell people what Pivot-Tables are, and demonstrate PivotTables to their fullest, it is truly a rewarding experience.

If you're wondering what qualifies me to write a book on PivotTables, perhaps I can share a portion of my work experience with you. I started my career in Microsoft Office when I joined the Microsoft Office User Assistance team more than four years ago. Microsoft had recently shipped Office 2000 and we were setting our sights on creating Microsoft Office XP. My first job was to go through all of the Office 2000 Visual Basic Language Reference documentation, including the documentation for Microsoft Excel, and prepare it for the next version of Office. During that time I learned the ins and outs of the Excel programmatic object model, along with the other Office applications.

After Office XP shipped, I moved over to become the editor for the Office Developer Center on the Microsoft Developer Network Web site. Around that time, I began teaching developers how to extend their customized Excel solutions and other Office solutions with Visual Basic for Applications and later Microsoft Visual Basic .NET and Microsoft Visual C# .NET.

At the same time, I saw a big gap between Office end users (we sometimes referred to them in Office as *information workers*) and Office solution developers. To help information workers who wanted to go deeper in their understanding of Excel and the other Office applications without becoming professional programmers, I founded the Office Power User Corner column on the Microsoft Office Online Web site.

As others and I began publishing monthly installments for the Office Power User Corner, we were overwhelmed by the positive customer response. We discovered that tens of thousands of folks each month visited the Office Power User Corner, and dozens of folks e-mailed us daily with kind words of appreciation and encouragement to continue.

Of the various subjects we wrote about, what really stood out for me in our e-mail feedback was the general lack of readers' understanding of what PivotTables were and how they could be used. A little over a year-and-a-half ago, I met with Apress founder Gary Cornell to discuss the opportunity of writing a book that shares my PivotTable skills with you to help you become a more productive Excel user.

I hope you enjoy reading this book as much as I enjoyed writing it. I hope you will find this book to be a great training resource and an indispensable ongoing technical reference.

Warmest regards,

Paul Cornell

Acknowledgments

First and foremost, I want to thank my wife, Shelley, for being my greatest encourager, a sounding board, an ongoing support, and the voice of common sense over these past 15-plus years. She is my everything. Without her, there's no way this book could have ever been written.

I also want to thank my two daughters for giving up a lot of their time spent with Daddy.

I want to thank Apress founder Gary Cornell for the opportunity to write this book, as well as the staff at Apress who helped me get this book into your hands: Dominic Shakeshaft, Lead Editor; Tracy Brown Collins, Project Manager; Andy Pope, Technical Reviewer; Julie McNamee, Copy Editor; and Glenn Munlawin, Product Manager. Also thanks to Beckie Stones, Tina Nielsen, Kelly Winquist, and several others at Apress for their help. The folks at Apress have truly been a joy to work with.

I want to thank my parents, Paul and Darlean, for their ongoing love and support.

Finally, I want to thank God for helping me acquire the knowledge and skills I needed to be able to write this book.

Introduction: PivotTables Are Powerful!

This book is designed to help you understand what PivotTables are. You'll learn how to get the most out of PivotTables to make your work tasks easier, which will make you more valuable to your organization. It doesn't matter whether you're a corporate data analyst, an information worker for a large- or medium-sized company, a small business owner, a student researcher, or anyone else who works with numbers. PivotTables will help reduce the time you spend analyzing data to spot trends, patterns, and problems. PivotTables will also help you make data-based decisions faster and more confidently.

For instance, by now you've probably used Excel to

- Work with the Insert Function dialog box to specify functions to report the sum of a column of numbers, find the lowest value in a column, and compute the average of a row of numbers.

- Subtotal a series of facts and figures by geographical region, date, or a person's name.

- Create a graph or chart to provide a visual representation of facts and figures.

These tasks aren't terribly difficult, but they aren't trivial either. Also, moving from one of these tasks to another means you have to use a different set of data analysis skills.

With PivotTables, you'll be able to perform these tasks easier:

- PivotTables provide standard functions such as Sum, Min, and Max that can be quickly calculated across a wide range of summarized data with just a few mouse clicks.

- PivotTables calculate subtotals automatically, based on logical categorizations of facts and figures, with no additional effort on your part.

- You can create a chart based on a PivotTable with as little as one mouse click.

Let's face it; data is everywhere. You already know that as you skim through your morning paper, you are confronted with numerical data, trends, and patterns. As you page through weather forecasts, the business section, and even the sports reports, there is a mountain of numbers. Your checkbook register, your monthly credit statements, and your taxes all resound with numerical figure after figure. The working world thrives on making wise decisions based on data to serve customers, sell more goods and services, and maximize profits. PivotTables organize, categorize, and present data in a summarized manner to help you make sense of the vast quantities of data that come your way.

What You Will Learn

Before you get started, here's a brief outline of what you'll be learning in this book. To demonstrate how much better PivotTables are for analyzing data, we'll first review Excel's basic data analysis techniques. You'll then begin creating simple PivotTables. From there, you'll practice using more advanced PivotTable features. You'll put your new skills to use right away by using PivotTables in real-world scenarios. You'll move from PivotTables to PivotCharts, and then into more advanced data-analysis scenarios by using PivotTables and PivotCharts to analyze multidimensional data. Finally, you'll use Visual Basic for Applications (VBA) code to programmatically automate PivotTables and PivotCharts. This book's chapters are organized to follow this outline, starting with basic data-analysis techniques and then moving to more advanced data-analysis techniques.

In *Chapter 1, What Are PivotTables?*, you are introduced to PivotTables. You learn why PivotTables are so valuable after you first try analyzing data using less sophisticated and less integrated Excel data analysis techniques, including visual inspection of long data lists, the use of summary functions, and concluding with the use of crosstab tables. By the end of this chapter, you'll begin to see how PivotTables bring together all these other data-analysis techniques into one cohesive tool. A PivotTable is like a Swiss Army knife for robust data analysis!

In *Chapter 2, Creating PivotTables*, you learn how to quickly create simple PivotTables with the PivotTable and PivotChart Wizard, which you later extend using other tools and techniques. You discover how to work with data sources other than data in Excel workbooks. You learn how to create data in external data sources. You also discover how to format PivotTables for more professional presentation. You finish the chapter by creating a PivotTable on your own using the wizard.

In *Chapter 3, Working with PivotTable Components*, you begin pivoting data quickly using row, column, data, and page fields. *Pivoting* allows you to look at your data from different perspectives, which enables you to quickly spot trends and anomalies, and helps provide answers to questions about your data. You also begin using the PivotTable Field List to customize PivotTables. You round out the chapter by working with the PivotTable toolbar and PivotTable menu to further extend PivotTables.

In *Chapter 4, Using PivotTables in the Real World*, you see how three fictional companies could use PivotTables to help increase their employees' data-analysis productivity, which allows their employees to make better business decisions faster. You are introduced to three companies: Fabrikam Interiors, Tailspin Toys, and Contoso Publishing Ltd. Each of these companies use PivotTables in a slightly different scenario. You can use these real-world scenarios to give you ideas and leverage best practices as you begin to use PivotTables in your organization.

In *Chapter 5, Working with PivotCharts*, you learn why *PivotCharts* are a powerful companion to PivotTables. As its name suggests, PivotCharts allow you to present data in a more graphically and visually friendly way. This makes data even more meaningful and also allows for even better and quicker decisions based on data than with PivotTables alone.

In *Chapter 6, Analyzing Multidimensional Data with PivotTables*, you are introduced to the concept of multidimensional data. This type of data basically deals with exponentially huge amounts of data that are interrelated in many complex ways. You discover how PivotTables can chew through these huge warehouses of information, summarizing the data for you in a more approachable and understandable manner.

In *Chapter 7, Programming PivotTables*, you learn how to extend Pivot-Tables even further through Visual Basic for Applications (VBA) code. This allows you to build more sophisticated PivotTable solutions than using the PivotTable wizard, toolbar, and menu alone.

Because this book discusses PivotTables and PivotCharts from an Excel 2003 perspective, it's important for you to understand how to adapt the descriptions and exercises if you're using an earlier Excel version. Therefore, an appendix is also included, which lists the primary differences between Excel 2000, Excel 2002, and Excel 2003 for features described throughout this book.

Outcome

By the time you finish this book, you should be able to

- Understand PivotTables, what they're used for, and the best scenarios in which to use them.

- Be very comfortable using the PivotTable and PivotChart Wizard with Excel data and other types of data to create and customize your own PivotTables.

- Feel confident using row, column, page, and data fields; the PivotTable toolbar and menus; and the PivotTable Field List to quickly rearrange PivotTables and bring new perspectives to data.

- Leverage best practices and case studies in real-world scenarios to help you apply PivotTables to your current data and business problems.

- Be at ease using PivotCharts to add visual perspective and depth to data in PivotTables.

- Have a good understanding of multidimensional data.

- Use PivotTables to analyze enormous collections of complex interrelated data, including online analytical processing (OLAP) data.

- Begin to build customized PivotTable solutions using VBA code.

- Understand the key differences between PivotTable features in different Excel versions.

Using the Try It! Exercises

Throughout this book, beginning in Chapter 1, several sections begin with the phrase *Try It!*. These sections provide opportunities for you to use Pivot-Tables and PivotCharts to help you more easily understand the concepts throughout this book. To access the business data used in these Try It! sections, visit the Apress Web site Downloads section at `http://www.apress.com`. This book uses Microsoft Office Excel 2003 as the basis of the Try It! sections. For information on the features that work on earlier Excel versions, see the appendix at the end of this book. The appendix lists some of the differences between Excel 2000, Excel 2002, and Excel 2003 that apply to concepts and exercises shared in this book.

What You Should Already Know

Before you begin using this book, you should have a good general understanding of Excel already. You should know about Excel terms such as *workbooks, worksheets, cells, formulas,* and the like. If you haven't guessed by now, this book only covers how to use PivotTables, not how to use the rest of Excel. You should already know how to use Excel's core user interface, including navigating the Excel menu bars, using and customizing Excel toolbars, and other Excel user interface components such as wizards. More specifically, you should know how to

- Add and delete worksheets in Excel workbooks.

- Import and export data to and from Excel.

- Format data such as currency and dates in worksheet rows and columns.

- Work with worksheet formulas.

- Format charts.

If you want to learn how to use Excel or brush up on your existing Excel skills, see the Microsoft Office Online Web site at `http://www.microsoft.com/office`, as well as the documentation included with Excel.

As you begin to master Excel, you might want to consider becoming certified as a Microsoft Office Specialist. When compared with those that aren't Office-certified, being a Microsoft Office Specialist can set you apart in the job market, increase your employment opportunities, give you the opportunity to increase your earning potential, and enhance career advancement. Not only that, you can also potentially increase your credibility with fellow coworkers, students, and customers. As an added benefit, you'll learn more about Excel, obviously increasing your satisfaction and skill level with the product. For more information about the Microsoft Office Specialist Certification, visit the Microsoft Office Specialist Web site at `http://www.microsoft.com/learning/mcp/officespecialist`.

While this book does contain a chapter about programming PivotTables, this is not a book on programming the rest of Excel. Before you read Chapter 7, you should already have an introductory understanding of Excel VBA. For more information on Excel programming, see the following Apress books:

- *Definitive Guide to Excel VBA Second Edition* by Michael Kofler (Apress, 2003)

- *Microsoft Office Programming: A Guide for Experienced Developers* by Rod Stephens (Apress, 2003)

If you're interested in other Office books by Apress, see *Office 2003 XML for Power Users* by Matthew MacDonald (Apress, 2004).

1

....

What Are PivotTables?

PivotTables are a feature of Excel that allows you to see patterns and trends of large amounts of data in a short amount of time. You can take lots of pieces of information and get insights about how the data is related. If you want to look at the same data insights from additional perspectives, you simply rearrange, or *pivot*, the data in the PivotTable accordingly so that additional insights swing into view.

As you use PivotTables to help you analyze and compare information, you begin to make sense of what at first seems like unrelated information, turning data into the fuel that helps you make key decisions in faster time.

For example, using PivotTables, you can take thousands of individual sales transactions and present them in a table that provides a summary view of sales by calendar month that fits nicely within your computer screen without scrolling. You could then quickly transform the summary view into sales by geographical store location for comparison. Lastly, you could quickly compare sales by both calendar month and store location at the same time with just a few mouse clicks.

You could get answers to questions such as

- What are my sales totals for each geographic region? Which product line sold the best and at which time of the year?

- When is the best day of the week for customers to visit my Web site? Which portion of the Web site attracts the most visitors during that day?

- In which academic quarter, and in which subjects during the quarter, did students score the best on their exams?

These somewhat involved data analysis questions are easy to figure out with a PivotTable. For instance, to get sales totals for each geographic region, you could simply drag a few items around in an Excel workbook. The resulting PivotTable could calculate all of the sales totals automatically. Likewise, with a few mouse clicks, you could quickly and easily determine which product sold the best based on a certain date.

Other Ways to Analyze Data in Excel

There are certainly other ways of analyzing Excel information. However, none of them have the benefits of PivotTables previously mentioned. To begin your PivotTable journey, you'll look at a few of these data analysis tools individually and then compare them to PivotTables. By the end of this chapter, you'll see that PivotTables provide a more integrated and powerful way to analyze data than each of the following data analysis approaches by themselves. Now you'll look at some of Excel's data analysis techniques individually.

Subtotals

You could use subtotals to analyze your data. Subtotaling is a fast and easy method of grouping similar data and summarizing it. Subtotaling data by time, location, person, subject, and so on are common data analysis tasks. To use subtotals, you simply select a cell in the column that you want to subtotal, choose Data ➤ Subtotals, and follow the directions in the Subtotal dialog box. An example of some data to be subtotaled is shown in Figure 1-1.

	A	B	C
1	Record Store Number	Music Genre	Albums In Stock
2	7846	Classical	95
3	7847	Classical	50
4	7848	Classical	100
5	7849	Classical	75
6	7846	Country	305
7	7847	Country	295
8	7848	Country	315
9	7849	Country	290
10	7846	Jazz	170
11	7847	Jazz	195
12	7848	Jazz	120
13	7849	Jazz	185
14	7846	Rock	385
15	7847	Rock	390
16	7848	Rock	340
17	7849	Rock	300

FIGURE 1-1
Example data to be subtotaled

An example of the Subtotal dialog box is shown in Figure 1-2.

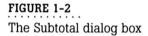

FIGURE 1-2

The Subtotal dialog box

At each change in music genre in the data as shown in Figure 1-1, a subtotal will be calculated for all albums in stock for that genre across all music stores.

Figure 1-3 shows the result of applying the subtotals.

	A	B	C
1	Record Store Number	Music Genre	Albums In Stock
2	7846	Classical	95
3	7847	Classical	50
4	7848	Classical	100
5	7849	Classical	75
6		**Classical Total**	320
7	7846	Country	305
8	7847	Country	295
9	7848	Country	315
10	7849	Country	290
11		**Country Total**	1205
12	7846	Jazz	170
13	7847	Jazz	195
14	7848	Jazz	120
15	7849	Jazz	185
16		**Jazz Total**	670
17	7846	Rock	385
18	7847	Rock	390
19	7848	Rock	340
20	7849	Rock	300
21		**Rock Total**	1415
22		**Grand Total**	3610

FIGURE 1-3

Subtotals applied to the data in Figure 1-1

However, this approach alone is insufficient as a robust data analysis solution. Unless your data is presented in a way that allows for easy subtotaling, for example listing time-based numbers by geographical region instead, using subtotals can yield odd results, which might force you to spend a lot of time reorganizing your data to get the subtotaling just the way you want. Also, every time you want to change the way your subtotals are calculated, you might have to remove the existing subtotals and go through the subtotaling process from the beginning all over again.

In contrast, PivotTables allow you to quickly rearrange numbers so that subtotals can be quickly recalculated, without having to rearrange the source data on which the PivotTables are based. Figure 1-4 shows a PivotTable based on the data in Figure 1-1.

Sum of Albums In Stock	
Music Genre ▾	Total
Classical	320
Country	1205
Jazz	670
Rock	1415
Grand Total	3610

FIGURE 1-4

A PivotTable based on the data in Figure 1-1

If you're unfamiliar with Excel's subtotaling feature, you can practice using it in the "Analyze Data Using Subtotals" section later in this chapter.

Worksheet Formulas

You could also use worksheet formulas to summarize data. Excel has hundreds of worksheet formula types covering simple calculations such as addition and averages all the way up to advanced statistical analysis. However, worksheet formulas can be unstable and error-prone.

The most frequent problem occurs when the worksheet locations of the numbers that a worksheet formula depends on change, such as when lists are sorted or grouped. When this happens, worksheet formulas that rely on numbers to be in a specific worksheet location could be rendered invalid or return the wrong results. One example is a simple function that sums three numbers. If one of these numbers is changed or removed from the group, the function will only report the results that include the new changed number or of the remaining two numbers if one of the numbers is missing. To see what this looks like in a worksheet, start with the scenario in Figure 1-5.

	C19	▼	*fx* =SUM(C2,C6,C10,C14)	
	A	B		C
1	Record Store Number	Music Genre		Albums In Stock
2	7846	Classical		95
3	7847	Classical		50
4	7848	Classical		100
5	7849	Classical		75
6	7846	Country		305
7	7847	Country		295
8	7848	Country		315
9	7849	Country		290
10	7846	Jazz		170
11	7847	Jazz		195
12	7848	Jazz		120
13	7849	Jazz		185
14	7846	Rock		385
15	7847	Rock		390
16	7848	Rock		340
17	7849	Rock		300
18				
19		Sales Albums In Stock for Store 7846		955

FIGURE 1-5

Sample data and formula with numbers in fixed positions on the worksheet.
Note that the formula in cell C19 depends on the values in rows C2, C6, C10,
and C14.

Now, move the numbers around in the column, as shown in Figure 1-6.

	C19	▼	*fx* = SUM(C2,C6,C10,C14)	
	A	B		C
1	Record Store Number	Music Genre		Albums In Stock
2	7846	Classical		95
3	7846	Country		305
4	7846	Jazz		170
5	7846	Rock		385
6	7847	Classical		50
7	7847	Country		295
8	7847	Jazz		195
9	7847	Rock		390
10	7848	Classical		100
11	7848	Country		315
12	7848	Jazz		120
13	7848	Rock		340
14	7849	Classical		75
15	7849	Country		290
16	7849	Jazz		185
17	7849	Rock		300
18				
19		Sales Albums In Stock for Store 7846		320

FIGURE 1-6

Sample data with a different result after values are moved from their previous
fixed positions. Notice that the result in cell C19 is incorrect because the values
in rows C2, C6, C10, and C14 are not the same as in Figure 1-5.

Notice how the result has changed because the numbers changed absolute positions in the column. Refer to Figure 1-4 earlier to see how these numbers would look in a PivotTable. Even if the numbers are moved around in the same column, the PivotTable's results should not change.

Additionally, more complex worksheet functions require an understanding of the functions' inputs. If you input the wrong information to a function, the function will, of course, return the wrong results. One of these functions, for example, is the Subtotal function. The first input to this function is a number from 1 to 111 that represents the intersection of a worksheet function such as Average, Min, or Var, along with whether the worksheet function recognizes or ignores hidden values. Obviously, this algorithm is not intuitive for most Excel users.

Worksheet functions in PivotTables are very flexible; because you're rearranging a copy of the source data and not the data itself, the worksheet functions can better rely on stationary source data. Additionally, PivotTable worksheet functions are self-contained. In other words, you don't have to learn how to craft formulas. You can spend your time doing direct data analysis instead.

The "Analyze Data Using Worksheet Functions" section later in this chapter gives you an opportunity to practice using worksheet functions if you're unfamiliar with this Excel feature.

Filters

Filters are also tools for analyzing data. Filters allow you to exclude numbers that don't meet particular criteria that you choose in advance. For example, you can use a filter to only view students' test results that exceed a given limit, say 85%.

Filters have the same issues as subtotals, however, in that if you want to apply different filters, you need to sometimes experiment with the AutoFilter buttons to get the right combination of filters on the correct rows and/or columns. Also, again, worksheet formulas can break or show the wrong results if they rely on unfiltered data only. For example, say you want to show albums in stock for only store 7847, as shown in Figure 1-7.

	A	B	C
1	Record Store Number ▾	Music Genre ▾	Albums In Stock ▾
6	7847	Classical	50
7	7847	Country	295
8	7847	Jazz	195
9	7847	Rock	390

FIGURE 1-7

Using a filter to show albums in stock for only store 7847

Next, say you want to show rock albums in stock for all stores. So, as shown in Figure 1-8, you attempt to set the filter for only showing rock albums. However, you forgot to turn off the filter for the store number column.

	A	B	C
1	Record Store Number ▾	Music Genre ▾	Albums In Stock ▾
9	7847 Rock		390

FIGURE 1-8

Using a filter to show only rock albums in stock for only store 7847. To show only rock albums in stock for all stores, you must remember to remove the filter from the store number column as well.

Getting all of these filters set correctly can be time consuming. PivotTables make this type of mistake much easier to spot, as shown in Figure 1-9.

Sum of Albums In Stock		
Record Store Number ▾	Music Genre ▾	Total
7846	Rock	385
7847	Rock	390
7848	Rock	340
7849	Rock	300
Grand Total		1415

FIGURE 1-9

A PivotTable, based on the scenario in Figures 1-7 and 1-8. It's easy to see that all store numbers are represented here.

In the "Analyze Data Using AutoFilter" section later in this chapter, you can practice filtering data, if you're not already familiar with this Excel feature.

Data Validation and Conditional Formatting

Validating data and applying conditional formatting to data are good basic indicators of data anomalies and trends.

You can validate data to make sure it falls within a specific numerical range of values, for example, ensuring that only valid calendar dates are entered for a sales transaction date.

You can use conditional formatting to change the visual display of the data, for instance coloring cells red if the number of albums in stock for any cell is 100 or less. An example of this is shown in Figure 1-10.

	A	B	C
1	Record Store Number	Music Genre	Albums In Stock
2	7846	Classical	95
3	7846	Country	305
4	7846	Jazz	170
5	7846	Rock	385
6	7847	Classical	50
7	7847	Country	295
8	7847	Jazz	195
9	7847	Rock	390
10	7848	Classical	100
11	7848	Country	315
12	7848	Jazz	120
13	7848	Rock	340
14	7849	Classical	75
15	7849	Country	290
16	7849	Jazz	185
17	7849	Rock	300

FIGURE 1-10

Dark red cells highlight cells in which albums in stock is 100 or less.

As with the other methods previously mentioned, validating data and applying conditional formatting works well for single pieces of data. However, when data is filtered or moved around, validation rules and conditional formatting can become inoperable, display incorrect results, or trigger the wrong outcomes. Also, validating data and applying conditional formatting doesn't help filter or group data. So, these methods are not good ways of performing robust data analysis on very large groups of data.

When used with PivotTables, data validation and conditional formatting take on greater meaning by providing additional data integrity and insights to already-summarized data, as shown in Figure 1-11.

Sum of Albums In Stock	Music Genre ▼				
Record Store Number ▼	Classical	Country	Jazz	Rock	Grand Total
7846	95	305	170	385	955
7847	50	295	195	390	930
7848	100	315	120	340	875
7849	75	290	185	300	850
Grand Total	320	1205	670	1415	3610

FIGURE 1-11

A PivotTable based on the data in Figure 1-11. Dark red cells highlight cells in which albums in stock is 100 or less.

If you're not familiar with how to use Excel's conditional formatting feature, you can practice using it in the "Analyze Data Using Conditional Formatting" section later in this chapter.

Dynamic Lists

Beginning in Excel 2003, you can organize data into dynamic lists. These lists support built-in filtering, sorting, and a limited set of worksheet functions, and the data in lists can be moved around as a discrete unit. An example of a dynamic list is shown in Figure 1-12.

	A	B	C
1	Record Store Number ▾	Music Genre ▾	Albums In Stock ▾
2	7846	Classical	95
3	7846	Country	305
4	7846	Jazz	170
5	7846	Rock	385
6	7847	Classical	50
7	7847	Country	295
8	7847	Jazz	195
9	7847	Rock	390
10	7848	Classical	100
11	7848	Country	315
12	7848	Jazz	120
13	7848	Rock	340
14	7849	Classical	75
15	7849	Country	290
16	7849	Jazz	185
17	7849	Rock	300
18	*		
19		Total	3610
20	List		▾ ×
21			
22	List ▾	Σ Toggle Total Row	

FIGURE 1-12
An example of a dynamic list based on the data in Figure 1-1

However, dynamic lists don't provide any additional built-in data analysis functionality on their own, such as subtotals and grouping, data validation, and conditional formatting.

PivotTables are superior to dynamic lists in that they add subtotals and grouping, as previously shown in Figure 1-4.

In the "Try It! Analyze Data with a List" exercises later in this chapter, you can practice using dynamic lists if you're not already familiar with how to use them.

Crosstab Tables

Lastly, you can create crosstab tables, which are summarized lists of subtotals, averages, or other types of calculations for numbers that are usually grouped in row-and-column format. One specific numerical dimension (such as sales by salespeople's names) is listed down the table's rows, and another specific numerical measurement (such as sales by calendar month) is listed across the table's columns. An example of a crosstab table is shown in Figure 1-13.

	A	B	C	D	E	F
1			Music Genre			
2	Music Store Number	Classical	Country	Jazz	Rock	Totals
3	7846	95	305	170	385	955
4	7847	50	295	195	390	930
5	7848	100	315	120	340	875
6	7849	75	290	185	300	850
7	Totals	320	1205	670	1415	3610

FIGURE 1-13
An example of a crosstab table

Although powerful, creating crosstab tables can be tedious and prone to error. Tedious because the summarized data in crosstab tables is frequently typed by hand and prone to error because crosstab tables' results are often based on worksheet formulas referring to highly volatile data or frequently moving cell positions. Additionally, crosstab tables usually address only one type of data analysis scenario at a time. To address additional data analysis scenarios, crosstab tables either need to be substantially modified, consisting of a complicated series of tasks, or the original crosstab tables must be replaced altogether by new sets of crosstab tables.

PivotTables use a unique series of rows, columns, row and column nesting, and pages to quickly present data views in three, four, or even more perspectives as your data analysis needs become more sophisticated, as previously shown in Figure 1-4.

If you're unfamiliar with using crosstab tables, the "Try It! Analyze Data with Crosstab Tables" exercises later in the chapter give you the opportunity to create and use crosstab tables.

Good Uses for PivotTables

To help you understand the scenarios that PivotTables are best used for, assume the facts and numbers in Figure 1-14 consist of hundreds or even thousands of rows of data like sales transactions for a given calendar year spread out over several sales outlets in a large geographical area.

	A	B	C
1	Record Store Number	Music Genre	Albums In Stock
2	7846	Classical	95
3	7846	Country	305
4	7846	Jazz	170
5	7846	Rock	385
6	7847	Classical	50
7	7847	Country	295
8	7847	Jazz	195
9	7847	Rock	390
10661	10511	Classical	110
10662	10511	Country	310
10663	10511	Jazz	195
10664	10511	Rock	425

FIGURE 1-14

An example of a very large set of data in an Excel worksheet (panes have been split for readability). Notice that there are well over 10,000 rows of data.

How would you begin to make sense of all of that data?

It would be hard to visually and mentally process thousands of rows of data, not to mention tens of thousands or hundreds of thousands of rows. Summing or averaging the rows is usually not enough. Outlining in Excel is not very flexible either. You will most likely need to organize related data together along several groupings.

When you want to look at the data from a different perspective, you need to start over and organize the data into different groupings. These groupings don't necessarily follow the pattern of the data as it's presented in the worksheet.

The nice thing about PivotTables is that changing the groupings of data is quick. You can quickly rearrange, or *pivot*, the data to see information from whole new perspectives. You can ask all sorts of questions about your data without affecting the underlying data itself.

Following are good candidates for data that can be measured by PivotTables:

- Data that is presented in rows with the same number of columns per row. For example, the geographical location that applies to each fact and figure is placed in the first column, the date that each fact and figure was collected is placed in the second column, and so on.

- Numerical data or columnar text that is restricted to predictable lists of choice or values; for example, true/false, male/female, only the numbers 1 through 10, north/south/east/west, and so on.

- Data that is separated into, and organized by, logical relationships; for example, time (years, months, weeks, days, hours, minutes, and seconds), geography (continents, countries, regions, zones, states, cities, and communities), and so on.

- Data that is measured consistently; for example, the same currency, date formatting, metric measurement system, and so on.

Try It! Work with Data Analysis Features

To further introduce you to PivotTables, here's a series of Try It! exercises to get you familiar with the different methods that you can use to analyze data.

In these exercises, you'll start by analyzing data in a somewhat manual fashion, and then you'll move to analyzing data with a dynamic list. You'll also analyze data using crosstab tables and a PivotTable.

By the end of these exercises, you'll be able to bring several techniques to bear to analyze your data, as well as learn why PivotTables make your data analysis tasks so much quicker and easier.

For these Try It! exercises, you'll first need to download the Visitors.xls workbook from the Apress Web site's Downloads section for this book at http://www.apress.com. This workbook consists of a simple set of data representing the number of visitors to a group of specialty gift boutique stores for a given calendar week located throughout a given geographical area. The data is organized by geographic region, then by store number in each region, then by day of the week, and then finally by the number of visitors.

Try It! Analyze Data Manually

Before you start using PivotTables, you should feel comfortable subtotaling, filtering, and formatting data. If you're already comfortable with these data analysis methods, you might want to go directly to the "Try It! Analyze Data with a PivotTable" exercises later in this chapter. If you're uncomfortable with these data analysis methods, however, you should stay in this section and work through the following exercises step by step. In this exercise, you'll use the following data analysis methods:

- Subtotals and other worksheet functions

- Filters

- Conditional formats

These data analysis methods can be collectively thought of as *manual data analysis* because you are mainly involved in manually inspecting data and then applying formulas, formats, and other behaviors to the data, which can be tedious and somewhat inflexible when compared to PivotTables.

Analyze Data Using Subtotals

First group the data by using subtotals to answer the question, "For the week, how many customers visited stores in each of the four geographic regions?"

Display Subtotals by Region

After you open the Visitors.xls workbook in Excel 2003 (File ➤ Open), select the Data worksheet tab.

> **NOTE** If a menu command is not visible, double-click the menu, or click the Expand icon at the bottom of the menu, to show all hidden menu commands.

1. Make sure you select one of the nonblank cells on the worksheet, for example, cell A1.

2. Click Data ➤ Subtotals.

3. Click OK. The data is grouped, and outline symbols are displayed in the left-hand margin.

4. Click the outline symbol numbered 2 to display the totals by region. To help you check your work as you go, see the results of Figure 1-15.

1 2 3		A	B	C	D
	1	Region	Store	Day	Visitors
+	16	North Total			2225
+	38	South Total			3520
+	60	East Total			2610
+	75	West Total			2680
−	76	Grand Total			11035

FIGURE 1-15
Visitor subtotals by geographic region

Display Subtotals by Day

Using subtotals is good in this case to subtotal data by region, but what if you want to subtotal data by day? The results aren't very good without some extra work:

1. Clear the current totals from the previous exercise by choosing Data ➤ Subtotals ➤ Remove All.

2. Click Data ➤ Subtotals again.

3. In the At Each Change In list, select Day.

4. Click OK. The data is grouped, but this time as shown in Figure 1-16, there is a subtotal after every row, which doesn't provide any additional useful information.

1 2 3		A	B	C	D
	1	Region	Store	Day	Visitors
	2	North	101	Friday	175
	3			Friday Total	175
	4	North	101	Monday	150
	5			Monday Total	150
	6	North	101	Saturday	275
	7			Saturday Total	275
	8	North	101	Sunday	250
	135			Sunday Total	300
	136	West	402	Thursday	145
	137			Thursday Total	145
	138	West	402	Tuesday	150
	139			Tuesday Total	150
	140	West	402	Wednesday	100
	141			Wednesday Total	100
	142			Grand Total	11035

FIGURE 1-16
Visitor subtotals by day before sorting the data (panes have been split for readability)

Display Subtotals by Day after Sorting the Data

The reason the results from the previous section don't look very good is because you must first sort your list so that the rows you want to subtotal are grouped together. By sorting your list, it makes subtotaling a lot easier:

1. Clear the current totals from the previous exercise by choosing Data ➤ Subtotals ➤ Remove All.

2. Click Data ➤ Sort.

3. In the Sort By list, select Day, and make sure that the other Then By boxes are blank.

4. Next to the Sort By list, click Ascending.

5. Click Options.

6. In the First Key Sort Order list, click the item starting with Sunday, Monday, Tuesday, Wednesday.

   NOTE If you don't see an item starting with Sunday, Monday, Tuesday, Wednesday, you'll need to add the item to the list before you can select it. To add the item to the list, click Tools ➤ Options ➤ Custom Lists. If you're not sure how to create a custom list, press F1 for help, or see the "Create, Change, Or Delete A Custom Fill Series" topic in Excel 2003 Help.

7. Click OK, and click OK again. The data is sorted by day.

8. Click Data ➤ Subtotals.

9. Click OK. The data is grouped, and outline symbols are displayed in the left margin.

10. Click the outline symbol numbered 2 to display the totals by day, as shown in Figure 1-17.

1 2 3		A	B	C	D
	1	Region	Store	Day	Visitors
+	12			Sunday Total	2360
+	23			Monday Total	1390
+	34			Tuesday Total	1270
+	45			Wednesday Total	780
+	56			Thursday Total	1185
+	67			Friday Total	1590
+	78			Saturday Total	2460
−	79			Grand Total	11035

FIGURE 1-17

Visitor subtotals by day after sorting the data. It's easy to see each day's total visitors.

As you have experienced, using subtotals, groups, outlines, and resorting lists requires a lot of steps. As you'll see later, PivotTables reduce these steps considerably, as well as provide an easier way to subtotal and sort data.

Analyze Data Using Worksheet Functions

Let's try something different. Can you spot the lowest and highest numbers in the Visitors column? You can use a couple of worksheet functions to figure this out.

Use the Min Worksheet Function

Follow these steps to show the lowest number in the Visitors column:

1. Clear the current totals from the previous exercise by choosing Data ➤ Subtotals ➤ Remove All.

2. Return the list to its presorted state by choosing Data ➤ Sort. Select Store in the Sort By list, and click OK.

3. Select cell D72.

4. Click Insert ➤ Function. The Insert Function dialog box appears.

5. In the Search For A Function box, type **MIN**, as shown in Figure 1-18. Click Go, and then click OK.

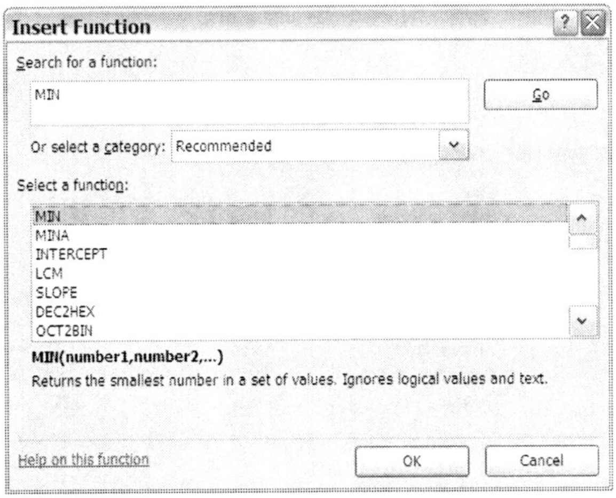

FIGURE 1-18
The Insert Function dialog box with MIN selected

6. Click OK again.

7. The number 50 appears in cell D72. This number represents the lowest number in the Visitors column.

Use the Max Worksheet Function

Now that you've shown the lowest number in the Visitors column, repeat the process to show the highest number in the Visitors column:

1. With cell D72 selected, press the Delete key.

2. Click Insert ➤ Function.

3. In the Search for a Function box, type **MAX**, click Go, and click OK.

4. Click OK again.

5. The number 300 appears in cell D72. This number represents the highest number in the Visitors column.

   Inserting worksheet formulas takes several steps. As you'll see later, PivotTables reduce these steps. PivotTables let you choose from a list of pre-defined functions with just a few mouse clicks, or you can create your own formulas very easily.

Analyze Data Using AutoFilter

In the "Analyze Data Using Subtotals" section previously in this chapter, you used subtotals to summarize data. But what if you wanted to select a few facts and figures out of the list that match certain criteria? For example, without using subtotals, can you quickly answer questions such as how many visitors were there on Sunday for stores in the South? You can use the AutoFilter feature to narrow down the data to determine this, as shown in the next section.

Show Visitors for Southern Stores on Sunday

Follow these steps to figure out how many visitors there were on Sunday for stores in the South:

1. Clear the worksheet function from the previous exercise by selecting cell D72 and pressing the Delete key.

2. Click cell A1.

3. Click Data ➤ Filter ➤ AutoFilter.

4. Click the AutoFilter button in cell C1, and select Sunday from the list, as shown in Figure 1-19.

FIGURE 1-19

Selecting an item from the AutoFilter list

5. Click the AutoFilter button in cell A1, and select South from the list.

6. Select the three numbers in the Visitors column. The sum, 645, appears in the status bar.

TIP If the status bar is not visible, click View ➤ Status Bar. If the sum is not visible on the status bar, right-click the status bar and click Sum, as shown in Figure 1-20.

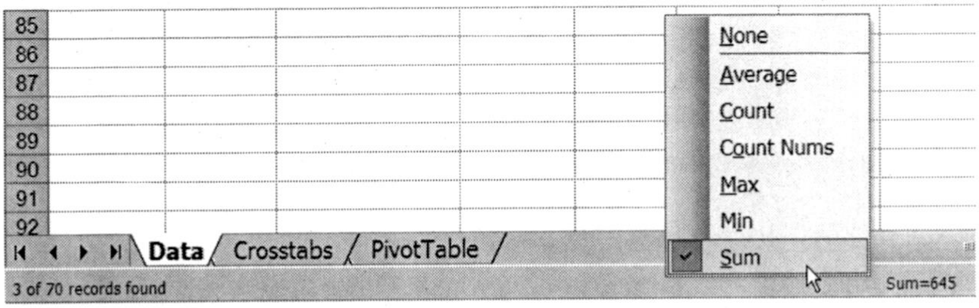

FIGURE 1-20

Selecting Sum from the status bar is faster than inserting the Sum formula into a worksheet.

Show Visitors for Eastern Stores on Wednesday

Now use filters to figure out how many visitors there were on Wednesday for stores in the East:

1. Click the AutoFilter button in cell C1, and select Wednesday from the list.

2. Click the AutoFilter button in cell A1, and select East from the list.

3. Select the three numbers in the Visitors column. The sum, 155, appears in the status bar.

Although filters are powerful, if you wanted to figure out how many visitors for each day of the week and then how many visitors for each store for each day of the week, you'd have to repeat these steps more than 70 times. As you can see, these steps can get tedious if you have to apply more than a few filters. As you'll see later, PivotTables allow you to apply multiple filters in faster time in many cases.

Analyze Data Using Conditional Formatting

As you read in the "Data Validation and Conditional Formatting" section earlier in this chapter, you can use conditional formatting to add visual highlights to specific facts and figures that meet certain criteria. In the next section, you'll use conditional formatting to highlight specific visitor totals. Conditional formatting works the same for both data lists and PivotTables.

Conditional Format Low Visitor Totals

Follow these steps to highlight visitor totals under 100:

1. Clear the filters from the previous exercise by choosing Data ➤ Filter ➤ Show All.

2. Select cells D2 through D71.

3. Click Format ➤ Conditional Formatting. The Conditional Formatting dialog box appears.

4. In the second list from the left, select Less Than.

5. In the third list from the left, type **100**.

6. Click Format.

7. Click the Patterns tab.

8. Click the red box, and then click OK. Compare your results to Figure 1-21.

FIGURE 1-21

The Conditional Formatting dialog box colors all cells red that are less than 100.

9. Click OK again. The cells of all visitor totals under 100 are shaded red, as shown in Figure 1-22.

	A	B	C	D
1	Region	Store	Day	Visitors
2	North	101	Sunday	250
3	North	101	Monday	150
4	North	101	Tuesday	110
5	North	101	Wednesday	75
6	North	101	Thursday	100
7	North	101	Friday	175
8	North	101	Saturday	275
9	North	102	Sunday	290
10	North	102	Monday	130
11	North	102	Tuesday	130
12	North	102	Wednesday	90
13	North	102	Thursday	110
14	North	102	Friday	150
15	North	102	Saturday	190
16	South	201	Sunday	225
17	South	201	Monday	110
18	South	201	Tuesday	145
19	South	201	Wednesday	95
65	West	402	Sunday	300
66	West	402	Monday	195
67	West	402	Tuesday	150
68	West	402	Wednesday	100
69	West	402	Thursday	145
70	West	402	Friday	180
71	West	402	Saturday	285

FIGURE 1-22

Results of applying conditional formatting. All cells that are less than 100 are colored red (panes have been split for readability).

Conditional Format High Visitor Totals

Next, use conditional formatting to highlight any visitor totals over 250:

1. With cells D2 through D71 still selected, click Format ➤ Conditional Formatting.

2. Click Add.

3. In the Condition 2 row, in the second list from the left, select Greater Than.

4. In the third list from the left, type **250**.

5. Click Format.

6. Click the Patterns tab.

7. Click the green box, and then click OK. Compare your results with Figure 1-23.

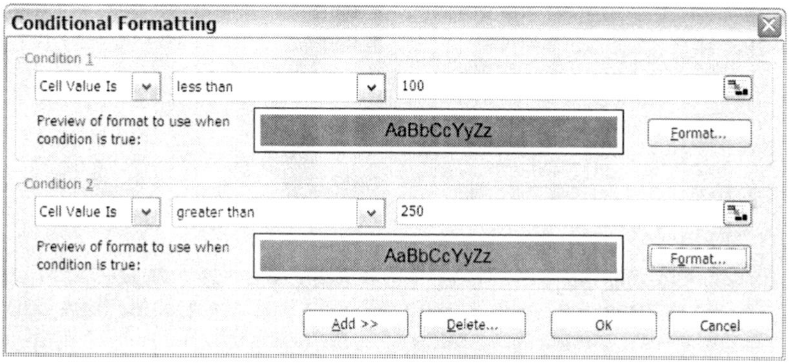

FIGURE 1-23

The Conditional Formatting dialog box colors all cells green that are greater than 250.

8. Click OK again. The cells of all visitor totals over 250 are shaded green, as shown in Figure 1-24.

	A	B	C	D
1	Region	Store	Day	Visitors
2	North	101	Sunday	250
3	North	101	Monday	150
4	North	101	Tuesday	110
5	North	101	Wednesday	75
6	North	101	Thursday	100
7	North	101	Friday	175
8	North	101	Saturday	275
9	North	102	Sunday	290
10	North	102	Monday	130
11	North	102	Tuesday	130
12	North	102	Wednesday	90
13	North	102	Thursday	110
14	North	102	Friday	150
15	North	102	Saturday	190
16	South	201	Sunday	225
17	South	201	Monday	110
18	South	201	Tuesday	145
19	South	201	Wednesday	95
65	West	402	Sunday	300
66	West	402	Monday	195
67	West	402	Tuesday	150
68	West	402	Wednesday	100
69	West	402	Thursday	145
70	West	402	Friday	180
71	West	402	Saturday	285

FIGURE 1-24

Results of applying conditional formatting. All cells that are less than 100 are colored red. Additionally, all cells that are greater than 250 are colored green (panes have been split for readability).

TIP To find cells with conditional formatting, click Edit ➤ Go To ➤ Special. Select the Conditional Formats option, and click OK.

Try It! Analyze Data with a List

Lists are self-contained units of related data rows in Excel. Excel 2003 enhances the notion of lists to add dynamic features such as enabling AutoFilter by default and displaying total rows.

Lists also make the creation of PivotTables even easier. Building off the previous exercises, let's see how easy it is to work with data in lists.

Create a List

Begin by creating a list out of the existing data:

1. Clear conditional formatting from the previous exercise by selecting cells D2 through D71, and choosing Format ➤ Conditional Formatting. Click Delete, select the Condition 1 and Condition 2 check boxes, click OK, and click OK again.

2. Click Data ➤ List ➤ Create List.

3. Select cells A1 through D71.

4. Select the My List Has Headers check box.

5. Click OK. A self-contained list is created. The list is bordered by a thick, blue line and AutoFilter buttons appear in the list's first row, as shown in Figure 1-25.

	A	B	C	D
1	Region ▼	Store ▼	Day ▼	Visitors ▼
2	North	101	Sunday	250
3	North	101	Monday	150
4	North	101	Tuesday	110
5	North	101	Wednesday	75
6	North	101	Thursday	100
7	North	101	Friday	175
8	North	101	Saturday	275
66	West	402	Monday	195
67	West	402	Tuesday	150
68	West	402	Wednesday	100
69	West	402	Thursday	145
70	West	402	Friday	180
71	West	402	Saturday	285
72	*			

FIGURE 1-25

A list in Excel 2003 with AutoFilter enabled by default (panes have been split for readability)

As you can see, automatic AutoFilter buttons are shown by default. This makes filtering data very quick and easy.

Use Worksheet Functions in a List

Let's see how much easier it is to display the minimum and maximum values of the Visitors column in a dynamic list, using the scenario from the "Analyze Data Using Worksheet Functions" exercise earlier in this chapter.

1. If a Total row (a row beginning with the word Total) is not visible in row D73, click Toggle Total Row on the List toolbar.

   TIP If the List toolbar is not visible, make sure you have selected at least one cell in the list. If the List toolbar is still not visible, click View ➤ Toolbars ➤ List.

2. Click the total in cell D73.

3. Click the arrow next to cell D73.

4. Select Min in the list. The number 50, representing the smallest number in the list, appears, as shown in Figure 1-26.

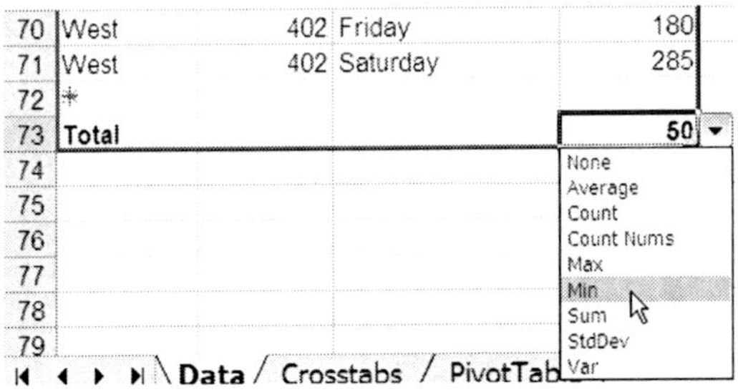

FIGURE 1-26

A list summarized by the Min function

5. Next, click the arrow next to cell D73 again.

6. Select Max in the list. The number 300, representing the largest number in the list, appears, as shown in Figure 1-27.

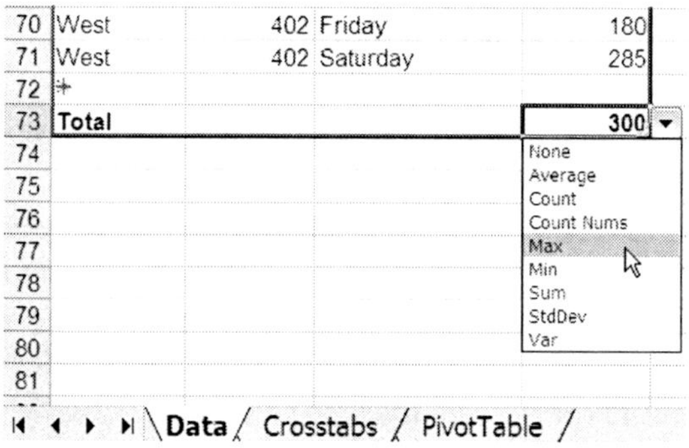

FIGURE 1-27
A list summarized by the Max function

As you can see, other functions such as Average and Count are easily available.

> **TIP** You can also display worksheet functions for other list columns. For example, you can click cell A73, click the arrow next to cell A73, and select Count from the list to display the count of rows in the column, and so on.

Use AutoFilter in a List

Now let's see how easy it is to use AutoFilter by using the scenario from the "Analyze Data Using AutoFilter" exercise earlier in this chapter:

1. In the list you created in the "Create a List" exercise earlier in this chapter, click the AutoFilter button in cell C1, and select Sunday from the list.

2. Click the AutoFilter button in cell A1, and select South from the list.

> **NOTE** If you didn't change the Total row from the previous exercise, the number 225 appears in the Total row, representing the largest number in the list of numbers currently displayed.

3. Click the AutoFilter button in cell C1, and select Wednesday from the list.

4. Click the AutoFilter button in cell A1, and select East from the list.

> **TIP** To hide the Total row, on the List toolbar, click Toggle ➤ Total Row.

Try It! Analyze Data with Crosstab Tables

So far, you've worked with simple lists of numbers. You've used subtotals to provide sums of groups of numbers, and you've used worksheet functions to find results such as the smallest and largest numbers in a list.

Crosstab tables allow you to take the next step in grouping and summarizing data. Crosstab tables also allow you to visually and mentally spot overall trends and anomalies with data much faster than some of the other data analysis methods that you've tried so far in this chapter. Crosstab tables display a sum, average, or other type of total for data that is most always grouped in two dimensions: one down the left side of the table and another across the top.

To get familiar with some crosstab tables, click the Visitor.xls workbook's Crosstabs worksheet tab. Two crosstab tables are displayed, showing visitors by store and day, as well as visitors by region and day, as shown in Figures 1-28 and 1-29.

	A	B	C	D	E	F	G	H	I
1					Visitors By Store and Day				
2					Day				
3	Store	Sunday	Monday	Tuesday	Wednesday	Thursday	Friday	Saturday	Totals
4	101	250	150	110	75	100	175	275	1135
5	102	290	130	130	90	110	150	190	1090
6	201	225	110	145	95	135	175	265	1150
7	202	205	140	145	80	140	170	275	1155
8	203	215	175	150	85	145	175	270	1215
9	301	195	100	100	50	95	125	205	870
10	302	190	105	105	50	90	130	215	885
11	303	195	95	95	55	85	130	200	855
12	401	295	190	140	100	140	180	280	1325
13	402	300	195	150	100	145	180	285	1355
14	Totals	2360	1390	1270	780	1185	1590	2460	11035

FIGURE 1-28

The Visitors By Store and Day crosstab table

16					Visitors By Region and Day				
17					Day				
18	Region	Sunday	Monday	Tuesday	Wednesday	Thursday	Friday	Saturday	Totals
19	North	540	280	240	165	210	325	465	2225
20	South	645	425	440	260	420	520	810	3520
21	East	580	300	300	155	270	385	620	2610
22	West	595	385	290	200	285	360	565	2680
23	Totals	2360	1390	1270	780	1185	1590	2460	11035

FIGURE 1-29

The Visitors By Region and Day crosstab table

Looking at the Visitors By Store and Day crosstab table first, you'll notice that the table's numbers look very similar to the numbers on the Data worksheet. That's because the numbers were just reorganized so that they're presented in a similar series of rows and columns. In fact, this crosstab table is fairly easy to create.

Resort the Numbers on the Data Worksheet

First, you simply sort the numbers on the Data worksheet, and then you copy the numbers over. Follow these steps to re-sort the numbers on the Data worksheet for this purpose:

1. If the data on the Data worksheet is contained in a dynamic list as a result of the "Create A List" exercise earlier in this chapter, convert the dynamic list to a range by clicking anywhere inside of the dynamic list and then clicking Data ➤ List ➤ Convert To Range.

2. On the Data worksheet, click a nonblank cell, such as cell A1.

3. Click Data ➤ Sort.

4. In the Sort By list, select Day.

5. In the Then By list, select Store.

6. Click Options.

7. In the First Key Sort Order list, select the entry that begins with Sunday, Monday, Tuesday, Wednesday, and so on, and click OK.

   NOTE If you don't see an item starting with Sunday, Monday, Tuesday, Wednesday, you'll need to add the item to the list before you can select it. To add the item to the list, click Tools ➤ Options ➤ Custom Lists. If you're not sure how to create a custom list, press F1 for help, or see the "Create, Change, Or Delete a Custom Fill Series" topic in Excel 2003 Help.

8. Click OK again. The list is sorted by day and then by store, as shown in Figure 1-30.

	A	B	C	D
1	Region	Store	Day	Visitors
2	North	101	Sunday	250
3	North	102	Sunday	290
4	South	201	Sunday	225
5	South	202	Sunday	205
6	South	203	Sunday	215
7	East	301	Sunday	195
8	East	302	Sunday	190
65	South	202	Saturday	275
66	South	203	Saturday	270
67	East	301	Saturday	205
68	East	302	Saturday	215
69	East	303	Saturday	200
70	West	401	Saturday	280
71	West	402	Saturday	285

FIGURE 1-30

Visitors sorted by day and then by store (panes have been split for readability)

As you can see, cells D2 through D11 were copied into the Crosstabs worksheet in cells B4 through B13 and so on for each day's numbers.

Create the Totals Row

Now that you have the individual numbers copied over into the crosstab table, creating the Totals row to summarize the numbers in the crosstab table is straightforward as well:

1. On the Crosstabs worksheet, select cells B14 through H14 and click Edit ➤ Clear ➤ All.

2. Click cell B14 again.

3. Click Insert ➤ Function.

4. Type **SUM**, click Go, and click OK.

5. Click OK again. The sum of 2,360 is displayed.

6. Select cells B14 through H14, and click Edit ➤ Fill ➤ Right. The sums for columns C through H are displayed.

7. Select cells I4 through I14 and click Edit ➤ Clear ➤ All.

8. Click cell I4 again.

9. Click Insert ➤ Function.

10. Type **SUM**, click Go, and click OK.

11. Select cells B4 through H4, and click OK. The sum of 1,135 is displayed.

    TIP You didn't need to select cells B13 in step 5, but you had to select cells B4 through H4 in step 11. This is because Excel interpreted the store number of 101 in cell A4 as a visitor subtotal. By selecting cells B4 through H4, you exclude counting the store number as a visitor subtotal in row 4.

12. Select cells I4 through I14, and click Edit ➤ Fill ➤ Down. The sums for rows 4 through 14 are displayed.

    TIP The green triangles in the upper-left corners of cells I4 through I13 indicate that the subtotals don't include the numbers in column A. That's okay in this case because the numbers in column A are store numbers and not visitor subtotals. If you want to get rid of the green triangles, select cells I4 through I13 and click Tools ➤ Error Checking, and then keep clicking Ignore Error until all of the green triangles are gone. You can also select cells I4 through I13, point at the Error Checking Options button, click the arrow, and click Ignore Error.

This crosstab table is interesting to look at, but doesn't give you much more information than what you started with. Let's summarize this data by moving to a crosstab table showing visitors by region and day.

Re-create the Visitors By Region and Day Crosstab Table

A more interesting crosstab table is Visitors By Region and Day, which summarizes more data. Creating this report from scratch is much harder. The following sections show you how you would do it.

Calculate the Subtotals

Calculating the subtotal for cell B19, as an example, is rather involved:

1. Click cell B19 and click Edit ➤ Clear ➤ All.

2. Click Insert Function.

3. Type **SUM**, and then click Go.

4. Click OK.

5. On the Data worksheet, while pressing and holding the Ctrl key, select the cells in the Visitors column in the rows that contain the value North in the Region column and Sunday in the Day column. These should be the cells with the values 250 and 290.

6. Click OK again. The value 540 appears in cell B19.

This process can get quite tedious and error-prone for the remaining 27 cells in the crosstab report. However, after you finish the previous steps for each cell, as well as add row and column totals similar to the previous exercise, the results are very insightful. You can begin to make quicker and more valuable data analysis observations with this summarized data, as shown in the next section.

Analyzing the Crosstab Reports' Subtotals

As one example of making some quick data analysis observations, you can spot the following subtotals quite easily in the Visitors By Region and Day crosstab report as shown in the beginning of the "Try It! Analyze Data with Crosstab Tables" exercises earlier in this chapter.

- Wednesday had the least visitors with 780.

- Saturday had the most visitors with 2,460.

- North had the least visitors with 2,225.

- South had the most visitors with 3,520.

- East had the least visitors on Wednesday with 155.

- South had the most visitors on Saturday with 810.

You can use the Visitors By Store and Day to take this analysis even further:

- Store 303 had the least visitors with 855.

- Store 402 had the most visitors with 1,355.

- Stores 301 and 302 had the least visitors on Wednesday, each with 50.

- Store 402 had the most visitors on Sunday with 300.

You can select groups of cells and use the status bar to get additional information with very little extra effort. (If you're not sure how to use the status bar, see the "Analyze Data Using AutoFilter" section earlier in this chapter.) Selecting the following cells yields the following averages when you click the status bar and select Average:

- Cells B4 through H13, representing average visitors per store per day: about 158.

- Cells B19 through H22, representing average visitors per region per day: about 394.

- Cells B4 through H4, representing average visitors for store 101 per day: about 162, just slightly greater than the average of all stores.

- Cells E4 through E13, representing average visitors per store on Wednesday: 78, slightly less than half of the average of all stores.

- Cells B22 through H22, representing average visitors for the West region per day: about 383, slightly less than the average of all stores.

- Cells G19 through G22, representing average visitors for all regions on Friday: about 398, slightly greater than average.

You can easily perform additional data analysis on these crosstab tables, such as sorting, filtering, conditionally formatting, and so on, by selecting cells A3 through H13 or cells A18 through H22 and performing many of the exercises presented earlier in this chapter. You can also turn these crosstab tables into lists to enable easy sorting and filtering using the techniques presented in preceding exercises.

Crosstab Report Drawbacks

Even with all of these data analysis techniques, however, it's hard to avoid the fact that crosstab tables are lacking in flexibility, and many data analysis tasks are just too tedious and error-prone for crosstab tables alone. The following is one simple scenario in which this is the case.

As the number of crosstab table cells increase, the opportunity for data-entry or data-calculation errors greatly increases. For example, a somewhat simple crosstab table displaying each calendar month across the columns and each of the 50 United States down the rows would of course result in 600 row-and-column intersections alone, a more than eight-fold increase in row-and-column intersections over the Visitors By Store and Day crosstab table. Repeating the previous data calculation steps 600 times is certainly inconvenient, to say the least.

Continuing this scenario, the act of changing the crosstab table layout so that calendar months are displayed down the rows and each of the 50 United States are displayed across the columns would be easier by creating a new crosstab table, but then you'd also need to copy the numbers from the previous crosstab table to the new crosstab table. Copying all of the data is also very inconvenient.

Try It! Analyze Data with a PivotTable

Now that you're comfortable with manual data analysis methods and crosstab tables, it's finally time to begin taking a look at PivotTables. You'll see how easy it is to perform many of the data analysis techniques that you've practiced so far in this chapter. You'll begin to see data trends virtually "jump off the screen" with little additional effort.

Create a PivotTable
Now, you'll create the PivotTable using the PivotTable and PivotChart Wizard:

1. In the Visitors.xls workbook, click the PivotTable worksheet tab.

2. Select cell A1.

3. Click Data ➤ PivotTable And PivotChart Report.

4. Click Next.

5. Click the Data worksheet tab.

6. Select cells A1 through D71.

   NOTE You cannot select cells A1 through D1 unless AutoFilter is turned off. To turn off AutoFilter, click Data ➤ Filter ➤ AutoFilter.

7. Click Finish. A blank PivotTable appears on the PivotTable worksheet tab, as shown in Figure 1-31.

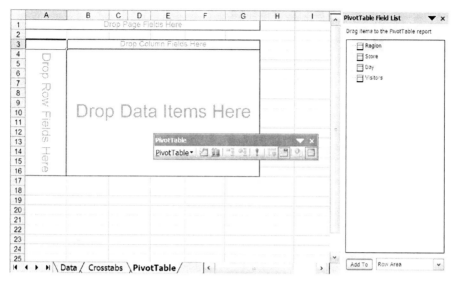

FIGURE 1-31
A blank PivotTable

Use Subtotals in a PivotTable

Now you'll see how much easier it is to not only recreate the subtotals as we did in the "Analyze Data Using Subtotals" exercise earlier in this chapter, but see the PivotTable create additional subtotals automatically for us as we go.

Show Visitor Subtotals by Region

First, display visitor subtotals for each of the four geographic regions.

1. In the PivotTable Field List, click Region.

2. In the Add To list, select Row Area.

3. Click Add To.

> **TIP** If the PivotTable Field List is not visible, click anywhere inside of the PivotTable's blue boundaries. If the PivotTable Field List is still not visible, on the PivotTable toolbar, click Show Field List. If the PivotTable toolbar is not visible, click View ➤ Toolbars ➤ PivotTable.

4. In the PivotTable Field List, click Visitors.

   5. In the Add To list, select Data Area.

   6. Click Add To. Visitor subtotals are displayed by region, as shown in Figure 1-32.

	A	B
1	Drop Page Fields Here	
2		
3	Sum of Visitors	
4	Region ▾	Total
5	East	2610
6	North	2225
7	South	3520
8	West	2680
9	Grand Total	11035

FIGURE 1-32
Visitor subtotals by geographic region

Show Visitor Subtotals by Day

Now show visitor subtotals by day:

   1. Right-click the Region field in cell A4, and click Hide.

   2. In the PivotTable Field List, click Day.

   3. In the Add To list, select Row Area.

   4. Click Add To. Visitor subtotals are displayed by day, as shown in Figure 1-33.

	A	B
1	Drop Page Fields Here	
2		
3	Sum of Visitors	
4	Day ▾	Total
5	Sunday	2360
6	Monday	1390
7	Tuesday	1270
8	Wednesday	780
9	Thursday	1185
10	Friday	1590
11	Saturday	2460
12	Grand Total	11035

FIGURE 1-33
Visitor subtotals by day

As you can clearly see, with just a few mouse clicks, subtotals are automatically generated for us without ever having to use the Sort or Subtotals dialog boxes. Neither did we have to click outline symbols nor pick a sort order key.

Use Worksheet Functions in a PivotTable

Now you'll see how easy it is for Excel to automatically calculate the results of worksheet functions in a PivotTable to spot the lowest number and highest number in the Visitors field.

Show the Lowest Number of Visitors

To show the lowest number of visitors, follow these steps:

1. Right-click the Day field in cell A4, and click Hide.

2. Right-click the Sum Of Visitors field in cell A3, and click Field Settings.

3. In the Summarize By list, select Min, and click OK. The lowest number in the Visitors field, 50, appears, as shown in Figure 1-34.

	A	B
1	Drop Page Fields Here	
2		
3	Min of Visitors	Total
4	Total	50

FIGURE 1-34
The lowest number in the Visitors field

Show the Highest Number of Visitors

To find the highest number in the Visitors field, follow these steps:

1. Right-click the Min Of Visitors field in cell A3, and click Field Settings.

2. In the Summarize By list, select Max, and click OK. The highest number in the Visitors field, 300, appears.

Selecting predefined calculations in this exercise and the preceding one is much easier than using the Insert Formula dialog box as described in the "Analyze Data Using Worksheet Functions" exercise earlier in this chapter. You didn't need to remove subtotals or re-sort any data for this to work either. You don't have to insert formulas for any of the cells yourself. You simply select the function and Excel automatically calculates everything for you.

Use AutoFilter in a PivotTable

Using AutoFilter in a PivotTable is similar to using AutoFilter elsewhere in Excel. Let's practice this by determining how many visitors there were on particular days for specific regions, as you did in the "Show Visitors for Southern Stores on Sunday" exercise earlier in this chapter.

Show Visitor Subtotals for Southern Stores on Sunday

To display the visitor subtotals for southern stores on Sunday, follow these steps:

1. Let's display visitor subtotals again by right-clicking the Max Of Visitors field in cell A3, clicking Field Settings, selecting Sum in the Summarize By list, and clicking OK.

2. In the PivotTable Field List, click Region.

3. In the Add To list, select Row Area, and click Add To.

4. In the PivotTable Field List, click Day.

5. In the Add To list, select Row Area, and click Add To.

6. Click the AutoFilter button in the Region field in cell A4. Clear the (Show All) check box, select the South check box, and click OK, as shown in Figure 1-35.

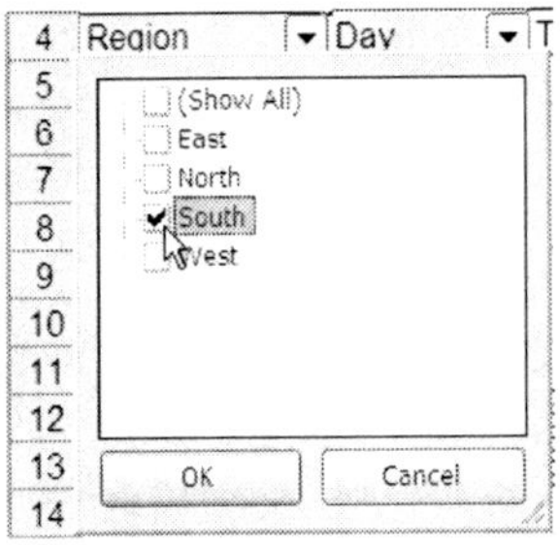

FIGURE 1-35
Working with the AutoFilter choices list in a PivotTable

7. Click the AutoFilter button in the Day field in cell B4. Clear the (Show All) check box, select the Sunday check box, and click OK. The total number of visitors for Southern stores for Sunday, 645, appears as shown in Figure 1-36.

	A	B	C
1	Drop Page Fields Here		
2			
3	Sum of Visitors		
4	Region ▾	Day ▾	Total
5	South	Sunday	645
6	South Total		645
7	Grand Total		645

FIGURE 1-36

Total number of visitors for Southern stores on Sunday

Show Visitor Subtotals for Eastern Stores on Wednesday

You can use filters to figure out how many visitors there were on Wednesday for stores in the East, as you did in the "Show Visitors for Eastern Stores on Wednesday" exercise earlier in this chapter.

1. Select the AutoFilter button in the Region field in cell A4. Clear the South check box, select the East check box, and click OK.

2. Select the AutoFilter button in the Day field in cell B4. Clear the Sunday check box, select the Wednesday check box, and click OK. The total number of visitors for Eastern stores for Wednesday, 155, appears.

As you can see in this exercise and the previous exercise, using AutoFilter in PivotTables is similar to using AutoFilter elsewhere in Excel. Also, you don't have to use the status bar to view the results of calculations such as Sum, because PivotTables can quickly provide this information for you without any additional effort.

Next Steps

In this chapter, you began learning basic data analysis techniques by analyzing data using subtotals, worksheet functions, filters, and conditional formatting. From there, you used these basic data analysis techniques in conjunction with dynamic lists, which include built-in tools to make it easier to analyze facts and figures. Next, you extended your data analysis skills to work with more summarized data in crosstab tables spanning two dimensions. Finally, you brought all of your skills together to create a PivotTable and work with data even faster and easier.

Before you head into the next chapter, you might want to take a copy of some data in an Excel workbook that you currently use and apply the Try It! exercises in this chapter to the data in your workbook. This will help you solidify the skills that you learned in this chapter and help you to start conceptually visualizing the interrelationships of the facts and figures in your workbook.

The more you understand how your data is related and can be summarized, the better success you'll have in working with your data in different perspectives within PivotTables. As you learn additional PivotTable techniques and skills throughout this book, you can apply your newfound skills to your own data and see the results right away.

2

Creating PivotTables

Creating a PivotTable in Excel based on existing source data is very straightforward when you use the PivotTable and PivotChart Wizard. However, the first time that you use the wizard, some of the wizard's specific steps and terms can be a little confusing. In this chapter, you'll learn how to

- Use the PivotTable and PivotChart Wizard.

- Select existing source data for your PivotTable.

- Create a new connection to source data for your PivotTable.

- Set PivotTable report formatting and data presentation options.

- Create a PivotTable on your own using the PivotTable and PivotChart Wizard.

Using the PivotTable and PivotChart Wizard

You use the PivotTable and PivotChart Wizard in Excel to create PivotTables (and PivotCharts, which are explained in more detail in Chapter 5). You can start the wizard by simply clicking Data ➤ PivotTable and PivotChart Report.

The PivotTable and PivotChart Wizard consists of three basic steps for selecting data, specifying data details, and setting layout and formatting behaviors, in order to turn the data into a PivotTable (along with an optional PivotChart). Later in this chapter, you'll practice using the PivotTable and PivotChart Wizard in a Try It! exercise. For now, we'll introduce you gradually to the various PivotTable and PivotChart Wizard components, so that you'll be more comfortable with what each component does when you use them.

Begin exploring the PivotTable and PivotChart Wizard components by following these steps:

1. Start Excel, type some random data in cells A1 and A2, and then click Data ➤ PivotTable and PivotChart Report.

    The wizard's first step, shown in Figure 2-1, allows you to select the data that you want to analyze, as well as select the kind of report you want to create.

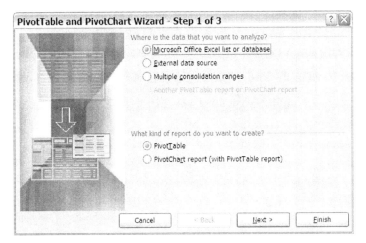

FIGURE 2-1

The first step of the PivotTable and PivotChart Wizard

The controls in the first step of the PivotTable and PivotChart Wizard allow you to

- Select a Microsoft Office Excel list or database as the PivotTable's data source.
- Select an external data source, such as a Microsoft Office Access database, as the PivotTable's data source.
- Select multiple cell groups on one or more Excel worksheets, as the PivotTable's data source.
- Select an existing PivotTable or PivotChart as the PivotTable's data source.
- Create a PivotTable only.
- Create a PivotTable and a PivotChart at the same time.

NOTE For more information on how to use this dialog box, see the "Selecting Existing Source Data" section later in this chapter.

2. Next, make sure the Microsoft Office Excel List Or Database and PivotTable options are selected, and then click Next.

In the wizard's second step, you provide specific details about the data that you want to analyze. The display of the wizard's second page depends on the options you selected in step 2. In this case, Figure 2-2 shows what the wizard's second step looks like if your source data is an Excel list or database, as you just selected.

FIGURE 2-2
The second step of the PivotTable and PivotChart Wizard, if your source data is an Excel list or database, as selected in the wizard's first step. You use this step if your source data consists of labeled rows and columns on a Microsoft Excel worksheet.

Options in this dialog box include

- The Range box allows you to type in a cell range (such as $A$1:$D$71 to represent cells A1 through D71) as the PivotTable's data source.

- You can also click the Browse button to select data in a file other than the current Excel workbook.

NOTE For details on how to use this dialog box, see the "Selecting an Excel List or Database" section later in this chapter.

3. Click Back.

4. Click External Data Source, and then click Next.

Figure 2-3 shows the wizard's second step if your source data is in an external data source, as you just selected.

FIGURE 2-3
The second step of the PivotTable and PivotChart Wizard, if your source data is in an external data source as selected in the wizard's first step. You use this step if your source data is stored in a file or database outside the current workbook or Excel.

When you click Get Data in this dialog box, the Choose Data Source dialog box appears. For more on how to use the Choose Data Source dialog box, see the "Selecting External Source Data" section later in this chapter.

5. Click Cancel, and then click Back.

6. Click Multiple Consolidation Ranges, and then click Next.

7. Click Create a Single Page Field For Me, as shown in Figure 2-4, and then click Next. (A *page field* is a logical organization of the data. You'll learn how to work with page fields in Chapter 3.)

FIGURE 2-4

The second step of the PivotTable and PivotChart Wizard if your source data is in cell ranges spanning one or more worksheets in one or more Excel workbooks

Figure 2-5 represents the wizard's second step if you selected a single page field, which you just did.

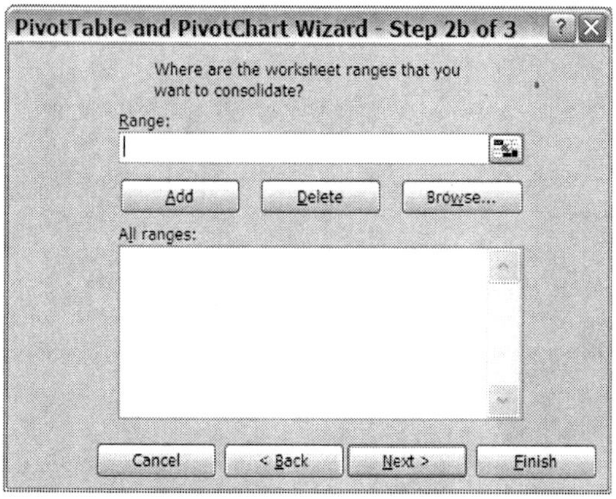

FIGURE 2-5

The second step of the PivotTable and PivotChart Wizard if your source data is in cell ranges spanning one or more worksheets in one or more Excel workbooks, and you want Excel to specify a single page field

The options in this dialog box include:

- The Range box allows you to type in a cell range (such as $A$1:$D$71 to represent cells A1 through D71) as the PivotTable's data source.

- The Add button adds your cell range to the list of cell ranges that serve as the PivotTable's data source.

- The Delete button removes the selected cell range from the list of cell ranges that serve as the PivotTable's data source.

- You can also click the Browse button to select data in a file other than the current Excel workbook.

NOTE For more details on how to use this dialog box, see the "Selecting a Consolidation Range" section later in this chapter.

8. Click Back.

9. Click I Will Create The Page Fields, and then click Next.

Figure 2-6 represents the wizard's second step if you selected the option for creating page fields on your own, which you just did.

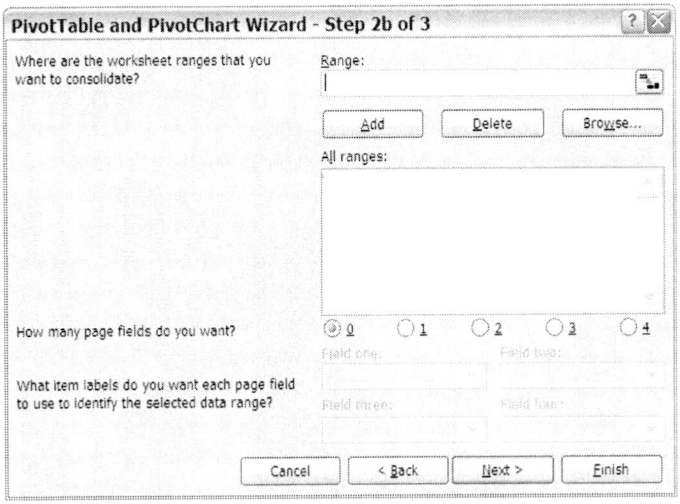

FIGURE 2-6

The second step of the PivotTable and PivotChart Wizard if your source data is in cell ranges spanning one or more worksheets in one or more Excel workbooks, and you want to create page fields on your own

The options toward the top of the dialog box are similar to those in Figure 2-5. Additional options include

- The options labeled 0, 1, 2, 3, and 4 allow you to specify up to four page fields.

- The Field One, Field Two, Field Three, and Field Four lists allow you to select the field in your data source that will serve as the page field for each of the four fields.

NOTE For more details on how to use this dialog box, see the "Selecting a Consolidation Range" section later in this chapter.

10. Click Back, and then click Back again.

Notice that you can't select the Another PivotTable Or PivotChart Report option because you don't have an existing PivotTable or PivotChart available. See Figure 2-7 for what the wizard's second step would look like if your data source were an existing PivotTable or PivotChart.

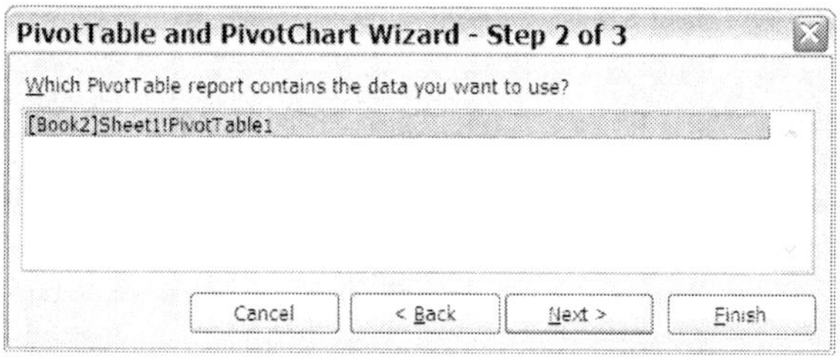

FIGURE 2-7

The second step of the PivotTable and PivotChart Wizard if your source data is in an existing PivotTable or PivotChart. You use this step if your source data is stored in another PivotTable report in the same workbook. Note that a PivotChart report must have an associated PivotTable report in the same workbook. If you specify a location in another workbook, the PivotChart report will also be created in that workbook.

NOTE For more information on how to use this dialog box, see the "Selecting an Existing PivotTable or PivotChart" section later in this chapter.

11. Click Microsoft Office Excel List Or Database.

12. Click Next, and then click Next again.

Figure 2-8 shows the wizard's third step, which allows you to provide your PivotTable's (and optional PivotChart's) layout and formatting options.

FIGURE 2-8

The third step of the PivotTable and PivotChart Wizard, which allows you to provide layout and formatting options for your PivotTable (and optional PivotChart)

13. Click Layout.

Figure 2-9 shows a dialog box that you can use to specify PivotTable layout options.

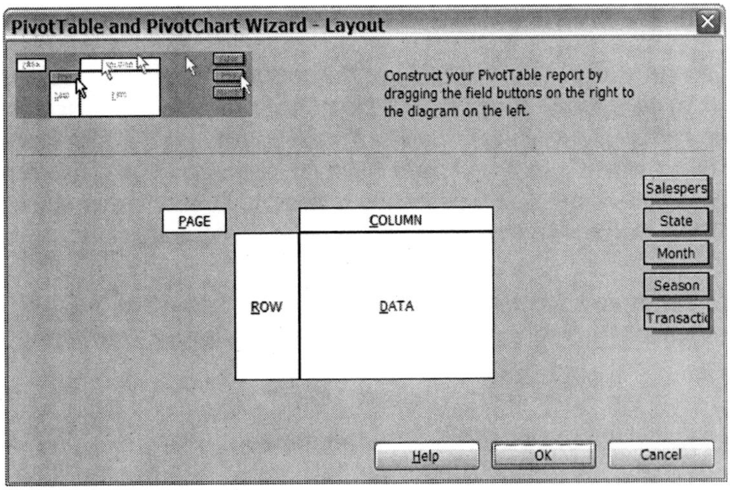

FIGURE 2-9

The PivotTable and PivotChart Wizard's Layout dialog box

This dialog box allows you to create your PivotTable by dragging field buttons on the right onto the PivotTable designer on the left. However, the PivotTable Field List dialog box is much easier and intuitive to use.

NOTE For more information on using the Layout dialog box and the PivotTable Field List dialog box, see Chapter 3.

14. Click Cancel.

15. Click Options.

Figure 2-10 shows a dialog box that you can use to specify PivotTable formatting options.

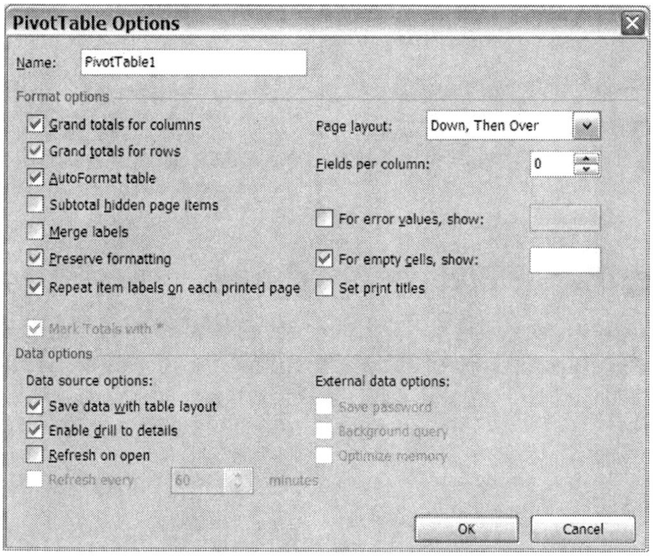

FIGURE 2-10

The PivotTable Options dialog box, which sets advanced formatting, layout, memory management, and external data options for your PivotTable or PivotChart report

NOTE More details on the options in this dialog box are described in the "Setting PivotTable Report Formatting and Data Presentation Options" section later in this chapter.

16. Click Cancel, and then click Cancel again to stop exploring the PivotTable and PivotChart Wizard.

Selecting Existing Source Data

Now that you've explored the PivotTable and PivotChart Wizard's main dialog boxes, let's examine each of these dialog boxes in more detail.

The first step in using the PivotTable and PivotChart Wizard is to tell the wizard where the underlying data is that the PivotTable will use. You can specify four categories of source data for the PivotTable (and optional PivotChart):

- An Excel *list* (a collection of Excel worksheet cells) or *database* (an Excel workbook)

- External source data

- Groups of cells in one or more worksheets spanning one or more Excel workbooks (called a *consolidation range*)

- An existing PivotTable or PivotChart

Let's look at each one of these four source data categories in more detail.

Selecting an Excel List or Database

The first source data category is a collection of Excel worksheet cells or an Excel workbook. Assume you have a simple list of facts and figures, as shown in Figure 2-11.

	A	B	C	D
1	City	State	Month	Average Temperature
2	Seattle	WA	January	45
3	Seattle	WA	February	49
4	Seattle	WA	March	52
5	Seattle	WA	April	57
6	Seattle	WA	May	64
7	Seattle	WA	June	69
8	Seattle	WA	July	75
9	Seattle	WA	August	75
10	Seattle	WA	September	70
11	Seattle	WA	October	59
12	Seattle	WA	November	51
13	Seattle	WA	December	46

FIGURE 2-11

Sample Excel list for the PivotTable and PivotChart Wizard

If you select an Excel list or database in the first step of the PivotTable and PivotChart wizard, you then see the dialog box as shown in Figure 2-12.

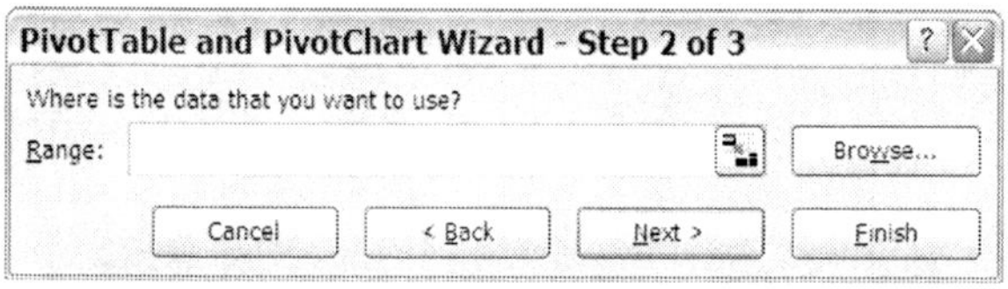

FIGURE 2-12

The second step of the PivotTable and PivotChart Wizard, if your source data is in an Excel list or database as selected in the wizard's first step

From there, it's very simple to select a range of cells in the current worksheet as your PivotTable source data. When you select cells A1 through D13, the dialog box will then look like Figure 2-13.

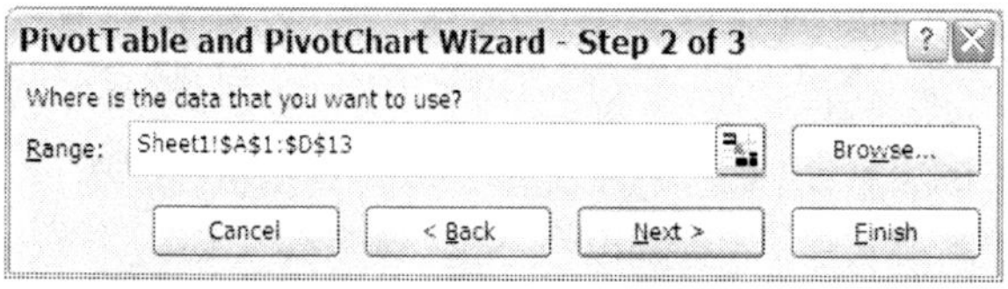

FIGURE 2-13

The second step of the PivotTable and PivotChart Wizard, after you select cells A1 through D13

It's important to note that if your data is not on the current worksheet, you select the worksheet and the range of cells on that worksheet for your source data. To specify an Excel list in another workbook, it's best to first open the other workbook before running the wizard. Also, by giving the Excel list a name (by clicking Insert ➤ Name ➤ Define to create a named range out of the list), you make it easier to update the resulting PivotTable. If the named Excel list's contents change, you can easily refresh the PivotTable to reflect these changes.

> **NOTE** When you create a PivotTable, Excel ignores any filters and subtotals you have applied to your source list. You should remove any filters, or copy the filtered information to a new list, as well as remove any subtotals on a list, before you create a PivotTable based on the list.

It's simple to demonstrate how to refer to data on a different worksheet than the worksheet on which the PivotTable will be created:

1. Type the data in a new Excel workbook as shown earlier in Figure 2-11.

2. Click File ➤ New.

3. Click Blank Workbook.

4. Click Data ➤ PivotTable and PivotChart Report, and then click Next.

5. With the Step 2 dialog box still visible, go to the Excel workbook with the data you typed in step 1.

6. Select cells A1 through D13.

7. Return to the blank workbook you created in step 3, and click Finish. A PivotTable is created.

If for some reason you don't want to follow the preceding steps, you can enter the worksheet and cell range manually in the Step 2 dialog box. To do so, you should use absolute, or fixed, cell references and refer to cells using these examples as a guide:

- For the range of cells in columns A through C and rows 1 through 20 in the same worksheet where the PivotTable is to be created, use $A$1:$C$20.

- For the range of cells in rows 15 through 30 and columns B through D in the same worksheet where the PivotTable is to be created, use $B$15:$D$30.

- For the range of cells A through F and rows 10 through 20 in a separate worksheet named Sales, use Sales!$A$10:$F$20.

- For the range of cells B through E and rows 1 through 15 in a separate workbook named RealEstate.xls and a worksheet in that workbook named Transactions, use [RealEstate.xls]Transactions!$B$1:$E$15.

Selecting External Source Data

The second data source category involves external data. If you select external source data in the first step of the PivotTable and PivotChart wizard, you then see the dialog box as shown in Figure 2-14.

FIGURE 2-14

The second step of the PivotTable and PivotChart Wizard, if your source data is in an external data source as selected in the wizard's first step

After you click the Get Data button, you then see the Choose Data Source dialog box. One of the choices in this dialog box is to choose from an existing data source type by clicking the Databases tab, as shown in Figure 2-15 (or create a new data source). You'll practice using this tab in the "Connecting to the Source Data" section of the Try It! exercise later in this chapter.

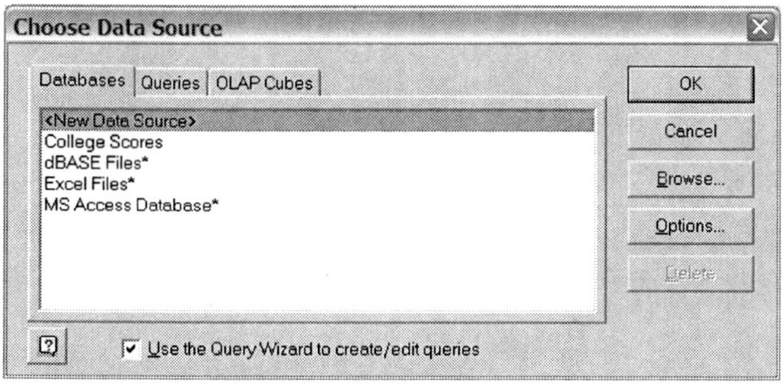

FIGURE 2-15

The Choose Data Source dialog box's Databases tab. Choose this tab if you have an existing data source defined.

Another choice is to use a data query as the basis of your data source by clicking the Queries tab, as shown in Figure 2-16.

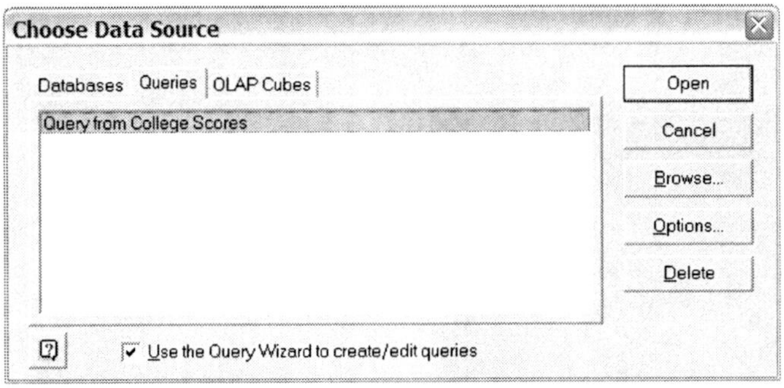

FIGURE 2-16

The Choose Data Source dialog box's Queries tab. Choose this tab if you have an existing query defined.

Finally, you can select an Online Analytical Processing (OLAP) cube by clicking the OLAP Cubes tab, as shown in Figure 2-17. Working with OLAP cubes is covered in Chapter 6.

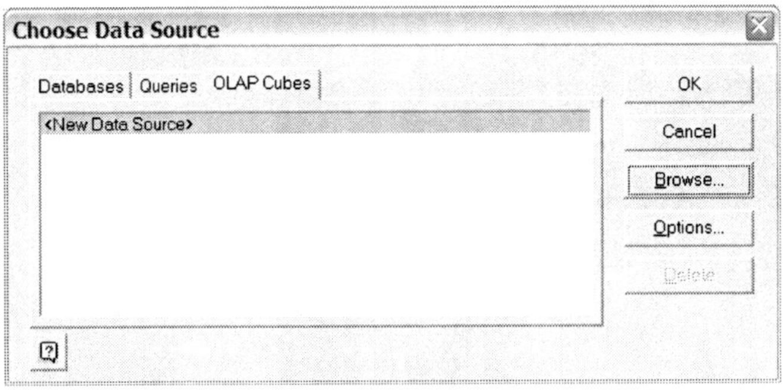

FIGURE 2-17

The Choose Data Source dialog box's OLAP Cubes tab. Choose this tab if you already have an existing OLAP cube available.

The existing types of data sources you can select include the following:

- Microsoft Access database files

- dBASE database files

- Microsoft FoxPro and Microsoft Visual FoxPro databases

- Microsoft Excel workbooks

- Oracle databases

- Paradox databases

- Microsoft SQL Server and Microsoft Analysis Services databases

- Text file databases, such as a list of comma-separated values

- Lists and document libraries on a Microsoft Windows SharePoint Services server

- Microsoft Business Solutions data running on a Windows SharePoint Services server

- Other data providers, if you have the data providers' driver installed. (For more information about drivers, contact your database provider.)

To select an external data source, select the external data source name on the Databases, Queries, or OLAP Cubes tab and then click OK. Based on the data source type, follow any onscreen directions to finish connecting to your external data source. For example, if you select Microsoft Access as the external data source type on the Databases tab, Excel prompts you to provide the location and name of the Access database file.

If your external data source isn't listed in the Choose Data Source dialog box, you'll need to create an external data source connection first. To do this, see the "Creating a New Data Source Connection" section later in this chapter.

NOTE If you want to reference external data using one of the following Excel data access methods, you should first import the external data into Excel by clicking Data ➤ Import External Data ➤ Import Data, before creating your PivotTable or PivotChart report. The Excel data access methods include

- Web page queries (by clicking Data ➤ Import External Data ➤ New Web Query).

- Parameter queries from a database server such as Microsoft SQL Server.

- Report templates (workbooks with the .xlt extension that already have your preferred formatting and text options).

- Query files and Office Data Connection files (files with the .dqy and .odc extensions, respectively). These files contain data source connectivity details and are most commonly created by clicking Data ➤ Import External Data ➤ Import Data.

After you import the external data, choose the Microsoft Office Excel List Or Database option in the PivotTable and PivotChart Wizard to refer to the imported data.

Selecting a Consolidation Range

The third data source category involves groups of cells in one or more worksheets spanning one or more Excel workbooks. These are more commonly referred to as *consolidation ranges*. If you select multiple consolidation ranges in the first step of the PivotTable and PivotChart wizard, you then see the dialog box as shown in Figure 2-18.

FIGURE 2-18

The second step of the PivotTable and PivotChart Wizard if your source data is in cell ranges spanning one or more worksheets in one or more Excel workbooks

Furthermore, if you let Excel create a single page field for you, you then see the dialog box as shown in Figure 2-19.

FIGURE 2-19

The second step of the PivotTable and PivotChart Wizard if your source data
is in cell ranges spanning one or more worksheets in one or more Excel
workbooks, and you want Excel to specify a single page field

Likewise, if you create the page fields yourself, you then see the dialog
box as shown in Figure 2-20. You'll practice using this dialog box in just a few
paragraphs.

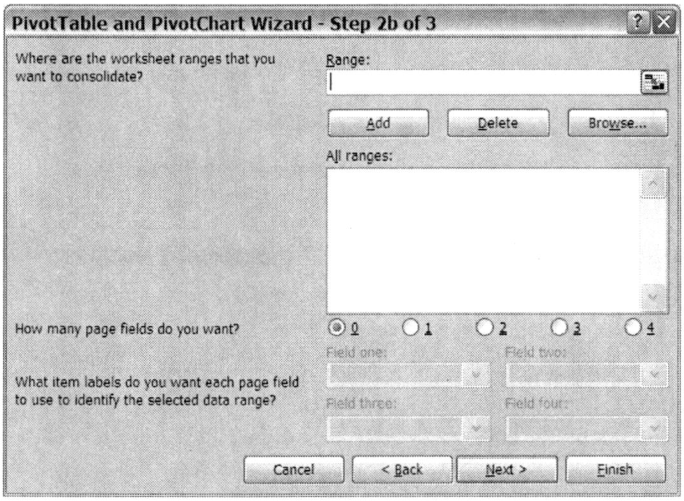

FIGURE 2-20

The second step of the PivotTable and PivotChart Wizard if your source data
is in cell ranges spanning one or more worksheets in one or more Excel
workbooks, and you want to create page fields on your own

As you can see by examining the two dialog boxes in Figures 2-19 and 2-20, they differ only when you elect to create the page fields yourself. If one of your ranges is in another workbook, it's best to first open the other workbook before running the wizard.

NOTE A page field allows you to filter the entire PivotTable report to display data for a single data subcategory. For example, you might want to view retail sales by geographic region across the rows and then by calendar month across the columns. The page field would allow you to filter the data even further, for example, viewing retail sales in the PivotTable by both geographic region and calendar month only for a particular product category.

To specify the ranges that you want to consolidate, select each range in turn and then click the Add button. If you select a range by mistake, you can remove it by clicking the Delete button.

Let's practice briefly using these dialog boxes, using the data as it's presented in Figure 2-21.

1. Type the data as shown in Figure 2-21 in a blank worksheet.

2. Click Data ➤ PivotTable and PivotChart Report.

3. Click Multiple Consolidation Ranges, and then click Next.

4. Click I Will Create The Page Fields, and then click Next.

5. With the dialog box still visible, select cells B2 through C10.

6. Select cells C13 through D21, and then click Add.

7. In the Field One list, type **1996**, compare your results to Figure 2-22, and then click Next.

8. Click New Worksheet, and then click Finish. Compare your results to Figure 2-23.

	B	C	D
1	2000 Games		
2		Medals	
3	Archery	2	
4	Baseball	7	
5	Basketball	6	
6	Boxing	4	
7	Diving	17	
8	Fencing	0	
9	Football	5	
10	Hockey	2	
11			
12		1996 Games	
13			Medals
14		Archery	1
15		Baseball	9
16		Basketball	5
17		Boxing	3
18		Diving	15
19		Fencing	2
20		Football	4
21		Hockey	5

FIGURE 2-21

Sample data in multiple consolidation ranges

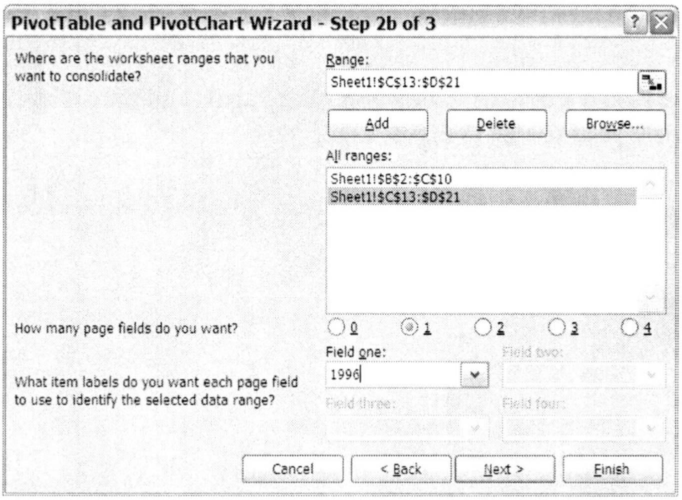

FIGURE 2-22

Completing the Step 2b dialog box to connect the PivotTable to the consolidation ranges

	A	B	C
1	Page1	(All) ▾	
2			
3	Sum of Value	Column ▾	
4	Row ▾	Medals	Grand Total
5	Archery	3	3
6	Baseball	16	16
7	Basketball	11	11
8	Boxing	7	7
9	Diving	32	32
10	Fencing	2	2
11	Football	9	9
12	Hockey	7	7
13	Grand Total	87	87

FIGURE 2-23

Creating an initial PivotTable based on the selected consolidation ranges

Let's clean up this PivotTable a bit so that it provides some more valuable data:

1. Right-click anywhere inside of the PivotTable, click Table Options, clear the Grand Totals For Columns and Grand Totals For Rows check boxes, and click OK.

2. Right-click the Row field button, click Field Settings, click None, and click OK.

3. In the PivotTable Field List dialog box, click Page1, and then click Add To. Compare your results to Figure 2-24.

	A	B	C
1	Drop Page Fields Here		
2			
3	Sum of Value		Column ▾
4	Row ▾	Page1 ▾	Medals
5	Archery	1996	1
6		2000	2
7	Baseball	1996	9
8		2000	7
9	Basketball	1996	5
10		2000	6
11	Boxing	1996	3
12		2000	4
13	Diving	1996	15
14		2000	17
15	Fencing	1996	2
16		2000	0
17	Football	1996	4
18		2000	5
19	Hockey	1996	5
20		2000	2

FIGURE 2-24

Displaying total medals for each of the Team sports

You're already learning how to use PivotTables! You can practice more of this in the Try It! exercise toward the end of this chapter.

Selecting an Existing PivotTable or PivotChart

The fourth and final data source category involves an existing PivotTable or PivotChart. If you select an existing PivotTable or PivotChart in the first step of the PivotTable and PivotChart wizard, you then see the dialog box as shown in Figure 2-25. Simply select the PivotTable or PivotChart from the list.

FIGURE 2-25

The second step of the PivotTable and PivotChart Wizard if your source data is in an existing PivotTable or PivotChart. You use this step if your source data is stored in another PivotTable report in the same workbook.

To use a PivotTable as the source data for another PivotTable, it's important to note that both PivotTables must reside in the same Excel workbook. If the source PivotTable is in a different workbook, you must first copy the source PivotTable to the Excel workbook where you want the new PivotTable to appear. This is because PivotTables (and PivotCharts) in different workbooks are separate, each having their own source data.

Other things to note:

- When you refresh the source data in either PivotTable in this scenario, Excel also updates the source data in the other PivotTable.

- When you group or ungroup items in one PivotTable, both PivotTables are affected.

- When you create calculated fields or calculated items in one PivotTable, both PivotTables are affected.

- When you make changes to a PivotChart in this scenario, the PivotTable is affected. Likewise, when you make changes to a PivotTable, the PivotChart is affected.

Try this using the PivotTable you created in the preceding section:

1. With the PivotTable visible that you created in the preceding section, click anywhere outside of the PivotTable, and then click Data ➤ PivotTable and PivotChart Report.

2. Click Another PivotTable Report or PivotChart Report, and then click Next.

3. Click Next again.

4. Click New Worksheet, and then click Finish.

A new PivotTable is created based on the existing PivotTable.

Creating a New Data Source Connection

If you are trying to connect a PivotTable to an external data source, you must tell Excel how to connect to the data source first. You must have a connection already defined, as described in the "Selecting External Source Data" section earlier. If that data source does not exist in the Choose Data Source dialog box as shown in Figure 2-26, you must create or reference the connection to the source data yourself.

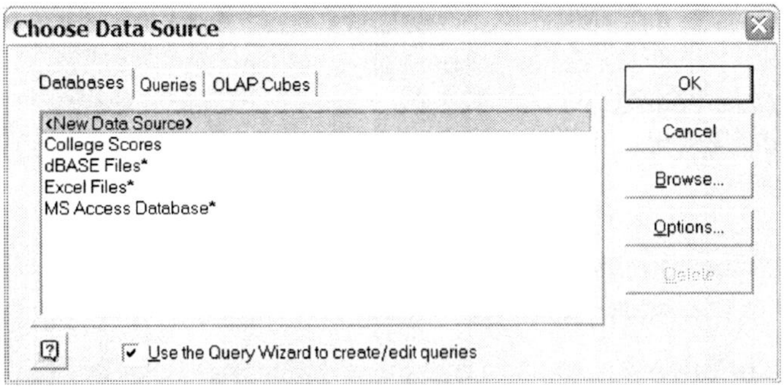

FIGURE 2-26

The Choose Data Source dialog box's Databases tab, used to connect a PivotTable to an external data source

To create a connection to source data, select a data source type in the Choose Data Source dialog box and then click OK. The Select <Data Source Type> dialog box then appears.

This dialog box's display varies depending on the source data type. For example, Figure 2-27 shows what the Select Database dialog box looks like when you select MS Access Database on the Databases tab.

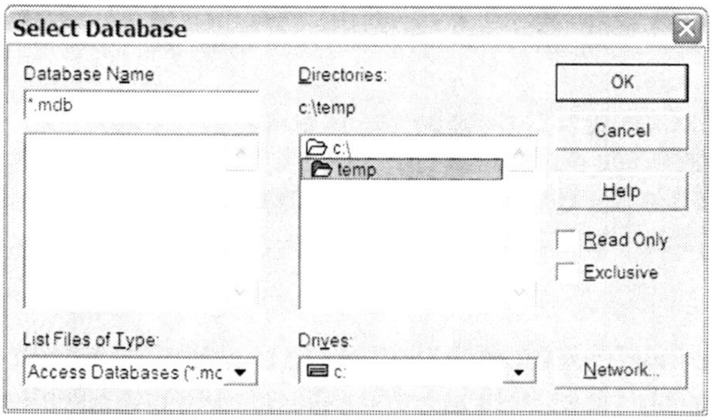

FIGURE 2-27
The Select Database dialog box when MS Access Database is selected on the Choose Data Source dialog box's Databases tab

Similarly, Figure 2-28 shows what the Select Workbook dialog box looks like when you select Excel Files on the Databases tab.

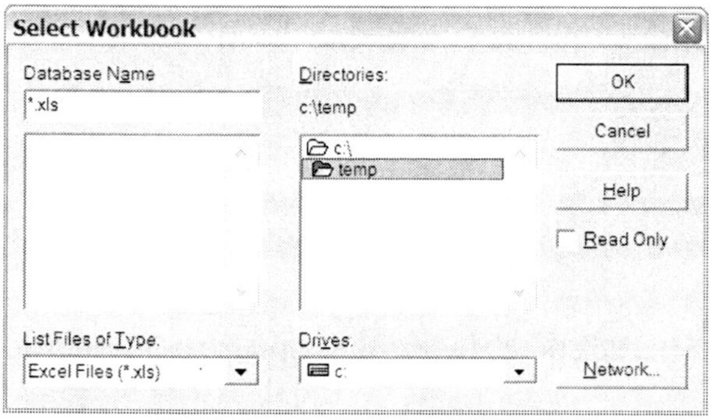

FIGURE 2-28
The Select Workbook dialog box when Excel Files is selected on the Choose Data Source dialog box's Databases tab

If you select the Use The Query Wizard To Create/Edit Queries check box before you create a new database connection on the Databases tab or choose an existing database connection on the Queries tab as shown in Figure 2-29, the Query Wizard is displayed when you click an entry on the Databases tab or Queries tab and click OK.

☑ Use the Query Wizard to create/edit queries

FIGURE 2-29

The Use The Query Wizard To Create/Edit Queries check box at the bottom of the Choose Data Source dialog box's Databases tab and Queries tab. Select this check box when you want to use the Query Wizard, an eaiser way to specify the data to which you want your PivotTable to connect.

The Query Wizard can be much easier for beginners to use then Microsoft Query, an advanced tool that can be used to import external data into Excel.

Let's try using the Query Wizard now. To do so, you'll need a copy of the sample Access Northwind database (Northwind.mdb), included with Access 2003.

1. With a blank worksheet visible, click Data ➤ PivotTable and PivotChart Report.

2. Click External Data Source, and then click Next.

3. Click Get Data.

4. On the Databases tab, click MS Access Database.

5. Make sure the Use The Query Wizard To Create/Edit Queries check box is selected, and then click OK.

6. In the Select Database dialog box, browse to and select the Northwind.mdb file, and then click OK. The Choose Columns page appears.

7. Click Customers, and then click the right arrow. Compare your results to Figure 2-30.

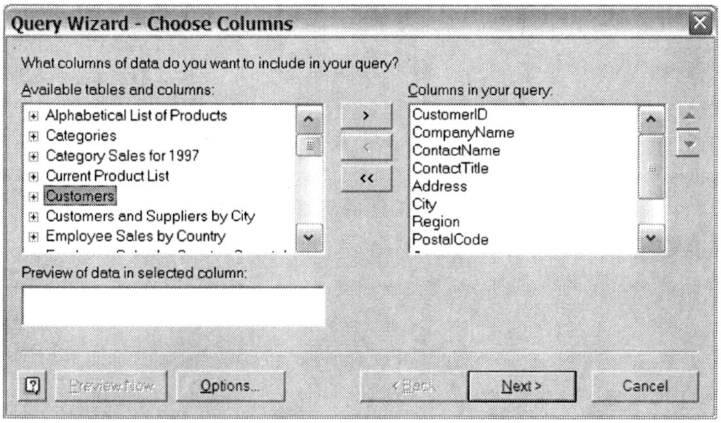

FIGURE 2-30

The Query Wizard's Choose Columns dialog box

8. Click Next. The Filter Data page appears.

9. Click Country, click Equals in the first row's left list, and click USA in the first row's right list, as shown in Figure 2-31.

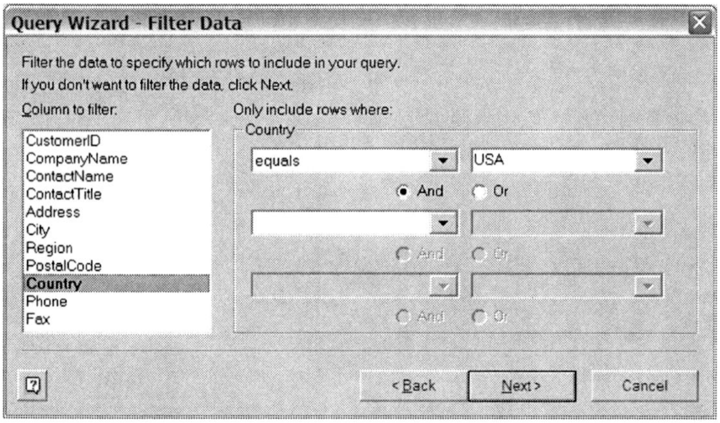

FIGURE 2-31

The Query Wizard's Filter Data dialog box

10. Click Next. The Sort Order page appears.

11. In the Sort By list, click CompanyName, as shown in Figure 2-32.

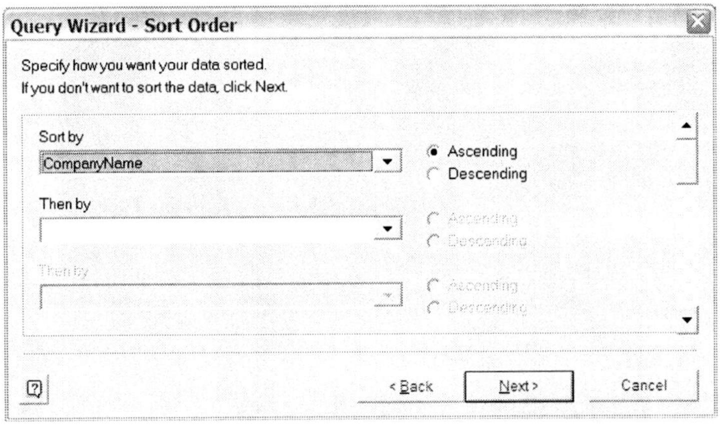

FIGURE 2-32

The Query Wizard's Sort Order dialog box

12. Click Next. The Finish page appears, as shown in Figure 2-33.

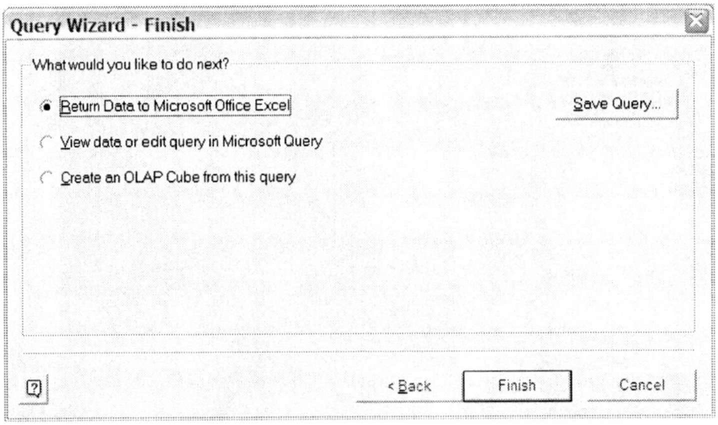

FIGURE 2-33

The Query Wizard's Finish dialog box

13. Click Finish, and click Finish again. The PivotTable is created, referencing only data for customers based in the United States of America.

As you've just seen, the Query Wizard is very intuitive to use. The same can't necessarily be said for Microsoft Query, as shown in Figure 2-34.

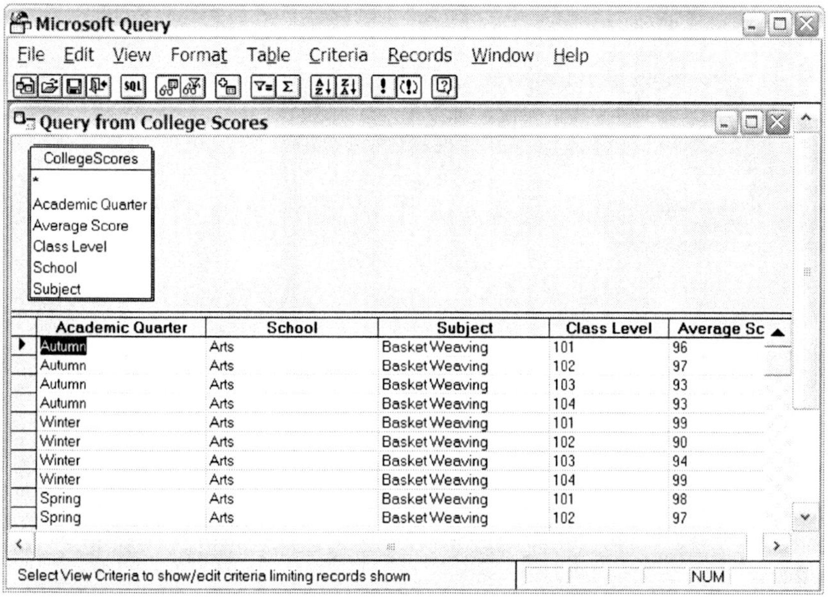

FIGURE 2-34
The Microsoft Query user interface

TIP You should use the Query Wizard when you want to

- Select entire data tables and/or entire columns only

- Perform simple data filtering and sorting

You should consider using Microsoft Query when you want to

- Reference data from two or more separate data sources

- Reference a database containing two or more data tables that are related to each other

- Set advanced data source connection or data retrieval options

- Issue advanced data retrieval commands using Structure Query Language (SQL)

- Perform a complicated filter or sort on the data, or you want to use more robust data filtering and sorting tools than the Query Wizard provides

To reference an existing data source connection, you can click Browse in the Choose Data Source dialog box. Data sources selected using this method typically have the extensions .udl, .dsn, .iqy, .dqy, and .oqy, as shown in Figure 2-35.

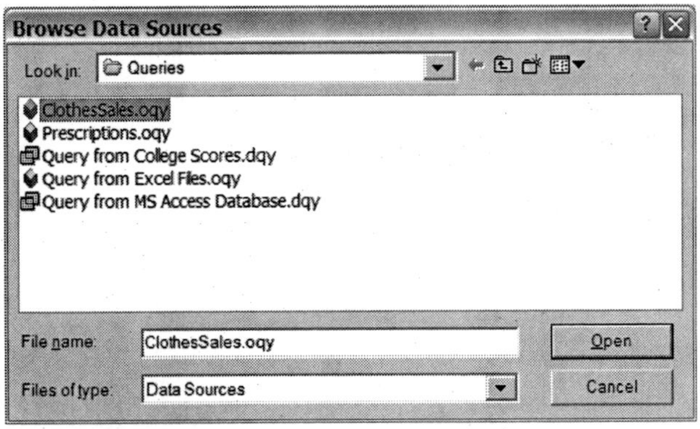

FIGURE 2-35

The Browse Data Source dialog box. Use this dialog box when you click Browse in the Data Source dialog box to reference an existing data source connection.

The two most common Excel data source connection files have either the .dqy extension (for database queries) or the .oqy extension (for OLAP cube files).

Setting PivotTable Report Formatting and Data Presentation Options

As you create PivotTables, you might want to change their formatting and data presentation styles. To do this as you create PivotTables, on Step 3 of the PivotTable and PivotChart Wizard, click Options. After you create PivotTables, you can click Table Options on the PivotTable menu of the PivotTable toolbar. In either case, the PivotTable Options dialog box appears, as shown in Figure 2-36.

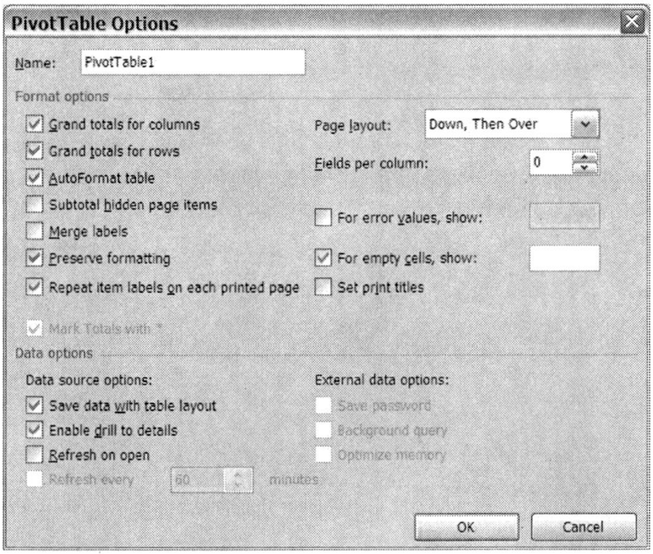

FIGURE 2-36

The PivotTable Options dialog box, which sets advanced formatting, layout, memory management, and external data options for your PivotTable or PivotChart

In the Name box at the top of the dialog box, you type the name that uniquely identifies the PivotTable, or you can leave the automatically generated PivotTable identifier, as shown in Figure 2-37. The next two sections describe the rest of the various choices in the PivotTable Options dialog box.

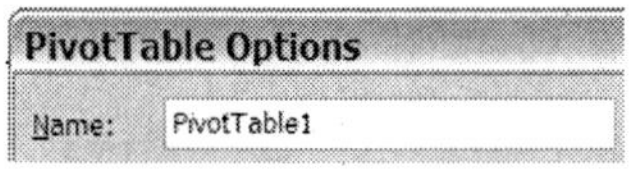

FIGURE 2-37

The PivotTable Options dialog box's Name box, which is used to uniquely identify the PivotTable

Format Options Area

The Format Options area's controls include the following, as shown in
Figure 2-38:

> **NOTE** Several terms are used in these descriptions (such as *items* and
> *page fields*) that might be unfamiliar to you. These terms will be defined in
> the next chapter.

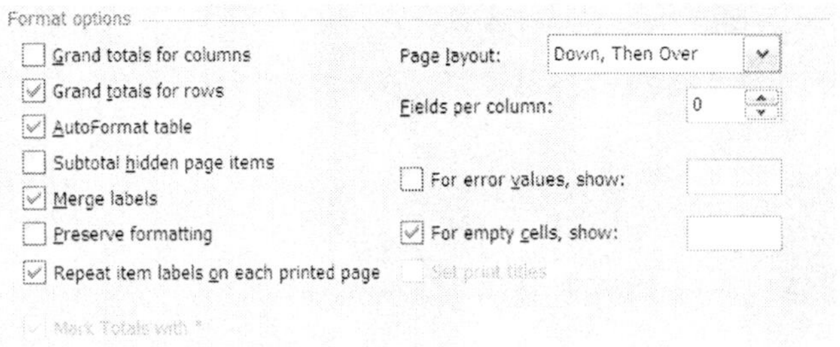

FIGURE 2-38

The PivotTable Options dialog box's Format Options area, which is used to
determine the PivotTable's visual format

- *Grand Totals For Columns check box*: Select this check box to display
  grand totals for each column in the PivotTable.

- *Grand Totals For Rows check box*: Select this check box to display grand
  totals for each row in the PivotTable.

- *AutoFormat Table check box*: If an AutoFormat has been applied to the
  PivotTable, clearing this check box removes the AutoFormat.

- *Subtotal Hidden Page Items check box*: Select this check box to subtotal
  any items that are hidden.

- *Merge Labels check box*: Select this check box to use merged cells for
  outer row and column (for example, to merge repeating values such as
  "Month" in the first several rows into a single cell titled "Month").

- *Preserve Formatting check box*: Select this check box to make sure that
  formatting will be preserved if you refresh the PivotTable's underlying
  data.

- *Repeat Item Labels On Each Printed Page check box*: Select this check
  box if you want to print a PivotTable, it has more than one row field, and
  you also want to repeat outer row field items on each page.

- *Mark Totals With * check box*: Select this check box to indicate that subtotals and grand totals in PivotTables include the values for all items in a field, including any items that you have hidden.

- *Page Layout list*: Select a choice in this list to determine whether a multiple-page PivotTable is printed top-to-bottom (Down, Then Over) or left-to-right (Over, Then Down).

- *Fields Per Column list*: Type the number of fields you want to show in each column of a PivotTable with multiple page fields.

- *For Error Values Show check box*: Select this check box to display or clear text in cells that contain errors, and then type the text you want to display instead of errors. To display errors as blank cells, delete any characters in the box to the right of the check box.

- *For Empty Values Show check box*: Select this check box to display or clear text in cells that contain empty values, and then type the text you want to display instead of empty values. To display empty values as blank cells, delete any characters in the box to the right of the check box.

- *Set Print Titles check box*: For a printed PivotTable, select this check box to repeat the row and column labels from the PivotTable on each printed page.

Data Options Area

The Data Options area's controls include the following, as shown in Figure 2-39:

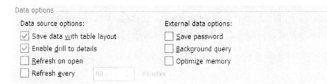

FIGURE 2-39

The PivotTable Options dialog box's Data Options area, which is used to determine the PivotTable's behaviors toward its data source and external data

- *Save Data With Table Layout check box*: Select this check box to save the data along with the PivotTable.

- *Enable Drill To Details check box*: Select this check box to enable drilling from summarized data into the underlying detailed data.

- *Refresh On Open check box*: Select this check box to automatically refresh the PivotTable with data from the underlying data source when the workbook is first opened.

- *Refresh Every check box*: Select this check box to refresh the PivotTable with data from the underlying data source on a given interval of minutes after the workbook is first opened.

- *Save Password check box*: Select this check box to save your password to access external data (if your external data source requires a password) with the workbook.

- *Background Query check box*: Select this check box to allow you to use Excel for other purposes while Excel retrieves your PivotChart's underlying data from an external data source.

- *Optimize Memory check box*: Select this check box to make the best use of computing memory when retrieving external data to summarize in a PivotTable.

Try It! Create a PivotTable Using the Wizard

Let's practice more of what you've learned so far. In this exercise, you'll use the PivotTable and PivotChart Wizard to create a PivotTable from an external data source, in this case summarizing a full academic year's worth of average test scores for all classes offered at a small liberal arts college.

Connecting to the Source Data

The data source in this exercise is a comma-separated value file that was exported from a file server. The file is named CollegeScores.csv and is available from the Apress Web site Downloads section at http://www.apress.com.
Use the PivotTable and PivotChart Wizard to connect to the comma-separated value file and then create a PivotTable based on the file's data:

1. Start Excel. A new blank workbook should be created for you already.

2. Click Data ➤ PivotTable and PivotChart Report.

3. Select the External Data Source option and then click Next.

4. Click Get Data.

5. Make sure the Use The Query Wizard To Create/Edit Queries check box is selected.

6. On the Databases tab, click <New Data Source>, and then click OK.

7. In the What Name Do You Want To Give Your Data Source box, type **College Scores**.

8. In the Select A Driver For The Type Of Database You Want To Access list, select Microsoft Text Driver (*.txt; *.csv).

9. Click Connect.

10. Clear the Use Current Directory check box.

11. Click Select Directory.

12. Browse to the directory containing the CollegeScores.csv file and then click OK. (For example, if the CollegeScores.csv file is in the root of your C:\ drive, browse to and select the C:\ drive in the Select Directory dialog box. The CollegeScores.csv file should then be visible in the File Name list.) The ODBC Text Setup dialog box should now look similar to Figure 2-40 (provided you also click the Options button).

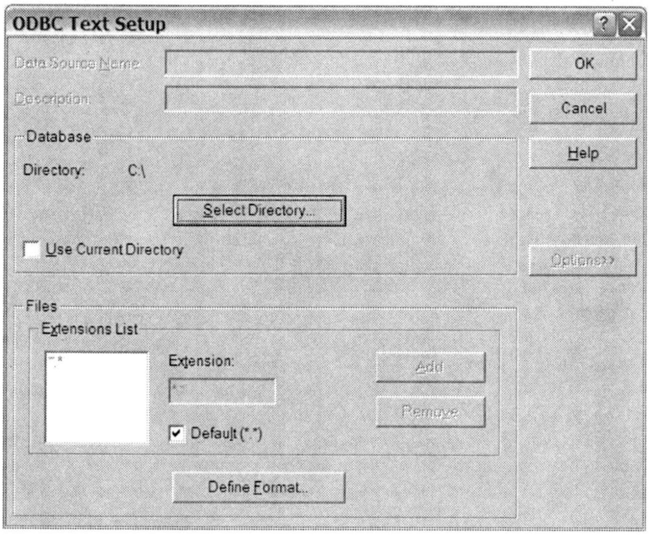

FIGURE 2-40
The ODBC Text Setup dialog box

13. Click OK.

14. In the Select A Default Table For Your Data Source list, select CollegeScores.csv. The Create New Data Source dialog box should now look similar to Figure 2-41.

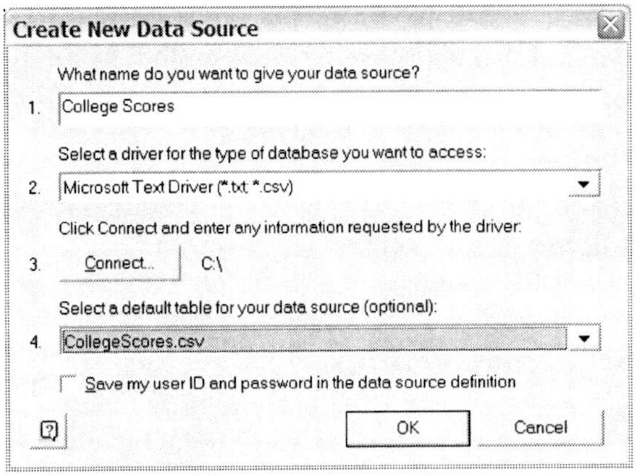

FIGURE 2-41
The Create New Data Source dialog box

15. Click OK.

16. Click OK again. The Choose Columns page of the Query Wizard appears.

17. Click the right arrow (>), and compare your results to Figure 2-42.

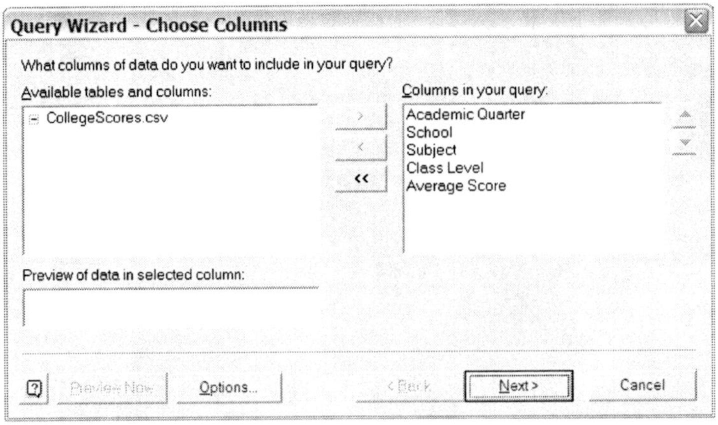

FIGURE 2-42
The Choose Columns dialog box, including all columns from the CollegeScores.csv file

18. Click Next. The Filter Data dialog box of the Query Wizard appears.

19. Because you don't want to filter the data right now, click Next. The Sort Order dialog box of the Query Wizard appears.

20. Again, because you don't want to sort the data right now, click Next.

21. Click Save Query.

22. Click Save.

23. Click Finish.

24. Click Next.

25. Click Finish. The PivotTable is created and looks similar to Figure 2-43.

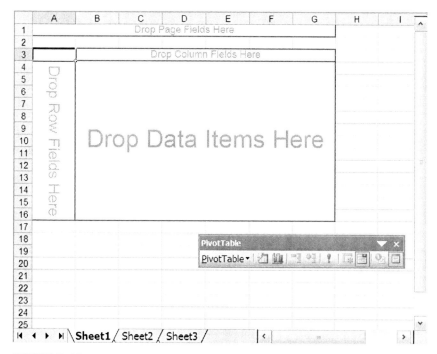

FIGURE 2-43
PivotTable for analyzing the college scores

Defining the PivotTable's Initial Layout

Now, customize the PivotTable that you just created:

1. In the PivotTable Field List dialog box, click School, and in the Add To list, select Page Area, as shown in Figure 2-44.

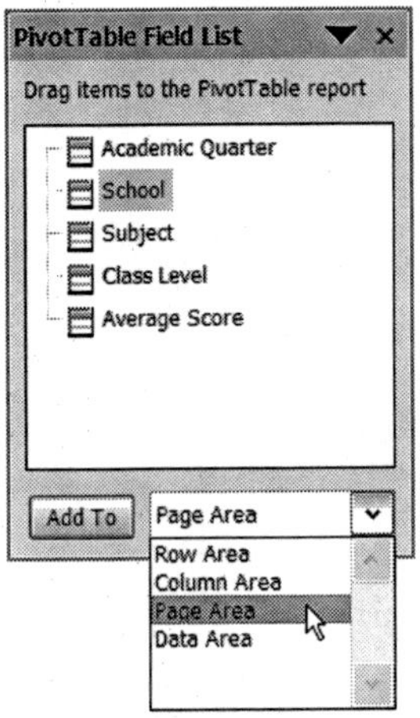

FIGURE 2-44

The PivotTable Field List dialog box, with the School field selected, about to be added to the Page Area

If the PivotTable Field List dialog box is not visible, on the PivotTable toolbar, click the Show Field List button, as shown in Figure 2-45. If the PivotTable toolbar is not visible, first click anywhere inside the PivotTable. If the PivotTable toolbar is still not visible, click View ➤ Toolbars ➤ PivotTable.

FIGURE 2-45

The PivotTable toolbar's Show Field List button

2. Click Add To.

3. In the PivotTable Field List, click Academic Quarter.

4. Click Add To.

5. In the PivotTable Field List, click Subject.

6. Click Add To.

7. In the PivotTable Field List, click Class Level. Compare your work to Figure 2-46.

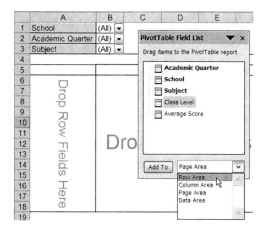

FIGURE 2-46

The PivotTable with the School, Academic Quarter, and Subject fields added to the page area. The Class Level is about to be added to the row area

8. In the Add To list, select Row Area, and then click Add To.

9. In the PivotTable Field List, click Average Score.

10. In the Add To list, select Data Area, and then click Add To. The Average Score field is added to the data area. The PivotTable should look similar to Figure 2-47.

	A	B
1	School	(All) ▾
2	Academic Quarter	(All) ▾
3	Subject	(All) ▾
4		
5	Sum of Average Score	
6	Class Level ▾	Total
7	101	5684
8	102	5714
9	103	5686
10	104	5681
11	Grand Total	22765

FIGURE 2-47

Initial layout for the PivotTable

Changing the Summary Function and Number Formatting

Now change the Sum Of Average Score field to an Average Of Average Score field. At the same time, change the number format to remove the fractional portion of the average scores.

1. Right-click cell A5 (the Sum Of Average Score field) and click Field Settings.

2. In the Summarize By list, select Average.

3. Click Number.

4. In the Category list, select Number.

5. In the Decimal Places box, click the Down button until the number zero (0) appears. The Format Cells dialog box should look similar to Figure 2-48.

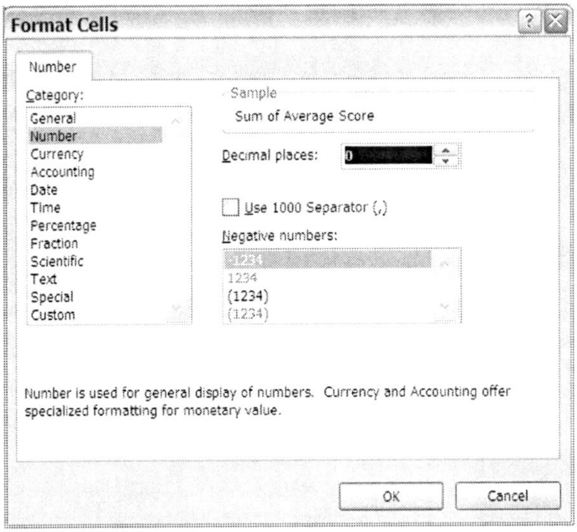

FIGURE 2-48
The Format Cells dialog box

6. Click OK. The PivotTable Field List dialog box appears. It should look similar to Figure 2-49.

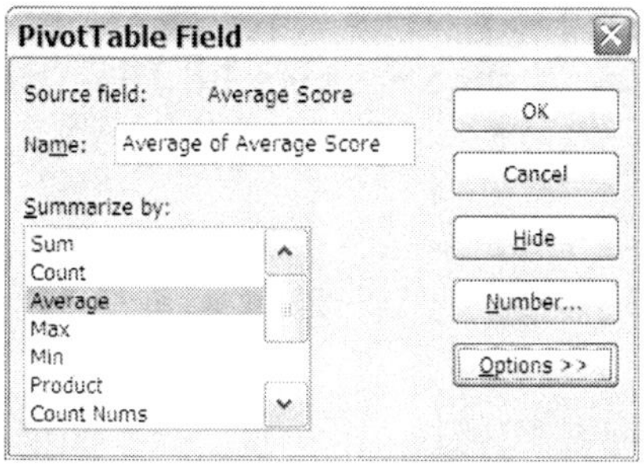

FIGURE 2-49
The PivotTable Field dialog box

7. Click OK. The PivotTable should look similar to Figure 2-50.

FIGURE 2-50
Average scores are displayed instead of score sums

Filtering the PivotTable's Data

Next, show average scores for Chemistry classes in the Sciences school for Autumn quarter:

1. Click the Filter button in cell B1 (the School field).

2. Click Sciences, and then click OK.

3. Click the Filter button in cell B2 (the Academic Quarter field).

4. Click Autumn, and then click OK.

5. Click the Filter button in cell B3 (the Subject field).

6. Click Chemistry, and then click OK. The PivotTable now displays average scores for Chemistry classes in the Sciences school for Autumn quarter, as shown in Figure 2-51.

	A	B
1	School	Sciences ▾
2	Academic Quarter	Autumn ▾
3	Subject	Chemistry ▾
4		
5	Average of Average Score	
6	Class Level ▾	Total
7	101	89
8	102	84
9	103	81
10	104	83
11	Grand Total	84

FIGURE 2-51

Average scores for Chemistry classes in the Sciences school for Autumn quarter

Now modify the PivotTable so that you can see average scores for all of the academic quarters for Geography in the Arts school at the same time:

1. In the PivotTable Field List dialog box, click Academic Quarter.

2. In the Add To list, select Row Area, and then click Add To.

3. In the PivotTable Field List dialog box, click Class Level.

4. In the Add To list, select Column Area, and then click Add To. Compare your results to Figure 2-52.

	A	B	C	D	E	F
1						
2	School	Sciences ▾				
3	Subject	Chemistry ▾				
4						
5	Average of Average Score	Class Level ▾				
6	Academic Quarter ▾	101	102	103	104	Grand Total
7	Autumn	89	84	81	83	84
8	Spring	88	81	87	81	84
9	Summer	86	82	85	84	84
10	Winter	81	84	84	81	83
11	Grand Total	86	83	84	82	84

FIGURE 2-52

Average scores for Chemistry classes by quarter and by class level

5. Click the Filter button in cell B2 (the School field).

6. Click Arts, and then click OK.

7. Click the Filter button in cell B3 (the Subject field).

8. Click Geography, and then click OK. The average scores in the PivotTable change to reflect the average scores for all of the academic quarters for Geography in the Arts school at the same time, as shown in Figure 2-53.

	A	B	C	D	E	F
1						
2	School	Arts ▾				
3	Subject	Geography ▾				
4						
5	Average of Average Score	Class Level ▾				
6	Academic Quarter ▾	101	102	103	104	Grand Total
7	Autumn	88	94	90	85	89
8	Spring	90	86	93	93	91
9	Summer	91	94	88	93	92
10	Winter	93	90	88	89	90
11	Grand Total	91	91	90	90	90

FIGURE 2-53

Average scores for Geography classes by quarter and by class level

Next Steps

In this chapter, you built on your existing skills by learning how to specify and connect to source data and create a PivotTable based on the data source connection. You also know how to create a new data source connection if you need to. You can set a PivotTable's report formatting and data presentation options. And, you can now create a PivotTable using the PivotTable and PivotChart Wizard.

Before you proceed with the next chapter, you might want to use the Try It! exercises in this chapter to connect to some of your organization's existing source data and practice turning the source data into a PivotTable using the PivotTable and PivotChart Wizard. The more comfortable you are with using the PivotTable and PivotChart Wizard, the easier time you'll have in working with the PivotTable Field List dialog box, toolbar, and menu in the next chapter. As you learn additional skills for working with PivotTables throughout this book, you can apply these skills to your own data and analyze your data even better than before.

3

Working with PivotTable Components

In the previous two chapters, you worked with the PivotTable and Pivot-Chart Wizard to create and customize simple and straightforward PivotTables. In this chapter, you'll learn more about working with PivotTable components such as *fields*, *drop areas*, and the PivotTable Field List dialog box. These components give you tools you need for more advanced data analysis tasks. Specifically, you'll

- Go farther in your understanding of how row, column, data, and page fields work. Knowing how to work with fields is the key to working with PivotTables.

- Learn how field items in row, column, data, and page areas work together to create more sophisticated PivotTables for deeper data analysis tasks.

- Learn how to use the PivotTable Field List dialog box, the PivotTable toolbar, and the PivotTable menu to quickly and easily change your PivotTables to show the results you want.

By the end of this chapter, you'll be able to create some fairly advanced PivotTables. You'll know how to move data around in PivotTables, show only the data you want, and analyze the data in ways you weren't easily able to do before.

Understanding Row, Column, Data, Page, and Calculated Fields and Field Items

You've run into the terms *row fields, column fields, data fields, page fields,* and *items* as you created and worked with PivotTables in the first two chapters. To help you better understand how to use the PivotTable components, let's review and define these five PivotTable terms, as well as other related terms. You'll need to understand these terms to complete this chapter's exercises.

Figure 3-1 represents source data for a PivotTable. Each row of facts and figures (also known as *data*) in this list (for example, cells A2 through C2) represents one *record* that the PivotTable can summarize. Each record consists of one or more *fields*. In this case, the fields are Date, Tide, and Height.

	A	B	C
1	Date	Tide	Height
2	1-Mar	High	10.3
3	1-Mar	Low	8.2
4	1-Mar	High	9.0
5	1-Mar	Low	0.7
6	2-Mar	High	10.8
7	2-Mar	Low	7.8
8	2-Mar	High	9.0
9	2-Mar	Low	0.3
10	3-Mar	High	11.2
11	3-Mar	Low	7.4
12	3-Mar	High	9.2
13	3-Mar	Low	0.0

FIGURE 3-1

Source data for a PivotTable. This data contains 12 records (rows 2 through 13). Each record contains three fields (columns A through C).

To better help you understand these terms, let's dive right in and create a PivotTable:

1. Create a new Excel workbook and type the data in Figure 3-1 in a blank worksheet.

2. Click Data ➤ PivotTable and PivotChart Report.

3. Make sure the Microsoft Office Excel List Or Database and PivotTable options are selected, and then click Next.

4. Select the cells you typed in step 1, and then click Next.

TIP You can quickly select a large group of cells by clicking the first cell, holding down the Shift key, and then clicking the last cell.

5. Make sure the New Worksheet option is selected, and click Finish.

Figure 3-2 represents a new blank PivotTable based on the source data in Figure 3-1.

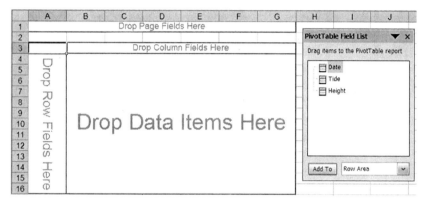

FIGURE 3-2

A new blank PivotTable based on the data in Figure 3-1

Now that you've create a new blank PivotTable, let's get more familiar with the PivotTable's *drop areas*.

Drop Areas

The areas labeled Drop Row Fields Here, Drop Column Fields Here, Drop Page Fields Here, and Drop Data Items Here in a PivotTable are collectively referred to as *drop areas*, as called out in Figure 3-3.

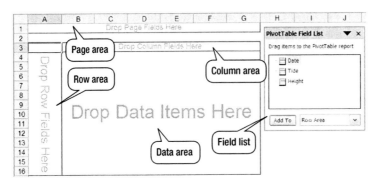

FIGURE 3-3
A PivotTable's drop areas and the field list. You drop fields from the field list onto the PivotTable's drop areas.

You drop fields from the PivotTable Field List dialog box on to these drop areas. Each of these drop areas are individually referred to as the *row area, column area, page area,* and *data area.*

Using the PivotTable shown in Figure 3-2, let's try this:

1. Drag the Date field from the PivotTable Field List dialog box to the row area, as shown in Figure 3-4.

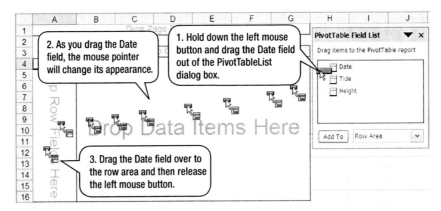

FIGURE 3-4
Dragging the Date field from the PivotTable Field List dialog box to the PivotTable's row area

2. Drag the Tide field from the PivotTable Field List dialog box to the column area.

3. Drag the Height field from the PivotTable Field List dialog box to the data area.

Figure 3-5 represents a PivotTable that summarizes the source data shown earlier in Figure 3-1.

	A	B	C	D
1	Drop Page Fields Here			
2				
3	Sum of Height	Tide ▾		
4	Date ▾	High	Low	Grand Total
5	1-Mar	19.3	8.9	28.2
6	2-Mar	19.8	8.1	27.9
7	3-Mar	20.4	7.4	27.8
8	Grand Total	59.5	24.4	83.9

FIGURE 3-5

A customized PivotTable based on the data in Figure 3-1

Let's explore the field list in more detail.

Field List

The PivotTable Field List, also referred to simply as the *field list*, displays all of the *fields* in the source data, as shown in Figure 3-6.

The data source's fields

When you click the Add To button, this is the drop area on the PivotTable onto which you want to place the selected field (or you can simply drag a field to the desired drop area on the PivotTable).

FIGURE 3-6

The PivotTable Field List dialog box. You drop fields from the field list onto the PivotTable's drop areas.

Any field name in the field list displayed in bold indicates the field already appears in the PivotTable. The field list is one of two tools that you can use to customize the layout of fields in PivotTables. (The other tool, the Layout page of the PivotTable and PivotChart Wizard, is explained later in this section.)

NOTE If the PivotTable Field List is not visible, click Show Field List on the PivotTable toolbar, or right-click a field in the PivotTable and select Show Field List. If the PivotTable toolbar is not visible, click View ➤ Toolbars ➤ PivotTable, or right-click a field in the PivotTable and select Show PivotTable Toolbar.

You can drop fields from the field list onto a PivotTable in two ways. The first way is to select a field in the field list, select a drop area in the list to the right of the Add To button, and then click the Add To button. The second way is to select a field in the field list, and then drag the selected field to the desired PivotTable drop area, as shown in Figures 3-7 and 3-8.

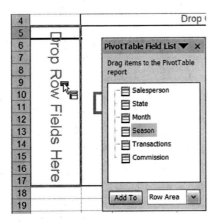

FIGURE 3-7

Actively dragging the Season field from the field list to the PivotTable's row area

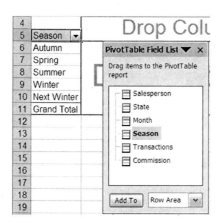

FIGURE 3-8

The result of dropping the Season field from the field list onto the PivotTable's row area

As you move the mouse pointer into the PivotTable, you'll see the mouse pointer change into one of the five icons shown in Table 3-1.

TABLE 3-1

Pointer Icons

Icon	Meaning
	The selected field is being dragged, but is not ready to be dropped onto the PivotTable.
	The selected field is ready to be dropped onto the row area.
	The selected field is ready to be dropped onto the column area.
	The selected field is ready to be dropped onto the data area.
	The selected field is ready to be dropped onto the page area.

To remove a field from the PivotTable, select the desired field button, drag the field outside of the PivotTable's boundaries until the icon looks like Figure 3-9, and then drop the field outside of the PivotTable.

FIGURE 3-9
The selected field is ready to be removed from the PivotTable

TIP You can also remove the field from the PivotTable by right-clicking the desired field button and clicking the Hide command from the context menu that appears.

NOTE Removing a field from the PivotTable does not remove the field from the field list nor the source data. You can then add the field back into the PivotTable if you want to by using the methods just described.

You can also lay out fields on a PivotTable another way, as you'll see next.

Using the Layout Page of the PivotTable and PivotChart Wizard

Sometimes, especially when working with source data that has several thousand rows or more, you'll discover that it takes a long time when you drop a field onto a PivotTable before you can perform other actions in Excel. In this case, you might be able to decrease your wait time by using the Layout dialog box of Step 3 of the PivotTable and PivotChart Wizard instead of using the field list.

You can get to Step 3 of the PivotTable and PivotChart Wizard as follows:

1. Click inside the boundaries of an existing PivotTable, and then do one of the following:

   - Click PivotTable ➤ PivotTable Wizard on the PivotTable toolbar.

   - Right-click a field button and click PivotTable Wizard from the context menu that appears.

   - Click Data ➤ PivotTable and PivotChart Report.

2. Click the Layout button to display the Layout dialog box of the PivotTable and PivotChart Wizard, as shown in Figure 3-10.

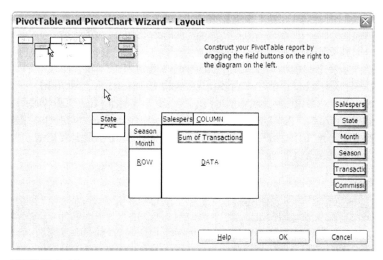

FIGURE 3-10

The Layout dialog box of the PivotTable and PivotChart Wizard. Use this dialog box to more quickly lay out fields with a lot of field items.

Using this dialog box is very straightforward. Simply drag the field buttons on the right to the drop areas in the diagram on the left. In Figure 3-10, the State field is in the page area, the Season and Month fields are in the row area, the Salesperson field is in the column area, and the Transactions field is in the data area. When you're finished using the Layout page, click OK and then click Finish to return to your PivotTable.

Field Buttons

In the PivotTable shown earlier in Figure 3-5, the Date field is a row field, the Tide field is a column field, and the Sum of Height field is a data field. Each field is represented by a gray *field button* containing the field's name. After you drop fields onto the PivotTable, you can drag the gray field buttons among a PivotTable's drop areas to change the PivotTable's layout. You can also right-click field buttons to change how the fields' data is displayed. In some cases, you can click a field button's arrow to restrict how much data is displayed.

Inner and Outer Row and Column Fields

Row fields and column fields can be related to each other and can be nested. In a PivotTable, the row field or column field closest in position to the data area is referred to as the *inner row field* (or *inner column field*, for column fields). The other row or column fields are referred to as *outer row fields* (or *outer column fields*, for column fields).

Fields can also be moved among the drop areas after the fields are added to a PivotTable. Let's try moving a column field to an inner row field.

Using the PivotTable shown earlier in Figure 3-5, drag the Tide field button to the right edge of the Date column. The mouse pointer changes its appearance and an "I-beam" appears between the Date column and data drop area, as shown in Figure 3-11.

	A	B	C	D
1	Drop Page Fields Here			
2				
3	Sum of Height	Tide ▼		
4	Date ▼	High	Low	Grand Total
5	1-Mar	19.3	8.9	28.2
6	2-Mar	19.8	8.1	27.9
7	3-Mar	20.4	7.4	27.8
8	Grand Total	59.5	24.4	83.9

FIGURE 3-11

Dragging a field to the row drop area as an inner row field. The I-beam provides a visual cue that the field will be added to the right of the existing row field.

When you release the left mouse button, the Tide field now becomes an inner row field, as shown in Figure 3-12. Accordingly, the Date field now becomes an outer row field.

	A	B	C
1	Drop Page Fields Here		
2			
3	Sum of Height		
4	Date ▾	Tide ▾	Total
5	1-Mar	High	19.3
6		Low	8.9
7	1-Mar Total		28.2
8	2-Mar	High	19.8
9		Low	8.1
10	2-Mar Total		27.9
11	3-Mar	High	20.4
12		Low	7.4
13	3-Mar Total		27.8
14	Grand Total		83.9

FIGURE 3-12

The Tide field is an inner row field. The Date field is now an outer row field.

Field Placement Restrictions

Fields in the field list can have one of three icons. The icons shown in Table 3-2 specify whether any restrictions apply to the drop areas in which the corresponding field can be placed in the PivotTable.

TABLE 3-2

Field Icons

Icon	Meaning
	Fields with this icon can be placed in any drop area.
	Fields with this icon can be placed only in row, column, and page areas.
	Fields with this icon can be placed only in the data area.

These icons help you more quickly determine in which PivotTable drop area you can place any particular field.

Field Items

Let's move from fields to field items. Each field contains one or more unique subcategories (also referred to as *members*) from the source data. These subcategories or entries are referred to as *items*. For example, using the Pivot-Table in Figure 3-13, the Date field is comprised of the 1-Mar, 2-Mar, and 3-Mar items. Similarly, the Tide field is comprised of the High and Low items.

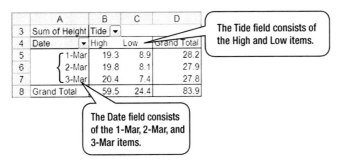

FIGURE 3-13

A field's unique subcategories or members are called *items*.

    It's important to note fields with text-based items (such as the Date and Tide fields) are good candidates for the row, column, and page areas, whereas fields with numbers (such as the Height field) are good candidates for the data area. When you drop a field containing numbers onto the data area, the Sum summary function is invoked by default. However, when you drop a field containing text onto the data area, the Count summary function is invoked instead. You can change these functions as you customize a PivotTable.

Item Filters

You can filter the fields in a PivotTable to display summarized data only for specific items. To do this, click the arrow in any field button for a row field, column field, or page field. A corresponding *field drop-down list* appears showing the items available for display in a field. Let's try using the fields' drop-down lists to show data only for the low tide for 2-Mar.

   1. Using the PivotTable in Figure 3-12, in the PivotTable Field List dialog box, click the Tide icon. In the list next to the Add To button, select Column Area, and then click OK. Then click the arrow in the Tide field button.

2. Clear the High check box, as shown in Figure 3-14, and then click OK.

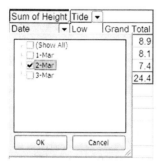

Sum of Height	Tide ▾	
Date ▾	☐ (Show All)	
1-Mar	High	
2-Mar	✔ Low	
3-Mar		
Grand Total		

OK   Cancel

FIGURE 3-14

The field drop-down list for the Tide column field. Only the Low item will be displayed.

3. Click the arrow in the Date field button.

4. Clear the (Show All) check box.

5. Select the 2-Mar check box, as shown in Figure 3-15.

Sum of Height	Tide ▾	
Date ▾	Low	Grand Total
☐ (Show All)		8.9
☐ 1-Mar		8.1
✔ 2-Mar		7.4
☐ 3-Mar		24.4

OK   Cancel

FIGURE 3-15

The field drop-down list for the Date column field. Only the 2-Mar item will be displayed.

6. Click OK. Compare your results to Figure 3-16.

Sum of Height	Tide ▾	
Date ▾	Low	Grand Total
2-Mar	8.1	8.1
Grand Total	8.1	8.1

FIGURE 3-16

PivotTable showing only data for the 2-Mar item

Any box with a check mark in it means that the corresponding item will be displayed in the PivotTable; any box without a check mark in it means that the corresponding item won't be displayed in the PivotTable. Placing a check mark in the (Show All) check box automatically places check marks in all of the boxes in a field drop-down list.

As noted in the previous exercise, you can quickly remove the check marks in all of the drop-down list boxes of a field by removing the check mark in the (Show All) box.

If a field is organized in levels of detail, you can click the plus or minus symbol next to a box to see which detail items are selected to display, as shown in Figure 3-17.

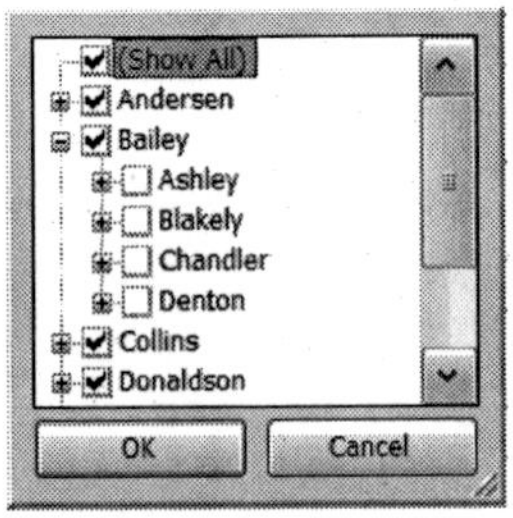

FIGURE 3-17

A field organized in levels of detail. Clicking a plus symbol displays lower levels of detail. Clicking a minus symbol hides lower levels of detail.

A double check mark in a box means that some or all of the detail items are displayed, as shown in Figure 3-18.

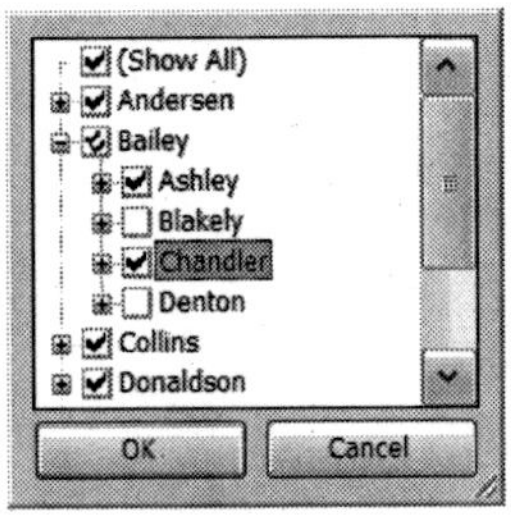

FIGURE 3-18

The double check mark in the Blakely check box means that one or more detail items (in this case, the Ashley and Chandler detail items) are selected.

This last type of field is primarily used in conjunction with OLAP-based PivotTables, as detailed in Chapter 6.

Calculated Fields and Items

You can also create your own data fields to perform custom calculations. These fields are called *calculated fields,* and they exist only for the duration of the PivotTable. Let's practice creating a calculated field, representing the clearance between the tide level and a reef line by using the PivotTable you created in Figure 3-16.

1. Click anywhere inside the PivotTable.

2. On the PivotTable toolbar, click PivotTable ➤ Formulas ➤ Calculated Field. The Insert Calculated Field dialog box displays, as shown in Figure 3-19.

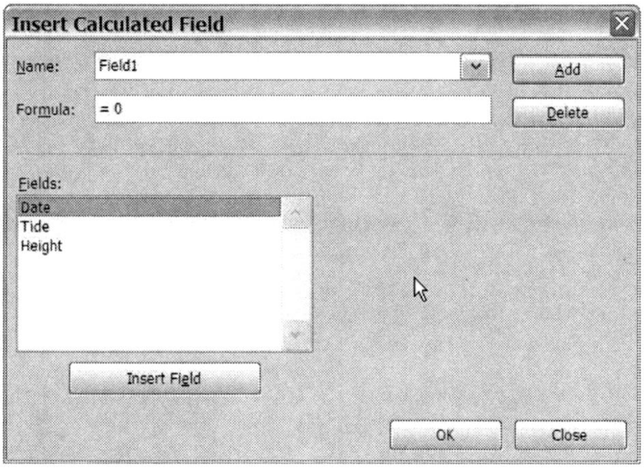

FIGURE 3-19
The Insert Calculated Field dialog box, which is used to create a calculated field containing a custom calculation

The options in the Insert Calculated Field dialog box include the following:

- The Name box allows you to rename the calculated field to something more that is easier to use.
- The Formula box allows you to type the custom calculation. For example, if you wanted a custom calculation that displayed the tide's height multiplied by 75%, you would type **=Height*.75** in the Formula box.
- The Insert Field button inserts the selection in the Fields list into the Formula box at the insertion point.
- The Add button adds the field in the Name box to the Fields list; the Delete button removes the field in the Name box from the Fields list.
- The OK button adds the field to the PivotTable's data area and the field list.

Let's finish creating the calculated field.

3. In the Name box, replace the text Field1 with the text **Reef Clearance**.

4. Click Height.

5. Click Insert Field.

6. After the text =Height, type **-5.0**. Compare your results with Figure 3-20.

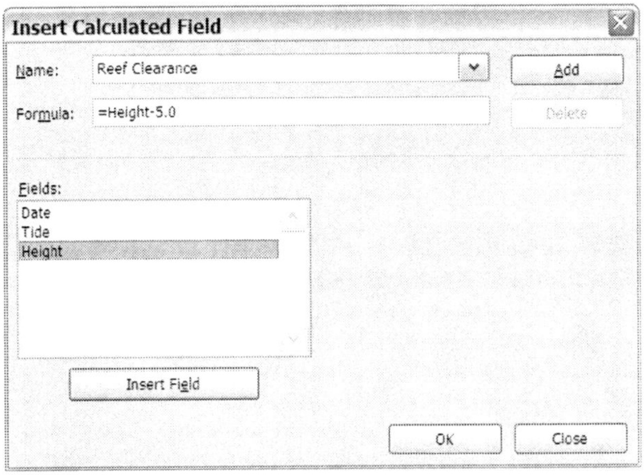

FIGURE 3-20

Completing the Insert Calculated Field dialog box. The Reef Clearance field consists of the Height field's value minus 5.0.

7. Click OK. Compare your results to Figure 3-21.

		Tide ▼	
Date ▼	Data ▼	Low	Grand Total
2-Mar	Sum of Height	8.1	8.1
	Sum of Reef Clearance	3.1	3.1
Total Sum of Height		8.1	8.1
Total Sum of Reef Clearance		3.1	3.1

FIGURE 3-21

The finished PivotTable containing the Sum of Reef Clearance
calculated field

For row and column fields, you can also create calculated items. Let's create a calculated item, representing a projected tide height for 4-Mar, using the PivotTable in Figure 3-21.

1. Click the Date field button.

2. On the PivotTable toolbar, click PivotTable ➤ Formulas ➤ Calculated Item. The Insert Calculated Item dialog box displays, as shown in Figure 3-22.

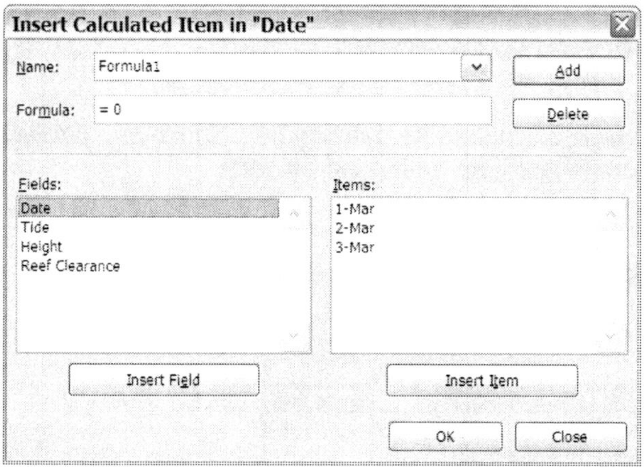

FIGURE 3-22

The Insert Calculated Item dialog box, which is used to create a
calculated item containing a custom calculation

TIP The Insert Calculated Item dialog box is similar to the Insert Calculated Fields dialog box, except that it also allows you to add items to your custom calculations.

3. In the Name box, replace the text Fomula1 with the text **4-Mar (Projected)**.

4. Click 3-Mar, and then click Insert Item.

5. After the text ='3-Mar', type ***0.75** and compare your results with Figure 3-23.

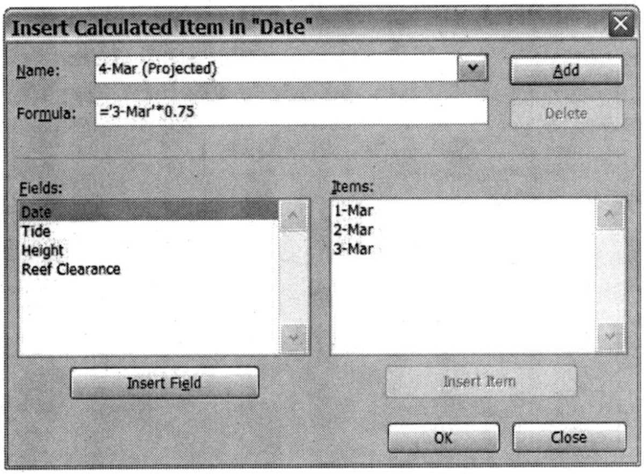

FIGURE 3-23

Completing the Insert Calculated Item dialog box. The 4–Mar (Projected) item consists of the 3–Mar item multiplied by 75%.

6. Click OK. Compare your results with Figure 3-24.

Date	Data	Tide Low	Grand Total
2-Mar	Sum of Height	8.1	8.1
	Sum of Reef Clearance	3.1	3.1
4-Mar (Projected)	Sum of Height	5.55	5.55
	Sum of Reef Clearance	0.6	0.6
Total Sum of Height		13.65	13.65
Total Sum of Reef Clearance		8.7	8.7

FIGURE 3-24

The finished PivotTable containing the 4–Mar (Projected) calculated item

Calculated fields and items allow you to add "what if" analysis to your PivotTables. You can dynamically create fields and items that contain custom calculations based on other information your PivotTable provides.

Now, let's move from talking about fields and items to exploring the PivotTable toolbar.

Working with the PivotTable Toolbar

The PivotTable toolbar, shown in Figure 3-25, allows you to perform common tasks for working with PivotTables, such as customizing how data is displayed and creating charts based on the source data.

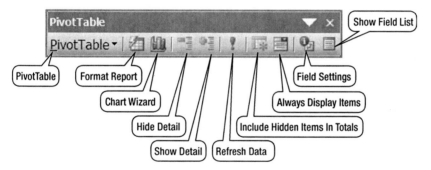

FIGURE 3-25

The PivotTable toolbar allows you to perform common tasks for working with PivotTables.

> **NOTE** If the PivotTable toolbar is not visible, click View ➤ Toolbars ➤ PivotTable, or right-click a field in the PivotTable and select Show PivotTable Toolbar. (Be aware that the PivotTable toolbar might be docked with other toolbars near the top of the Excel window.)

The toolbar's commands, from left to right, are as follows:

- *PivotTable button*: Displays the PivotTable menu, detailed in the next section.

- *Format Report button*: Displays the AutoFormat dialog box, which allows you to change the PivotTable's overall visual display format.

- *Chart Wizard button*: Creates a PivotChart with a default visual display format based on the current PivotTable.

- *Hide Detail button*: Hides detailed information in a PivotTable. For instance, clicking the Hide Detail button in the row area containing a Season outer row field and a Month inner row field hides the Month inner row field's details.

- *Show Detail button*: Shows detailed information in a PivotTable. Continuing the Hide Detail scenario, clicking the Show Detail button for the Season outer row field shows the Month inner row field's details. Clicking the Show Detail button for the Month inner row field allows you to show even more details, for instance month by salesperson, month by state, and so on, depending on the nature of your source data.

TIP Double-clicking an item in a row or column field shows details if they are hidden, hides details if they are displayed, or allows you to show even more details, depending on your PivotTable's field layout and the nature of your source data. Double-clicking a cell in the data area shows details for that data cell on a new worksheet (unless the Enable Drill To Details check box is cleared in the PivotTable Options dialog box).

- *Refresh Data button*: Updates the PivotTable's data based on the latest version of your source data, if any.

- *Include Hidden Items In Totals button*: Allows you to include (when selected, or not include when not selected) any hidden items when calculating subtotals and grand totals in PivotTables. If this button is not available, you can still include or not include hidden page items in subtotals; to do so, click the PivotTable button on the PivotTable toolbar, click the Table Options command, and then select or clear the Subtotal Hidden Page Items check box.

- *Always Display Items button*: Allows you to display (when selected, or hide if not selected) a field's items under certain circumstances. For instance, when Always Display Items is not selected and a field is added to the row area, none of the items are displayed until a field is added to the data area.

- *Field Settings button*: Displays the PivotTable Field dialog box, which is equivalent to double-clicking a field button in a row, column, data, or page area.

- *Show Field List* button: Displays (when selected, or hides if not selected) the PivotTable Field List dialog box.

Let's turn from working with the PivotTable as a whole to working with individual fields.

Understanding the PivotTable Field Dialog Box

The PivotTable Field dialog box is a powerful tool that allows you to control the layout and behavior of fields in a PivotTable. This dialog box is displayed when you do one of the following:

- Click the Field Settings button on the PivotTable toolbar.

- Double-click a field button in a row, column, data, or page area.

- Click the PivotTable toolbar's PivotTable button and then click the Field Settings command.

This dialog box and its child dialog boxes vary based on the type of field that you're working with:

- For column fields, you can specify if and how subtotals are displayed, show or hide items with no data, hide fields altogether, sort items, and show only the top or bottom number of items, as shown in Figures 3-26 and 3-27.

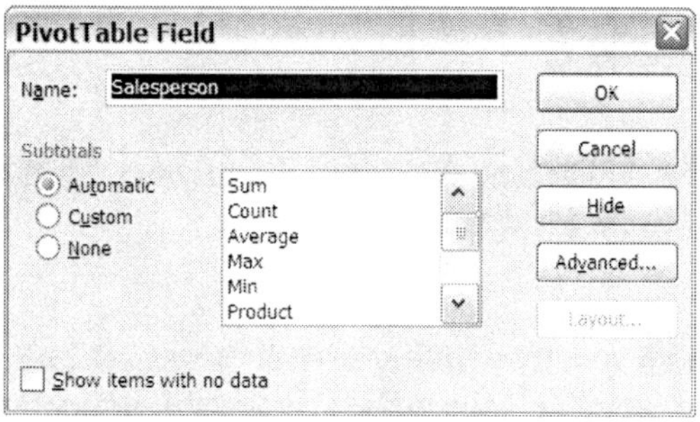

FIGURE 3-26

The PivotTable Field dialog box for column and row fields

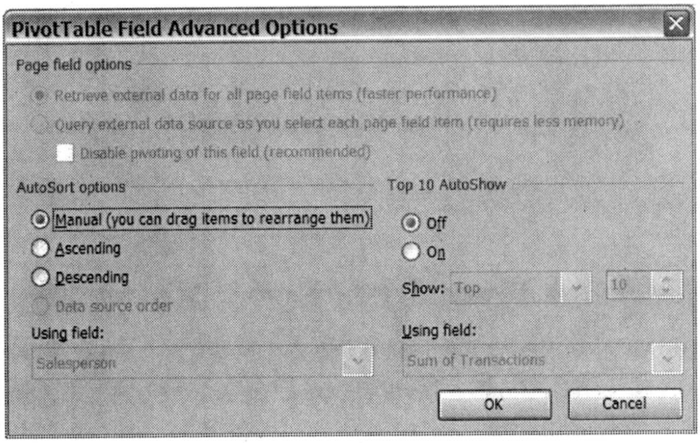

FIGURE 3-27

The PivotTable Field Advanced Options dialog box, displayed when you click the Advanced button on the PivotTable Field dialog box.

- For row fields, you can also specify whether items are displayed in tabular or outline format, insert a blank line after each item, and insert a page break after each item, as shown in Figure 3-28.

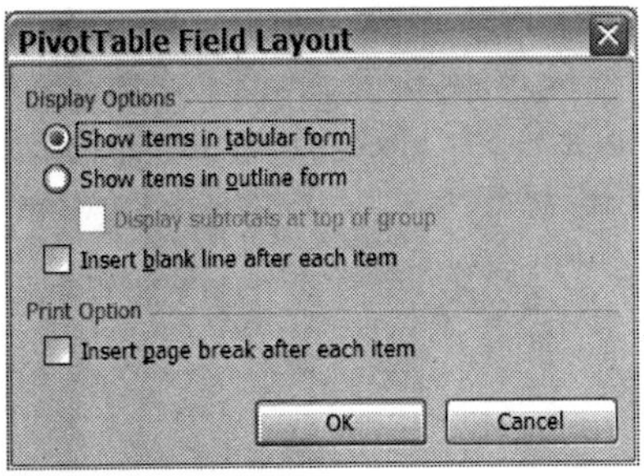

FIGURE 3-28

The PivotTable Field Layout dialog box, displayed when you click the Layout button on the PivotTable Field dialog box.

- For page fields, you can also specify whether certain items are hidden, as well as improve performance on source data retrieval for very large data sources, as shown in Figures 3-27 and 3-29.

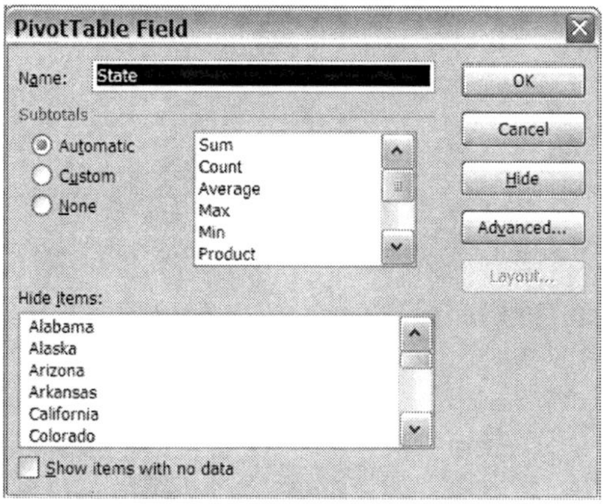

FIGURE 3-29

The PivotTable Field dialog box for page fields

- For data fields, the option for if and how to display subtotals is replaced with options for displaying summarized data, whether it's by Sum, Count, or Average, as well as whether the summarized data is based on other summarized data in the data area, whether the summarized data is displayed with currency or percentage symbols, and so on, as shown in Figures 3-30 and 3-31.

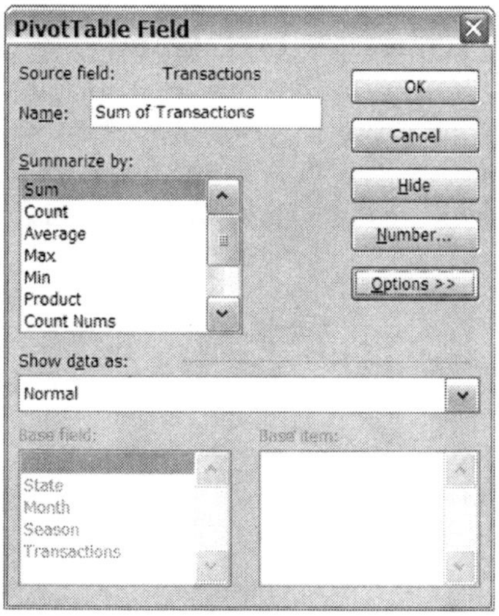

FIGURE 3-30

The PivotTable Field dialog box for data fields. Clicking the Options button displays the Show Data As, Base Field, and Base Item controls.

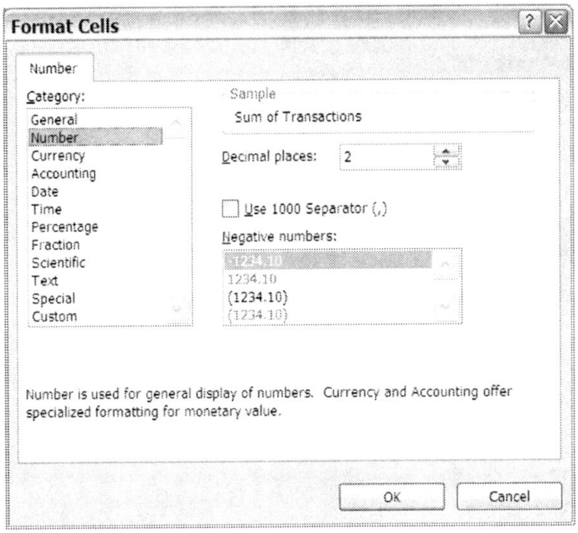

FIGURE 3-31

The Format Cells dialog box, displayed when the Number button is clicked on the PivotTable Field dialog box for data fields. The display of this dialog box depends on what you select in the Category list.

Next, let's look specifically at the Pivot Field dialog box for working with column and row fields.

Working with the PivotTable Field Dialog Box for Column and Row Fields

Figure 3-32 shows the PivotTable Field dialog box that displays when you right-click a column or row field button in a PivotTable, and then click Field Settings. This dialog box allows you to change the visual display of column and row fields.

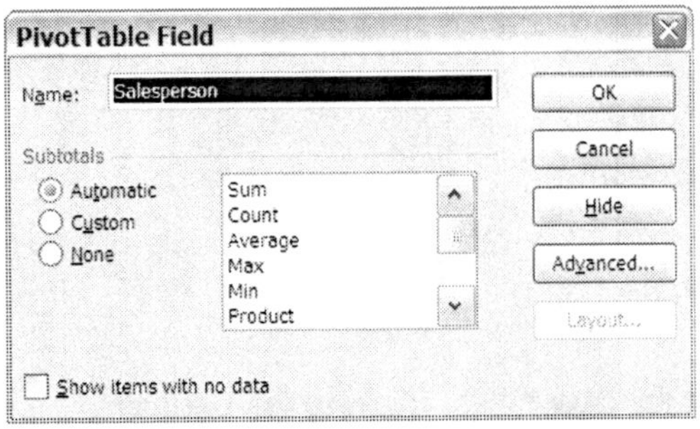

FIGURE 3-32

The PivotTable Field dialog box for column and row fields

This dialog box allows you to change field display names and how field values are subtotaled:

- The Name box allows you to specify a different display name for the field. This display name also appears in the field list.

- The Subtotals area allows you to specify Automatic subtotals for outer row and column fields, Custom subtotals for inner row and column fields (if available), or for no field subtotals. The subtotal type is specified in the corresponding list. The Show Items With No Data check box, when selected, allows you to show all items (if supported by your source data).

NOTE Hiding an item in a row field or column field removes it from the report, but the item still appears in the drop-down list for the field.

You should be aware of a few advanced field options for working with column, row, and page fields, as discussed in the next section.

Working with the PivotTable Field Advanced Options Dialog Box

When you right-click a column, row, or page field button in a PivotTable, click Field Settings, and then click the Advanced button, the PivotTable Field Advanced Options dialog box is displayed (see Figure 3-33). This dialog box allows you to sort and show specific items in the field, as well as control data retrieval options for page fields.

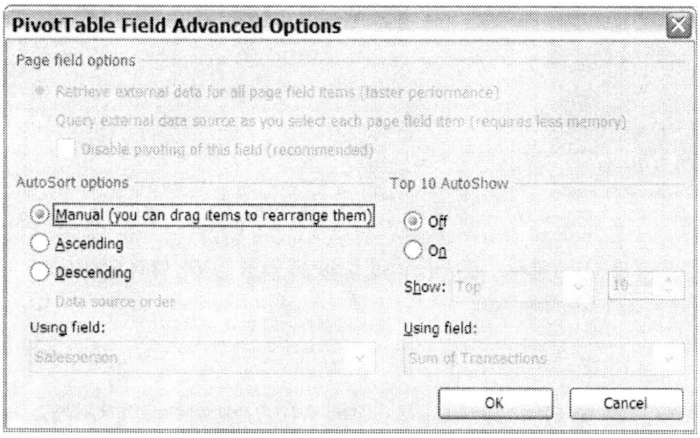

FIGURE 3-33

The PivotTable Field Advanced Options dialog box, displayed when you click the Advanced button on the PivotTable Field dialog box

Note that the Page Field Options controls in the preceding figure are only available when the field is a page field and the source data is not in the current or an external Excel workbook.

This dialog box allows you to sort items as well as show only the top or bottom number of items:

- The AutoSort Options area allows you to sort items in a Manual fashion, in Ascending order, or in Descending order, based on the selection in the Using Field list. You can also choose to use the Data Source Order to sort items, if the data source allows it.

- The Top 10 AutoShow area allows you to turn On or Off AutoShow behavior, showing the Top or Bottom number of items, based on the selection in the Using Field list.

You can set a few unique options when working with outer row fields, as described in the next section.

Working with the PivotTable Field Layout Dialog Box

When you right-click an outer row field button in a PivotTable, click Field Setting, and then click Layout, the PivotTable Field Layout dialog box is displayed (see Figure 3-34).

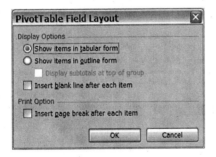

FIGURE 3-34
The PivotTable Field Layout dialog box, displayed when you click the Layout button on the PivotTable Field dialog box

This dialog box allows you to specify display and print options for outer row fields:

- The Display Options area allows you to Show Items In Tabular Form and Show Items In Outline Form (with an option to Display Subtotals At Top Of Group). You can also Insert Blank Line After Each Item.

- The Print Option area allows you to Insert Page Break After Each Item.

Page fields have some unique format settings, as we'll see in the next section.

Working with the PivotTable Field Dialog Box for Page Fields

When you right-click a page field button in a PivotTable and click Field Settings, Figure 3-35 shows the version of the PivotTable Field dialog box displays.

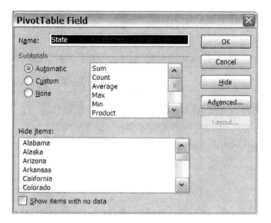

FIGURE 3-35

The PivotTable Field dialog box for page fields

This dialog box allows you to change field display names and subtotals, hide a field's items, and show items with no data:

- The Name box and Subtotals areas behave the same as its column and row field counterpart.

- The Hide Items list allows you to hide items from the page field. If the Hide Items list is missing, your source data always lists all available items in the drop-down list for the page field.

  NOTE Hiding an item in a page field removes it both from the report and from the drop-down list for the field.

- The Show Items With No Data check box behaves the same as its column and row field counterpart.

- The Subtotals area allows you to specify Automatic subtotals for outer row and column fields, Custom subtotals for inner row and column fields, or for no field subtotals. The subtotal type is specified in the corresponding list. The Show Items With No Data check box, when selected, allows you to show all items, even if they have no data associated with them.

NOTE The Page Field Options area of the PivotTable Field Advanced Options dialog box provides options to Retrieve External Data All Page Field Items, Query External Data Source As You Select Each Page Field Item, and Disable Pivoting Of This Field, if your external source data supports it (not applicable for external Excel workbook source data).

Data fields have some interesting visual display settings as well. Let's take a look at them in the next section.

Working with the PivotTable Field Dialog Box for Data Fields

When you right-click a data field button on a PivotTable and click Field Settings, the version of the PivotTable Field dialog box that displays is shown in Figure 3-36.

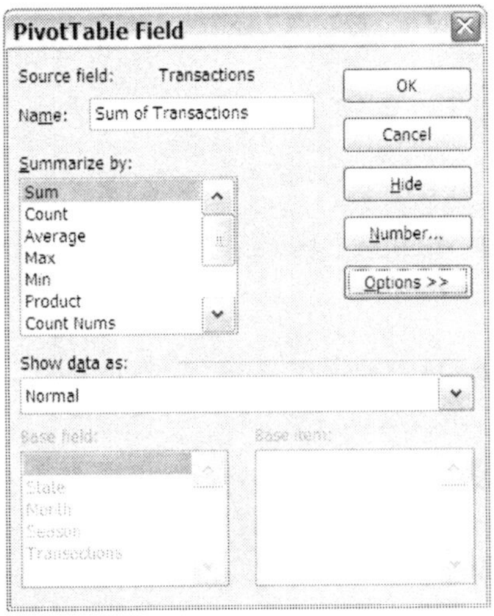

FIGURE 3-36

The PivotTable Field dialog box for data fields. The Show Data As, Base Field, and Base Item controls are displayed when you click the Options button.

This dialog box allows you to change the field's display name and summary calculation:

- The Name box behaves the same as its column, row, and page field counterparts.

- The Summarize By list allows you to choose the summary calculation for the data.

- The Show Data As list allows you to pick a custom calculation for the data, as described in Table 3-3.

TABLE 3-3

Custom Calculations and Their Results

Custom Calculation	Result
Difference From	Displays data as the difference from the value of the selection in the Base Item list in the selection in the Base Field list
% Of	Displays data as a percentage of the value of the selection in the Base Item list in the selection in the Base Field list
% Difference From	Displays data as the percentage difference from the value of the selection in the Base Item list in the selection in the Base Field list
Running Total In	Displays the data for successive items in the selection in the Base Item list as a running total
% Of Row	Displays the data in each row as a percentage of the total for the row
% Of Column	Displays all the data in each column as a percentage of the total for the column
% Of Total	Displays data as a percentage of the grand total of all the data in the report
Index	Calculates data as follows: ((value in cell) x (Grand Total of Grand Totals)) / ((Grand Row Total) x (Grand Column Total))

You can also format cells with numbers, such as adding currency symbols. Let's explore these options in the next section.

Working with the Format Cells Dialog Box

When you right-click a data field button in a PivotTable (or right-click any field button containing numeric items), click Field Settings, and then click Number, the Format Cells dialog box appears. You can use this dialog box to modify the number format for data cells, as shown in Figure 3-37.

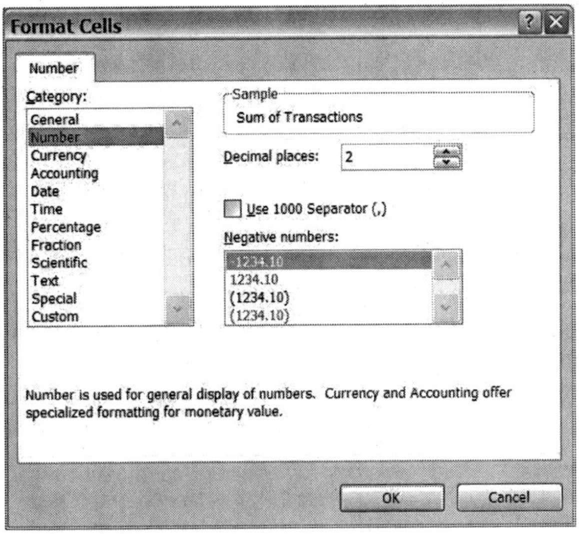

FIGURE 3-37

The Format Cells dialog box, displayed when you click the Number button on the PivotTable Field dialog box for data fields. The display of this dialog box depends on what you select in the Category list.

In this example, the Number category is selected. The formatting choices in this case include the number of decimal places, whether the 1000 separator is used, and how negative numbers are formatted.

Now that we've explored the PivotTable toolbar and its commands, let's drill into the PivotTable menu a bit.

Working with the PivotTable Menu

When you click the PivotTable menu on the PivotTable toolbar, additional PivotTable commands drop down, as shown in Figure 3-38.

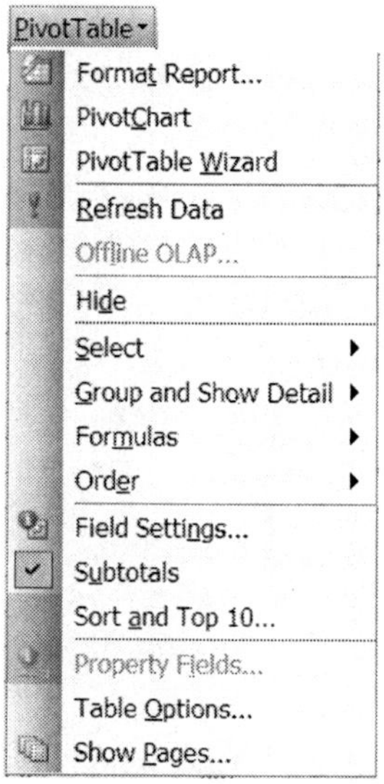

FIGURE 3-38

The PivotTable toolbar's PivotTable menu contains additional PivotTable commands.

Some of these commands are duplicates of other commands on the PivotTable toolbar, whereas some commands are new. The entire list of commands is described here.

- The Format Report command displays the AutoFormat dialog box, which allows you to change the PivotTable's overall visual display format. This command is equivalent to clicking the Format Report button on the PivotTable toolbar.

- The PivotChart command creates a PivotChart with a default visual display format based on the current PivotTable. This command is equivalent to clicking the Chart Wizard button on the PivotTable toolbar, or right-clicking a field on the PivotTable and clicking PivotChart.

- The PivotTable Wizard command displays the PivotTable and PivotChart Wizard, which allows you to place the PivotTable on a different worksheet, connect to different source data, and change PivotTable layout and other options. This command is equivalent to clicking Data ➤ PivotTable and PivotChart Wizard, or right-clicking a field on the PivotTable and clicking PivotTable Wizard.

- The Refresh Data command button updates the PivotTable's data based on the latest version of your source data, if any. This command is equivalent to clicking the Refresh Data button on the PivotTable toolbar, or right-clicking a field on the PivotTable and clicking Refresh Data.

- The Offline OLAP command allows you to connect to offline OLAP source data. For more information, see Chapter 6.

- The Hide command removes the selected field from the PivotTable, basically treating the field as if it never existed in the PivotTable. This is equivalent to right-clicking a field on the PivotTable and clicking Hide. You can still drag the field back onto the PivotTable.

- The Select command allows you to select all of the PivotTable's field buttons, data, both field buttons and data, or the entire PivotTable, if the Enable Selection command is selected first. This is equivalent to right-clicking a field on the PivotTable and clicking Select.

- The Group and Show Detail command allows you to hide and show detailed information in a PivotTable. This is equivalent to right-clicking a field on the PivotTable and clicking Group and Show Detail. The first two subcommands are equivalent to clicking the Hide Detail and Show Detail buttons on the PivotTable toolbar. The Group and Ungroup subcommands allow you to group related items together for easier placement and formatting in the PivotTable.

- The Formulas command allows you to create calculated fields, create calculated items, determine the solve order of calculated formulas, and list the calculated formulas that are available to the PivotTable.

- The Order command allows you to move items up and down and beginning to end in fields. This is equivalent to right-clicking a field on the PivotTable and clicking Order.

- The Field Settings command displays the PivotTable Field dialog box, which is equivalent to clicking the Field Settings button on the PivotTable toolbar, or right-clicking a field on the PivotTable and clicking Field Settings.

- The Subtotals command shows or hides subtotals for the selected field.

- The Sort and Top 10 command displays the PivotTable Sort and Top 10 dialog box.

- The Property Fields command allows you to access OLAP property fields. For more details, see Chapter 6.

- The Table Options command displays the PivotTable Options dialog box. This is equivalent to clicking the Options button in the last step of the PivotTable and Pivot Chart Wizard, or right-clicking a field on the PivotTable and clicking Table Options.

- The Show Pages command, when a page field is selected, creates one worksheet with a PivotTable on it per page field item.

Now let's bring all of these PivotTable components together in the following Try It! exercises.

Try It! Create and Customize a PivotTable

In this exercise, you'll create a basic PivotTable containing several row, column, data, and page fields. In later exercises, you'll use the PivotTable Field List dialog box, the PivotTable toolbar, and the PivotTable menu to further customize this basic PivotTable.

Connect to the Source Data

First create the PivotTable by connecting to the source data. The source data for this chapter's exercises are located in the Excel worksheet named HouseSales.xls available from the Apress Web site's Download section at http://www.apress.com. The source data represents financial transactions made by a home lending corporation over the course of a given year.

1. Start Excel.

2. Open the HouseSales.xls file.

3. Create a new blank workbook if you don't have one already available.

4. With the blank workbook visible, click Data ➤ PivotTable and PivotChart Report.

5. Make sure the Microsoft Office Excel List Or Database option and PivotTable option is selected, and then click Next.

6. With the PivotTable and PivotChart Wizard visible, switch back to HouseSales.xls.

7. On Sheet1, select cells A1 through E601, and then click Finish. A PivotTable based on the selected data is created in Sheet1 of Book1.

Add Fields to the Layout

Next, let's begin performing some data analysis tasks by adding some fields to the PivotTable:

1. In the PivotTable Field List dialog box, click State.

2. In the Add To list, select Page Area, as shown in Figure 3-39.

3. Click the Add To button. Compare your results to Figure 3-40.

4. In the field list, click Season.

5. In the Add To list, select Row Area.

6. Click the Add To button. Compare your results to Figure 3-41.

7. In the field list, click Month.

FIGURE 3-39

The PivotTable Field List dialog box, with the State field about to be added to the PivotTable's page area

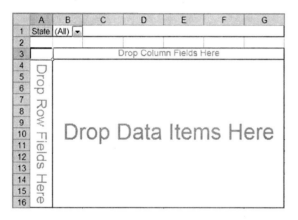

FIGURE 3-40

The PivotTable with the State field added to the page area

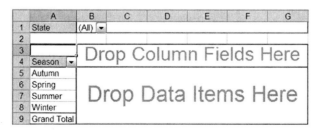

FIGURE 3-41

The PivotTable with the State field added to the page area and the Season field added to the row area

8. Make sure that Row Area is showing the Add To list. Click the Add To button. The Month field is added to the PivotTable as an inner row field. By default, the Season field becomes an outer row field, as shown in Figure 3-42.

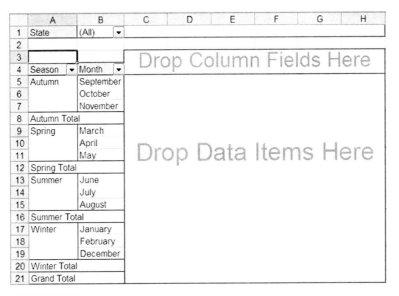

FIGURE 3-42

The PivotTable with the State field added to the page area, the Season field added to the row area as an outer row field, and the Month field added to the row area as an inner row field

9. In the field list, click Salesperson.

10. In the Add To list, select Column Area.

11. Click the Add To button. Compare your results to Figure 3-43.

12. In the field list, click the Transactions icon.

13. In the Add To list, select Data Area.

14. Click the Add To button. The Transactions field is added to the PivotTable as a data field. Your results should look like Figure 3-44.

Now that you've placed the fields on the PivotTable, what if you change your mind on where the fields are placed? We'll explore that next.

	A	B	C	D	E	I	J
1	State	(All)					
2							
3			Salesperson				
4	Season	Month	Crosby	Fisher	Johnson	Smith	Grand Total
5	Autumn	September					
6		October					
7		November					
8	Autumn Total						
9	Spring	March					
10		April					
11		May					
12	Spring Total						
13	Summer	June					
14		July					
15		August					
16	Summer Total						
17	Winter	January					
18		February					
19		December					
20	Winter Total						
21	Grand Total						

FIGURE 3-43

The PivotTable with the State field added to the page area, the Season field added to the row area as an outer row field, the Month field added to the row area as an inner row field, and the Salesperson column added to the column area (panes have been split for readability)

	A	B	C	D	E	I	J
1	State	(All)					
2							
3	Sum of Tran		Salesperson				
4	Season	Month	Crosby	Fisher	Johnson	Smith	Grand Total
5	Autumn	September	11654	5268	7838	600	35400
6		October	11634	5526	7878	500	35590
7		November	11748	5752	7496	594	35782
8	Autumn Total		35036	16546	23212	1694	106772
9	Spring	March	11604	5722	7750	544	35254
10		April	11566	5554	7778	618	35352
11		May	11754	5644	7654	534	35666
12	Spring Total		34924	16920	23182	1696	106272
13	Summer	June	35232	17484	23022	2010	107340
14		July	35274	16542	24264	1818	107994
15		August	35034	16536	22866	2280	106926
16	Summer Total		105540	50562	70152	6108	322260
17	Winter	January	6058	2790	3910	238	18032
18		February	6036	2834	3850	346	18033
19		December	5945	2627	3761	275	17596
20	Winter Total		18039	8251	11521	859	53661
21	Grand Total		193539	92279	128067	10357	588965

FIGURE 3-44

The PivotTable with the State field added to the page area, the Season field added to the row area as an outer row field, the Month field added to the row area as an inner row field, the Salesperson column added to the column area, and the Sum of Transactions field added to the data area (panes have been split for readability)

Move a Field to a Different Drop Area

You can move a field from one drop area to another drop area by following these steps:

1. In the field list, click the Season icon.

2. In the Add To list, select Page Area.

3. Click the Add To button. The Season field changes from a row field to a page field. Compare your results to Figure 3-45.

	A	B	C	D	H	I
1	State	(All)				
2	Season	(All)				
3						
4	Sum of Transactions	Salesperson				
5	Month	Crosby	Fisher	Johnson	Smith	Grand Total
6	January	6058	2790	3910	238	18032
7	February	6036	2834	3850	346	18033
8	March	11604	5722	7750	544	35254
9	April	11566	5554	7778	618	35352
10	May	11754	5644	7654	534	35666
11	June	35232	17484	23022	2010	107340
12	July	35274	16542	24264	1818	107994
13	August	35034	16536	22866	2280	106926
14	September	11654	5268	7838	600	35400
15	October	11634	5526	7878	500	35590
16	November	11748	5752	7496	594	35782
17	December	5945	2627	3761	275	17596
18	Grand Total	193539	92279	128067	10357	588965

FIGURE 3-45

The PivotTable with the State field and Season field added to the page area (panes have been split for readability)

Next, you'll learn how to show only specific data in the PivotTable.

Filter the PivotTable

Next, filter the PivotTable to show only specific data by following these steps:

1. Click the arrow in the Season field button, as shown in Figure 3-46.

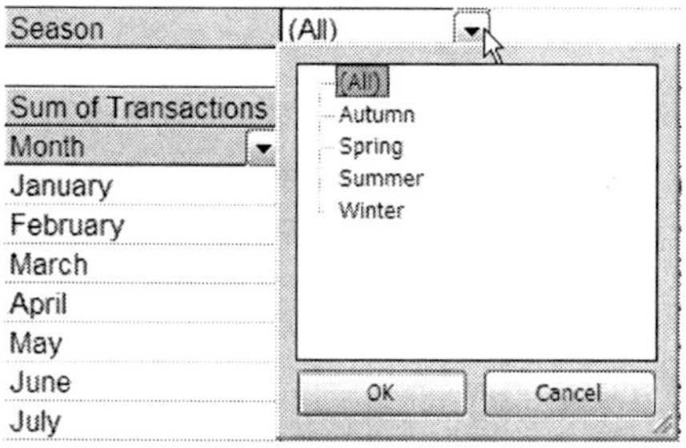

FIGURE 3-46

Click the arrow in the Season field button to show the field drop-down list.

2. Click Winter, and then click OK. The PivotTable now displays only data for Winter.

3. Click the arrow in the Salesperson field button.

4. Clear the (Show All) check box, select the Johnson and Lundgren check boxes, and click OK. The PivotTable now displays only data for Johnson and Lundgren for January, February, and December, as shown in Figure 3-47.

	A	B	C	D
1	State	(All)		
2	Season	Winter		
3				
4	Sum of Transactions	Salesperson		
5	Month	Johnson	Lundgren	Grand Total
6	January	3910	3325	7235
7	February	3850	3302	7152
8	December	3761	3219	6980
9	Grand Total	11521	9846	21367

FIGURE 3-47

Transactions for Johnson and Lundgren for January, February, and December

With just a few mouse clicks, you can zoom in on the data you're interested in. Now let's move to the next section and perform a "what if" analysis using a calculated field.

Create a Calculated Field

Next, create a calculated field that displays salespeople's transaction commissions of 3.5% and display only commission data in the PivotTable. Before you do this, first move the Season field back to the row area, as described in steps 1 through 4:

1. In the field list, click the Season icon.

2. In the Add To list, select Row Area.

3. Click the Add To button. The Season field changes from a page field to a row field.

4. Right-click the Season field button, and click Order ➤ Move Left from the context menu that appears, as shown in Figure 3-48.

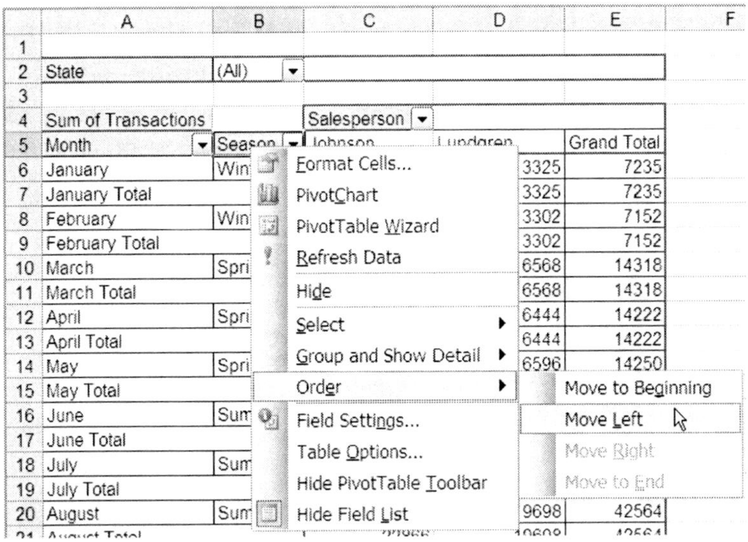

FIGURE 3-48

To move a field, right-click the field button, click Order, and click where to move the field (for example, Move Left).

Now, create the calculated field by following these steps:

1. In the PivotTable, click the Season field button.

2. On the PivotTable toolbar, click PivotTable ➤ Formulas ➤ Calculated Field.

3. In the Name box, type **Commission**.

4. Clear the contents of the Formula box.

5. In the Field list, click Transactions, and click Insert Field.

6. In the Formula box, append the text ***0.035**, as shown in Figure 3-49.

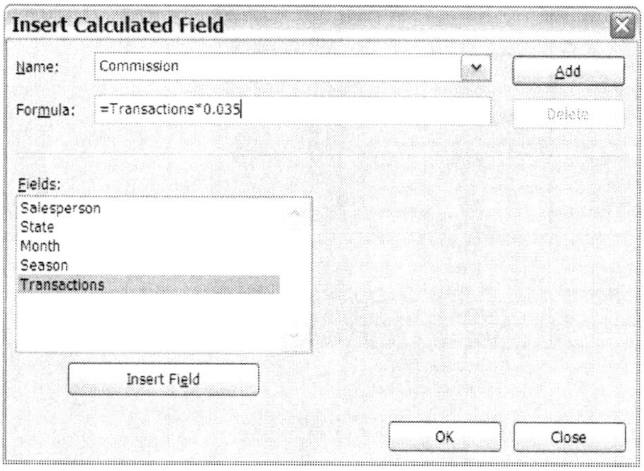

FIGURE 3-49

The Insert Calculated Field dialog box, reflecting a transaction commission of 3.5%

7. Click OK. The Commission calculated field is added to the PivotTable data area and the field list.

Next, let's show only data for the sum of commissions.

1. Click the arrow in the Data field button.

2. Clear the Sum Of Transactions check box, and then click OK. The PivotTable now displays only the commission data, as shown in Figure 3-50.

	A	B	C	D	E
1					
2	State	(All)			
3					
4	Sum of Commission		Salesperson		
5	Season	Month	Johnson	Lundgren	Grand Total
6	Autumn	September	274.33	226.59	500.92
7		October	275.73	227.5	503.23
8		November	262.36	233.17	495.53
9	Autumn Total		812.42	687.26	1499.68
10	Spring	March	271.25	229.88	501.13
11		April	272.23	225.54	497.77
12		May	267.89	230.86	498.75
13	Spring Total		811.37	686.28	1497.65
14	Summer	June	805.77	660.66	1466.43
15		July	849.24	688.59	1537.83
16		August	800.31	689.43	1489.74
17	Summer Total		2455.32	2038.68	4494
18	Winter	January	136.85	116.375	253.225
19		February	134.75	115.57	250.32
20		December	131.635	112.665	244.3
21	Winter Total		403.235	344.61	747.845
22	Grand Total		4482.345	3756.83	8239.175

FIGURE 3-50

Showing only commission data in the PivotTable

Let's do another type of "what if" by creating a calculated item, as described in the next section.

Create a Calculated Item

Add a calculated item that estimates what next year's Winter transactions would add at an estimated 3% transaction increase:

1. In the PivotTable, click the Season field button.

2. With the Season field selected in the PivotTable, on the PivotTable toolbar, click PivotTable ➤ Formulas ➤ Calculated Item.

3. In the Name box, type **Next Winter**.

4. Clear the contents of the Formula box.

5. In the Fields list, make sure that Season is selected.

6. In the Items list, click Winter, and then click Insert Item.

7. In the Formula box, append the text ***0.03**, as shown in Figure 3-51.

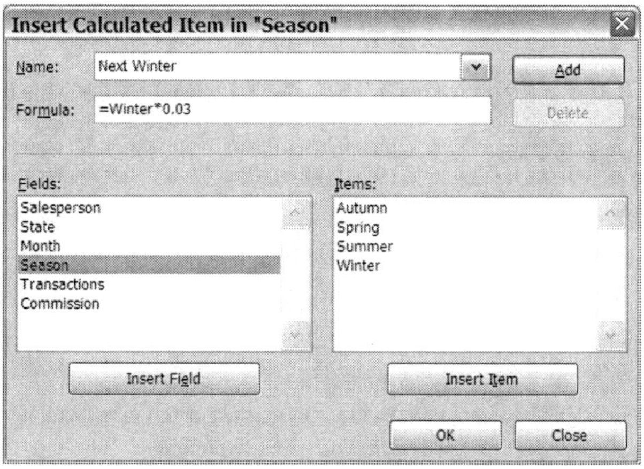

FIGURE 3-51
The Next Winter calculated item formula

8. Click OK. The Next Winter calculated item is added to the PivotTable, as shown in Figure 3-52.

	A	B	C	D	E
2	State	(All)			
3					
4	Sum of Commission		Salesperson		
5	Season	Month	Johnson	Lundgren	Grand Total
6	Autumn	September	274.33	226.59	500.92
7		October	275.73	227.5	503.23
8		November	262.36	233.17	495.53
22	Next Winter	January	4.1055	3.49125	7.59675
23		February	4.0425	3.4671	7.5096
24		March	0	0	0
25		April	0	0	0
26		May	0	0	0
27		June	0	0	0
28		July	0	0	0
29		August	0	0	0
30		September	0	0	0
31		October	0	0	0
32		November	0	0	0
33		December	3.94905	3.37995	7.329
34	Next Winter Total		12.09705	10.3383	22.43535
35	Grand Total		4494.44205	3767.1683	8261.61035

FIGURE 3-52
Showing the Next Winter calculated item in the PivotTable

Let's move on to working more deeply with the PivotTable Field List to customize the PivotTable's field layout.

Try It! Use the PivotTable Field List to Customize a PivotTable

In this exercise, you'll use the drag-and-drop features of the PivotTable Field List dialog box to re-create the PivotTable you created in the previous exercise. Follow these steps:

1. Using the PivotTable from the previous exercise, clear the existing fields from the PivotTable. To do so, right-click each field button and click the Hide command on the context menu that appears. When finished, you should have a blank PivotTable, as shown in Figure 3-53.

FIGURE 3-53

A blank PivotTable

2. Drag and drop the State icon from the field list to the Drop Page Fields Here area of the PivotTable.

3. Drag and drop the Season icon from the field list to the Drop Row Fields Here area of the PivotTable.

4. Drag and drop the Month icon from the field list to the Drop Row Fields Here area of the PivotTable. To make the Month field an inner row field, be sure to drop the field on top of and to the right edge of the Season field. You'll know when you're ready to drop the field correctly when an I-beam appears to the right edge of the Season field, as shown in Figure 3-54.

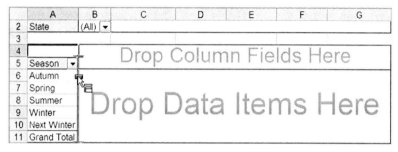

FIGURE 3-54

An I-beam indicates that if the field is dropped here, it will become an inner row field.

TIP To change an outer row field to an inner row field, drag and drop either the field button in the PivotTable or the field icon from the field list to the right edge of the row area. To create an inner column field, drag and drop the field on top of and to the bottom edge of the column area. Similarly, to change an outer column field to an inner column field, drag and drop either the field button in the PivotTable or the field icon from the field list to the bottom edge of the row area.

5. Drag and drop the Salesperson icon from the field list to the Drop Column Fields Here area of the PivotTable.

6. Drag and drop the Transactions icon from the field list to the Drop Data Items Here area of the PivotTable. By default, the Sum summary function is selected for numeric data, so the Sum Of Salesperson field is added to the PivotTable's data area.

NOTE To hide the Next Winter calculated item from the PivotTable, click the arrow in the Season field button in the PivotTable, clear the Next Winter check box, and then click OK.

Next, let's get more familiar working with the PivotTable toolbar to change the PivotTable's overall visual format, among other tasks.

Try It! Work with the PivotTable Toolbar

Let's quickly perform a few simple PivotTable actions from the PivotTable toolbar, including AutoFormat and Hide and Show Detail, to change the PivotTable's visual display and layout. From there, we'll move to working with the various versions of the PivotTable Field dialog box to customize the visual display of fields as well. For this exercise, continue using the PivotTable from a previous exercise. To begin this exercise, your PivotTable should look like Figure 3-55.

	A	B	C	F	G	H	I	J
1								
2	State	(All)						
3								
4	Sum of Transactions		Salesperson					
5	Season	Month	Crosby	Jones	Lundgren	McDonald	Smith	Grand Total
6	Autumn	September	11654	1398	6474	2168	600	35400
7		October	11634	1538	6500	2014	500	35590
8		November	11748	1458	6662	2072	594	35782
9	Autumn Total		35036	4394	19636	6254	1694	106772
10	Spring	March	11604	1312	6568	1754	544	35254
11		April	11566	1506	6444	1886	618	35352
12		May	11754	1422	6596	2062	534	35666
13	Spring Total		34924	4240	19608	5702	1696	106272
14	Summer	June	35232	4416	18876	6300	2010	107340
15		July	35274	4068	19674	6354	1818	107994
16		August	35034	4116	19698	6396	2280	106926
17	Summer Total		105540	12600	58248	19050	6108	322260
18	Winter	January	6058	710	3325	1001	238	18032
19		February	6036	721	3302	944	346	18033
20		December	5945	719	3219	1050	275	17596
21	Winter Total		18039	2150	9846	2995	859	53661
22	Grand Total		193539	23384	107338	34001	10357	588965

FIGURE 3-55

PivotTable before changing its visual format (panes have been split for readability)

In the next section, you'll jazz the PivotTable up a bit with some color.

Add Color to the PivotTable

Use colors and highlights for the salespersons' names, the subtotals, and the grand totals in the PivotTable:

1. On the PivotTable toolbar, click the Format Report button, as shown in Figure 3-56.

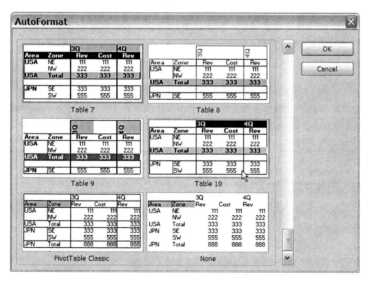

FIGURE 3-56

The PivotTable toolbar's Format Report button

2. The AutoFormat dialog box appears, as shown in Figure 3-57.

FIGURE 3-57

The AutoFormat dialog box allows you to quickly change a PivotTable's overall visual format.

3. In the dialog box, scroll down to and select the Table10 box, and then click OK. The color and highlighting is added to the PivotTable, as shown in Figure 3-58.

	A	B	C		F	G	H	I	J
1									
2	State	(All)	▼						
3									
4	Transactions		Salesperson ▼						
5	**Season** ▼	**Month** ▼	**Crosby**		**Jones**	**Lundgren**	**McDonald**	**Smith**	**Grand Total**
6	Autumn	September	11654		1398	6474	2168	600	35400
7		October	11634		1538	6500	2014	500	35590
8		November	11748		1458	6662	2072	594	35782
9	**Autumn Total**		**35036**		**4394**	**19636**	**6254**	**1694**	**106772**
10	Spring	March	11604		1312	6568	1754	544	35254
11		April	11566		1506	6444	1886	618	35352
12		May	11754		1422	6596	2062	534	35666
13	**Spring Total**		**34924**		**4240**	**19608**	**5702**	**1696**	**106272**
14	Summer	June	35232		4416	18876	6300	2010	107340
15		July	35274		4068	19674	6354	1818	107994
16		August	35034		4116	19698	6396	2280	106926
17	**Summer Total**		**105540**		**12600**	**58248**	**19050**	**6108**	**322260**
18	Winter	January	6058		710	3325	1001	238	18032
19		February	6036		721	3302	944	346	18033
20		December	5945		719	3219	1050	275	17596
21	**Winter Total**		**18039**		**2150**	**9846**	**2995**	**859**	**53661**
22	**Grand Total**		**193639**		**23384**	**107338**	**34001**	**10357**	**688966**

FIGURE 3-58

The PivotTable with the Table10 AutoFormat applied (panes have been split for readability)

Most PivotTable tasks are very straightforward with just a few mouse clicks. As you'll learn in the next section, you're just a few more mouse clicks away from hiding and showing field details.

Hide and Show Detail

Temporarily hide the detail for the Month field in the PivotTable and then show the detail again:

1. In the PivotTable, click the Season field button.

2. On the PivotTable toolbar, click the Hide Detail button. The Month field details are hidden.

3. On the PivotTable toolbar, click the Show Detail button. The Month field details are displayed.

Hiding and showing field details couldn't be easier!

Let's analyze the data more deeply in the next section by using the PivotTable Field dialog box.

Use the PivotTable Field Dialog Box

Let's now use the PivotTable Field dialog box to customize the PivotTable's layout and behavior.

Show Salespeople in Order of Transactions

Next, reorder the data by salesperson, with the salespersons having the highest total transactions listed first (toward the left edge of the data area):

1. Click the Salesperson field button.

2. On the PivotTable toolbar, click the Field Settings button.

3. In the Name box, type **Sales Associate**.

4. Click the Advanced button.

5. In the AutoSort Options area, click the Descending option.

6. In the Using Field list, select Sum Of Transactions, click the OK button, and then click the OK button again. The salespersons having the highest total transactions are listed first, as shown in Figure 3-59.

	A	B	C	G	H	I	J
1							
2	State	(All) ▾					
3							
4	Transactions		Sales Associate				
5	**Season** ▾	**Month** ▾	**Crosby**	**McDonald**	**Jones**	**Smith**	**Grand Total**
6	Autumn	September	11654	2168	1398	600	35400
7		October	11634	2014	1538	500	35590
8		November	11748	2072	1458	594	35782
9	Spring	March	11604	1754	1312	544	35254
10		April	11566	1886	1506	618	35352
11		May	11754	2062	1422	534	35666
12	Summer	June	35232	6300	4416	2010	107340
13		July	35274	6354	4068	1818	107994
14		August	35034	6396	4116	2280	106926
15	Winter	January	6058	1001	710	238	18032
16		February	6036	944	721	346	18033
17		December	5945	1050	719	275	17596
18	**Grand Total**		**193539**	**34001**	**23384**	**10357**	**588965**

FIGURE 3-59

The salespersons having the highest transactions are listed first (panes have been split for readability).

You now know the salesperson having the highest transactions. What's the top month for transactions in each season? Let's find out in the next section.

Show the Top Month for Transactions per Season

Show the top month for transactions in each season. First, for easier readability, let's remove the subtotals from the Season field:

1. Click the Season field button.

2. On the PivotTable toolbar, click the Field Settings button.

3. In the Subtotals area, click the None option, and then click OK.

4. Continuing on, click the Month field button.

5. On the PivotTable toolbar, click the Field Settings button.

6. Click the Advanced button.

7. In the Top 10 AutoShow area, click the On option.

8. In the box next to the Show Top box, type or select the number 1 in place of the default number 10.

9. In the Using Field list, select Sum Of Transactions, as shown in Figure 3-60.

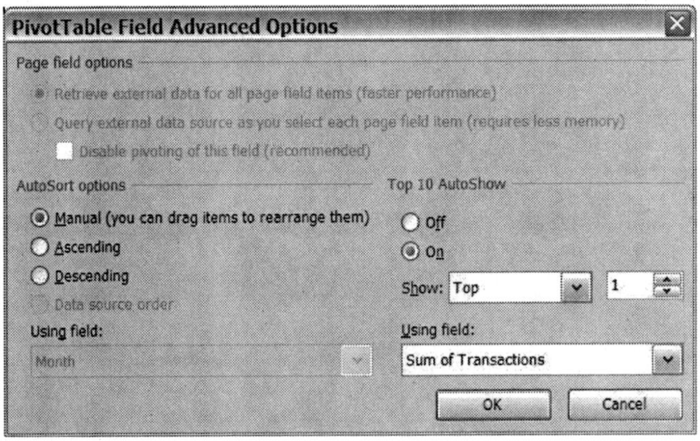

FIGURE 3-60

Completing the PivotTable Field Advanced Options dialog box. In this instance, the top item shows based on the Sum Of Transactions data.

10. Click the OK button, and then click the OK button again. The top month for each season in terms of transactions appears, as shown in Figure 3-61.

	A	B	J
1			
2	State	(All) ▾	
3			
4	Transactions		
5	**Season** ▾	**Month** ▾	**Grand Total**
6	Autumn	November	35782
7	Spring	May	35666
8	Summer	July	107994
9	Winter	February	18033
10	**Grand Total**		**197475**

FIGURE 3-61

The top month for each season in terms of transactions (panes have been split for readability)

Next, how would you show a month-to-month running total for the top month of each season, demonstrating how each salesperson did? You'll find out how to do this in the next section.

Show a Monthly Running Total for Transactions

Show a running total from month to month in the top month of each season showing how each salesperson contributed to the total transactions:

1. Click the Transactions field button.

2. On the PivotTable toolbar, click the Field Settings button.

3. Click the Options button.

4. In the Show Data As list, click Running Total In.

5. In the Base Field list, click Sales Associate.

6. Click OK. The PivotTable shows a running total from month to month in the top month of each season showing how each salesperson contributed to the total transactions, as shown in Figure 3-62.

	A	B	C	G	H	I	J
1							
2	State	(All) ▾					
3							
4	Transactions		Sales Associate ▾				
5	**Season** ▾	Month ▾	**Crosby**	**McDonald**	**Jones**	**Smith**	**Grand Total**
6	Autumn	November	11748	33730	35188	35782	
7	Spring	May	11754	33710	35132	35666	
8	Summer	July	35274	102108	106176	107994	
9	Winter	February	6036	16966	17687	18033	
10	**Grand Total**		**64812**	**186514**	**194183**	**197475**	

FIGURE 3-62

A running total from month to month in the top month of each season showing how each salesperson contributed to the total transactions (panes have been split for readability)

It would be nice to add some commas to the numbers to make them easier to read. Go to the next section to find out how to do this.

Format Transaction Data
Finally, format the transactions to show thousand separators:

1. Click the Transactions field button.

2. On the PivotTable toolbar, click the Field Settings button. The PivotTable Field dialog box appears.

3. Click the Number button. The Format Cells dialog box appears.

4. In the Category list, click Number.

5. In the Decimal Places box, type or select the number **0** in place of the default number 2.

6. Select the Use 1000 Separator check box, click the OK button, and click the OK button again. The transactions are formatted to show thousand separators, as shown in Figure 3-63.

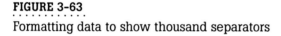

	A	B	C	G	H	I	J
1							
2	State	(All) ▼					
3							
4	Transactions		Sales Associate				
5	**Season** ▼	Month ▼	**Crosby**	**McDonald**	**Jones**	**Smith**	**Grand Total**
6	Autumn	November	11,748	33,730	35,188	35,782	
7	Spring	May	11,754	33,710	35,132	35,666	
8	Summer	July	35,274	102,108	106,176	107,994	
9	Winter	February	6,036	16,966	17,687	18,033	
10	**Grand Total**		**64,812**	**186,514**	**194,183**	**197,475**	

FIGURE 3-63
Formatting data to show thousand separators

As we draw this chapter to a close, you've done a lot! You've connected to a data source, added fields to a PivotTable and then moved the fields around, filtered data, created a calculated field and a calculated item, sorted items, displayed the top items in a field, and more!

Next Steps

In this chapter, you continued increasing your knowledge of PivotTables by understanding PivotTable terminology, working with row, column, data, page, and calculated fields and items; drop areas; the field list; field filters; and the PivotTable toolbar.

Before you proceed with the next chapter, you might want to use the Try It! exercise in this chapter in conjunction with the PivotTables you created in the previous two chapters. You should feel comfortable using the PivotTable Field dialog box to display different subtotal types, to use AutoSort and Top 10 AutoShow, to display custom calculations, and to change cell formatting with little effort. The more comfortable you are with using these features, the quicker you'll be able to analyze your data to make fast and intelligent decisions based on that data.

In the next chapter, you'll put your newfound skills to use in real-world data analysis scenarios.

4

Using PivotTables in the Real World

The previous chapters introduced you to the PivotTable and PivotChart Wizard, the PivotTable Field dialog box, the PivotTable toolbar, and the PivotTable menu so you could begin analyzing data from various sources. In this chapter, you'll use your new skills to analyze data for three different organizations:

- Fabrikam Interiors, a recreational furniture manufacturer
- Tailspin Toys, a toy distributor
- Contoso Publishing Limited, an academic book wholesaler

You'll play the role of a manufacturing manager, a survey analyst, and a product manager, as you analyze the data of these three organizations throughout the chapter. For example, you'll perform advanced data analysis tasks such as

- Displaying partial data as a running percentage of the entire data
- Performing "what if" data analysis by grouping similar items together
- Sorting, ordering, filtering, and showing items to find and rank data easier and faster

The data for all three of the following case studies are available in three Excel workbooks—FabrikamInteriors.xls, TailspinToys.xls, and Contoso-Publishing.xls—available from the Apress Web site Downloads section at http://www.apress.com.

Case Study 1: Fabrikam Interiors

Fabrikam Interiors manufactures recreational furniture such as deck chairs, outdoor folding chairs, weather-resistant side and end tables, deck loungers, outdoor dining sets, and other related accessories. Your job is to manage the manufacturing process for Fabrikam Interiors' complete line of recreational furniture. Part of your responsibilities include meeting quarterly with the warehouse manager to go over stock-keeping levels for the previous four calendar quarters.

You just received the warehouse manager's figures and you are meeting with her tomorrow. You want to do some analysis on her stock-keeping figures in advance of tomorrow's meeting.

The warehouse manager's figures consist of the following, as shown in Figure 4-1.

	A	B	C	D	E
1	Item	Category	Quarter	In Stock	On Order
2	Cross Back Chair	Other Chair	1	264	18
3	Arm Chair	Other Chair	1	218	15
4	Stacking Chair	Other Chair	1	276	18
5	Dining Chair	Other Chair	1	228	15
6	Curved Chair	Other Chair	1	217	14
7	Tall Folding Chair	Folding Chair	1	251	17
8	Short Folding Chair	Folding Chair	1	224	15
9	Poolside Chair	Folding Chair	1	273	18
10	Arm Chair	Folding Chair	1	274	18
11	Reclining Chair	Folding Chair	1	287	19
12	High Back Folding Chair	Folding Chair	1	260	17
115	Drink Table	Other Table	4	52	4
116	Steamer Lounger	Lounger	4	23	2
117	Sun Lounger	Lounger	4	25	1
118	Round Fixed Table with Dining Chairs	Dining Set	4	42	4
119	Folding Table with Wicker Chairs	Dining Set	4	35	3
120	Leaf Table with Reclining Chairs	Dining Set	4	42	4
121	Bar Arm Chair	Accessory	4	202	17
122	Rider Bar Chair	Accessory	4	264	22
123	Lamp	Accessory	4	243	20
124	Indoor Planter	Accessory	4	224	19
125	Foot Stool	Accessory	4	240	20

FIGURE 4-1

Fabrikam Interiors warehouse manager's figures to analyze (panes have been split for readability)

- The Item field contains individual products such as Arm Chair, Coffee Table, and Foot Stool.

- Each set of like products is contained within a Category field such as Extending Table, Folding Chair, and Accessory.

- Each of Fabrikam's fiscal periods is organized into Quarter 1, 2, 3, and 4.

- The In Stock field lists the number of individual products in the warehouse on the last day of a given fiscal period.

- Similarly, the On Order field lists the number of individual products that the warehouse manager has outstanding against the manufacturing department on the last day of a given fiscal period.

Create the PivotTable

Start by creating a PivotTable that connects to the warehouse manager's figures:

1. Start Excel.

2. Open the FabrikamInteriors.xls file.

3. Click File ➤ New.

4. In the New Workbook task pane, click Blank Workbook.

5. Click Data ➤ PivotTable and PivotChart Report.

6. Click Next.

7. Click Window ➤ FabrikamInteriors.xls.

8. Select cells A1 through E125 on the Sheet1 worksheet tab.

9. Click Finish. Compare your results to Figure 4-2.

FIGURE 4-2

A PivotTable connected to the Fabrikam Interiors warehouse manager's data

Now that you have your PivotTable, let's add some data to it!

Add Fields to the PivotTable

Continue by adding fields to the PivotTable. Start by examining the in-stock figures by category by quarter. Because the in-stock figures are a series of numbers, it makes sense to put them in the data area. We'll experiment with putting the Quarter and Category items in both the page and row areas.

Add fields to the PivotTable as follows:

1. Drag the In Stock field from the field list to the PivotTable's data area, as shown in Figure 4-3.

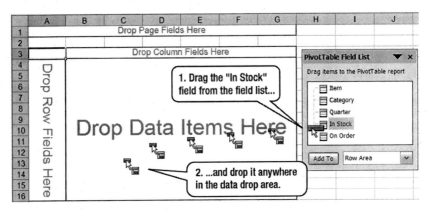

FIGURE 4-3
Dragging the In Stock field to the PivotTable's data area

2. Drag the Quarter field from the field list to the page area.

3. Drag the Category field from the field list to the page area. Compare your results to Figure 4-4.

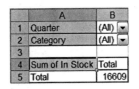

FIGURE 4-4
Initial PivotTable field layout

The data, a Sum Of In Stock field value of 16,609, doesn't really tell us much. Let's change the PivotTable fields' positions to understand just where the warehouse's stock is distributed.

Change Field Orientations

The PivotTable is beginning to take shape. However, getting a good handle on how the warehouse's stock is distributed would take a lot of work at this point unless you changed the PivotTable fields' positions. For instance, without moving any of the PivotTable's fields as they're placed now, you could change the Quarter field value to 1 and look at the Sum Of In Stock data value (which is 4,321), then change the Quarter field value to 2 and look at the Sum Of In Stock data value again (which is 3,769), and so on.

You could also do the same thing with each of the seven Category field values. For instance, you could change the Category field value to Accessory and look at the Sum Of In Stock data value (which is 3,658), then change the Category field value to Dining Set and look at the Sum Of In Stock data value again (which is 369), and so on. As you've probably figured out by now, making 28 field value changes for each combination of quarters and categories one field change at a time and noting the data values is extremely inconvenient. So, move the two page fields to the column and row areas so that you can see a lot more information at a glance:

1. Drag the Quarter field from the page area to the column area.

2. Drag the Category field from the page area to the row area. Compare your results to Figure 4-5.

	A	B	C	D	E	F
1						
2		Drop Page Fields Here				
3						
4	Sum of In Stock	Quarter ▾				
5	Category ▾	1	2	3	4	Grand Total
6	Accessory	997	710	778	1173	3658
7	Dining Set	83	87	80	119	369
8	Extending Table	205	194	167	240	806
9	Folding Chair	1569	1399	1250	1835	6053
10	Lounger	41	38	31	48	158
11	Other Chair	1203	1152	895	1498	4748
12	Other Table	223	189	149	256	817
13	Grand Total	4321	3769	3350	5169	16609

FIGURE 4-5

Changing the page fields to column and row fields

What initial analysis can you make from the PivotTable so far? Here are a few quick observations:

- The Accessory, Folding Chair, and Other Chair Category items have the largest in-stock numbers.

- The Dining Set and Lounger Category items have relatively small in-stock numbers.

- The Extending Table and Other Table Category items have similar in-stock numbers.

- Quarter 4 had the most items in stock, while Quarter 3 had the least items in stock.

Display Data by Category as a Percentage of Quarterly Totals

Seeing all of these in-stock numbers makes your analysis tasks a bit easier. Now make some additional observations by looking at the in-stock numbers by category as a percentage of the quarterly in-stock totals:

1. Right-click the Sum Of In Stock field button, and then click Field Settings.

2. Click Options.

3. In the Show Data As list, select % Of Column.

4. Click Number.

5. In the Decimal Places box, select or type the number **0**, click OK, and click OK again. Compare your results to Figure 4-6.

What additional analysis can you make from the PivotTable at this point? Here are a few more observations:

- The Accessory, Folding Chair, and Other Chair Category items each contribute between one-quarter and one-third of each quarter's in-stock numbers.

- The Other Table and Extending Table Category items each contribute about the same percentage (about 5%) to each quarter's in-stock numbers.

- The Lounger Category item comprises only a measly 1% of each quarter's in-stock numbers.

The Accessory, Folding Chair, and Other Chair Category items seem to comprise a majority of the warehouse's in-stock categories. In the next section, let's group these categories together to see how much they contribute to the warehouse's inventory.

	A	B	C	D	E	F
1						
2	Drop Page Fields Here					
3						
4	Sum of In Stock	Quarter ▾				
5	Category ▾	1	2	3	4	Grand Total
6	Accessory	23%	19%	23%	23%	22%
7	Dining Set	2%	2%	2%	2%	2%
8	Extending Table	5%	5%	5%	5%	5%
9	Folding Chair	36%	37%	37%	36%	36%
10	Lounger	1%	1%	1%	1%	1%
11	Other Chair	28%	31%	27%	29%	29%
12	Other Table	5%	5%	4%	5%	5%
13	Grand Total	100%	100%	100%	100%	100%

FIGURE 4-6

Data displayed by category as a percentage of quarterly totals

Grouping and Ungrouping Items

To show the magnitude of the collective in-stock ratio of the three highest in-stock categories each quarter, go back and add a grouped field that contains an item for the Accessory, Folding Chair, and Other Chair Category items as a single item. Also, add an item that groups the remaining Category items into another single item:

1. While holding down the Ctrl key, click the Accessory, Folding Chair, and Other Chair Category items.

2. Right-click the Other Chair Category item, and then click Group and Show Detail ➤ Group.

3. Right-click the Category field button and click Hide.

4. Click the Group1 item (in cell A6), press the F2 key, clear the text Group1, type **Top 3 Categories**, and press the Enter key. Compare your results to Figure 4-7.

	A	B	C	D	E	F
1						
2		Drop Page Fields Here				
3						
4	Sum of In Stock	Quarter				
5	Category2	1	2	3	4	Grand Total
6	Top 3 Categories	87%	87%	87%	87%	87%
7	Dining Set	2%	2%	2%	2%	2%
8	Extending Table	5%	5%	5%	5%	5%
9	Lounger	1%	1%	1%	1%	1%
10	Other Table	5%	5%	4%	5%	5%
11	Grand Total	100%	100%	100%	100%	100%

FIGURE 4-7

Top three Category items grouped into a single item

5. While holding down the Ctrl key, click the Dining Set, Extending Table, Lounger, and Other Table Category items.

6. Right-click the Other Table Category item, and then click Group and Show Detail ➤ Group.

7. Click the Group2 item (in cell A7), press the F2 key, clear the text Group2, type **Bottom 4 Categories**, and press the Enter key. Compare your results to Figure 4-8.

	A	B	C	D	E	F
1						
2		Drop Page Fields Here				
3						
4	Sum of In Stock	Quarter				
5	Category2	1	2	3	4	Grand Total
6	Top 3 Categories	87%	87%	87%	87%	87%
7	Bottom 4 Categories	13%	13%	13%	13%	13%
8	Grand Total	100%	100%	100%	100%	100%

FIGURE 4-8

Bottom four Category items grouped into a single item

8. Show the original items for each group by right-clicking the Category2 field button.

9. Click Group and Show Detail ➤ Show Detail.

10. Click Category, and click OK.

11. On the PivotTable toolbar, click PivotTable ➤ Subtotals. Compare your results to Figure 4-9.

	A	B	C	D	E	F	G
1							
2		Drop Page Fields Here					
3							
4	Sum of In Stock		Quarter ▾				
5	Category2 ▾	Category ▾	1	2	3	4	Grand Total
6	Top 3 Categories	Accessory	23%	19%	23%	23%	22%
7		Folding Chair	36%	37%	37%	36%	36%
8		Other Chair	28%	31%	27%	29%	29%
9	Top 3 Categories Total		87%	87%	87%	87%	87%
10	Bottom 4 Categories	Dining Set	2%	2%	2%	2%	2%
11		Extending Table	5%	5%	5%	5%	5%
12		Lounger	1%	1%	1%	1%	1%
13		Other Table	5%	5%	4%	5%	5%
14	Bottom 4 Categories Total		13%	13%	13%	13%	13%
15	Grand Total		100%	100%	100%	100%	100%

FIGURE 4-9
Showing details for the two grouped items

You can clearly see that the top three Category items comprise 87% of each quarter's in-stock number, whereas the bottom four Category items comprise the remaining 13%.

Now that we've looked at each inventory category as a percentage of the entire in-stock inventory in absolute terms, let's look at how in-stock numbers fluctuate as a running quarter-over-quarter percentage.

Display Data by Category as a Quarterly Differential Percentage

Now look at the in-stock percentages on a running quarter-by-quarter basis:

1. First, remove the grouped field from the PivotTable by right-clicking the Category2 field button and clicking Hide.

2. Right-click the Sum Of In Stock field button and click Field Settings.

3. In the Show Data As list, click % Difference From.

4. In the Base Field list, click Quarter.

5. In the Base Item list, click (Previous), and then click OK. Compare your results to Figure 4-10.

	A	B	C	D	E	F
1						
2			Drop Page Fields Here			
3						
4	Sum of In Stock	Quarter ▾				
5	Category ▾	1	2	3	4	Grand Total
6	Accessory		-29%	10%	51%	
7	Dining Set		5%	-8%	49%	
8	Extending Table		-5%	-14%	44%	
9	Folding Chair		-11%	-11%	47%	
10	Lounger		-7%	-18%	55%	
11	Other Chair		-4%	-22%	67%	
12	Other Table		-15%	-21%	72%	
13	Grand Total		-13%	-11%	54%	

FIGURE 4-10

Running quarter-by-quarter changes in in-stock percentages

You're looking at a change from one quarter to the next. Let's now look at a comparison to just Quarter 1:

1. Right-click the Sum Of In Stock field button and click Field Settings.

2. In the Base Item list, click 1, and then click OK. Compare your results to Figure 4-11.

	A	B	C	D	E	F
1						
2			Drop Page Fields Here			
3						
4	Sum of In Stock	Quarter ▾				
5	Category ▾	1	2	3	4	Grand Total
6	Accessory		-29%	-22%	18%	
7	Dining Set		5%	-4%	43%	
8	Extending Table		-5%	-19%	17%	
9	Folding Chair		-11%	-20%	17%	
10	Lounger		-7%	-24%	17%	
11	Other Chair		-4%	-26%	25%	
12	Other Table		-15%	-33%	15%	
13	Grand Total		-13%	-22%	20%	

FIGURE 4-11

Changes for in-stock percentages as compared to just Quarter 1

We can make several very straightforward conclusions here:

- In Figure 4-10, the second quarter's in-stock numbers fall by an average of 13% as compared to the first quarter, then fall another 11% in the third quarter, and then rise by a huge 54% in the fourth quarter.

- In Figure 4-11, the third quarter's in-stock numbers fall by an average of 22% as compared to the first quarter, and then rise by 20% in the fourth quarter as compared to the first quarter.

- In either case, a pattern emerges. In-stock numbers fall off from the first quarter to the second quarter, fall off even more from the second quarter to the third quarter, and rebound sharply from the third quarter to the fourth quarter.

You've looked only at in-stock numbers to this point. Let's now compare in-stock numbers to on-order numbers to determine whether any correlations exist between items in stock and items on order. As you'll practice in the next section, a good way to do this is to create a second PivotTable showing on-order numbers and place it next to the existing PivotTable that shows in-stock numbers. This makes visual comparisons quick and easy.

Creating a PivotTable Based on Another PivotTable's Source Data

Use another PivotTable to compare the in-stock numbers to the on-order numbers for replenishing warehouse stock:

1. To leave enough room for the first PivotTable, click cell A25.

2. Click Data ➤ PivotTable and PivotChart Report.

3. Click Another PivotTable Report Or PivotChart Report.

4. Click Finish. Another PivotTable, connected by default to the worksheet's existing PivotTable, is created below the existing PivotTable.

5. Drag the Category field from the field list to the new PivotTable's row area.

6. Drag the Quarter field from the field list to the new PivotTable's column area.

7. Drag the On Order field from the field list to the new PivotTable's data area. Compare your results to Figure 4-12.

	A	B	C	D	E	F
22						
23			Drop Page Fields Here			
24						
25	Sum of On Order	Quarter ▼				
26	Category ▼	1	2	3	4	Grand Total
27	Accessory	66	36	31	98	231
28	Dining Set	6	1	0	11	18
29	Extending Table	14	8	4	22	48
30	Folding Chair	104	70	50	153	377
31	Lounger	0	0	0	3	3
32	Other Chair	80	57	36	126	299
33	Other Table	15	8	3	22	48
34	Grand Total	285	180	124	435	1024

FIGURE 4-12

New PivotTable showing the warehouse's on-order figures

8. Right-click the Sum Of On Order field, and then click Field Settings.

9. Click Options.

10. In the Show Data As list, click % Difference From.

11. In the Base Field list, click Quarter.

12. In the Base Item list, click 1.

13. Click Number.

14. In the Category list, make sure Percentage is selected.

15. In the Decimal Places box, select or type the number **0**.

16. Click OK, and click OK again.

17. Right-click the Sum Of On Order field again, and then click Table Options.

18. Select the For Error Values Show check box.

19. In the box next to the For Error Values Show check box, type the number **0**.

20. Click OK, and compare your results to Figure 4-13.

	Sum of On Order	Quarter				
	Category	1	2	3	4	Grand Total
	Accessory		-45%	-53%	48%	
	Dining Set		-83%	-100%	83%	
	Extending Table		-43%	-71%	57%	
	Folding Chair		-33%	-52%	47%	
	Lounger		0%	0%	0%	
	Other Chair		-29%	-55%	58%	
	Other Table		-47%	-80%	47%	
	Grand Total		-37%	-56%	53%	

Drop Page Fields Here

FIGURE 4-13

Changes for on-order percentages as compared to just Quarter 1

Here are the conclusions that we can draw:

- The on-order numbers follow the same pattern as the in-stock numbers. On-order numbers fall off from the first quarter to the second quarter, fall off even more from the second quarter to the third quarter, and rebound sharply from the third quarter to the fourth quarter.

- The on-order changes from one quarter to the next are much more dramatic than the in-stock numbers. The second quarter's on-order numbers fall by an average of 37% as compared to the first quarter, the third quarter's in-stock numbers fall by an average of 56% as compared to the first quarter, and then rise by 53% in the fourth quarter as compared to the first quarter. Compare these to 13%, 22%, and 20% for the in-stock changes, respectively, and you can easily see the magnitude of the on-order changes from quarter to quarter.

Now that you know the percentages of the in-stock and on-order numbers each by themselves, you can figure out the ratio of in-stock numbers to on-order numbers. As you'll see in the next section, this is most easily accomplished by creating a calculated field that displays this ratio.

Create a Calculated Field

Create a calculated field that reflects the percentage ratio of in-stock to on-order furniture:

1. In the topmost PivotTable, click the Sum Of In Stock field button.

2. On the PivotTable toolbar, click PivotTable ➤ Formulas ➤ Calculated Field.

3. Clear the contents of the Name box, and then type **Stock Strength** in the Name box.

4. Clear the contents of the Formula box.

5. In the Fields list, double-click On Order.

6. In the Formula box, type a forward slash (/). The Formula box should now contain the text ='On Order'/.

7. In the Fields list, double-click In Stock. The Formula box should now contain the text ='On Order'/'In Stock'.

8. Click OK.

9. Click the Data field button's arrow.

10. Clear the Sum Of In Stock check box, and then click OK. Compare your results to Figure 4-14.

	A	B	C	D	E	F
1						
2		Drop Page Fields Here				
3						
4	Sum of Stock Strength	Quarter ▾				
5	Category ▾	1	2	3	4	Grand Total
6	Accessory	7%	5%	4%	8%	6%
7	Dining Set	7%	1%	0%	9%	5%
8	Extending Table	7%	4%	2%	9%	6%
9	Folding Chair	7%	5%	4%	8%	6%
10	Lounger	0%	0%	0%	6%	2%
11	Other Chair	7%	5%	4%	8%	6%
12	Other Table	7%	4%	2%	9%	6%
13	Grand Total	7%	5%	4%	8%	6%

FIGURE 4-14

Initial results of creating a calculated field in a PivotTable

11. Right-click the Sum Of Stock Strength field, and then click Field Settings.

12. Click Options.

13. In the Show Data As list, click % Difference From.

14. In the Base Field list, click Quarter.

15. In the Base Item list, click 1, and then click OK.

16. Right-click the Sum Of Stock Strength field again, and then click Table Options.

17. Select the For Error Values Show check box.

18. In the box to the right of the For Error Values Show check box, type the number **0**.

19. Click OK. Compare your results to Figure 4-15.

	A	B	C	D	E	F
1						
2		Drop Page Fields Here				
3						
4	Sum of Stock Strength	Quarter ▾				
5	Category ▾	1	2	3	4	Grand Total
6	Accessory		-23%	-40%	26%	
7	Dining Set		-84%	-100%	28%	
8	Extending Table		-40%	-65%	34%	
9	Folding Chair		-25%	-40%	26%	
10	Lounger		0%	0%	0%	
11	Other Chair		-26%	-40%	26%	
12	Other Table		-37%	-70%	28%	
13	Grand Total		-28%	-44%	28%	

FIGURE 4-15

Changes for stock strength percentages as compared to Quarter 1

Conclusions

As you prepare to meet with the warehouse manager, consider this suggested final analysis from these exercises that can serve as the beginnings of a meeting agenda:

- The top three furniture categories account for a whopping 87% (more than six out of every seven) of in-stock items for the preceding 12 months.

- The Dining Set and Lounger Category items have relatively small in-stock numbers. The Lounger category in particular comprises a miniscule 1% of each quarter's in-stock numbers.

- There is a clear pattern to the in-stock and on-order figures for the preceding 12 months. Both in-stock and on-order levels drop noticeably from the first quarter to second, drop even further from the second quarter to the third quarter, but rise very sharply from the third quarter to the fourth quarter. This pattern is especially pronounced for the on-order figures.

Case Study 2: Tailspin Toys

Tailspin Toys is a distributor of children's toys. Recently, the Tailspin Toys' board of directors gave tentative approval to begin distributing a line of plush stuffed animals, produced by an international toy manufacturer, to a chain of well-known local specialty toy stores. The decision is tentative by the board of directors pending the analysis of a demographic test study of local children with the stuffed animal product line. The test study was completed last week and you're just now receiving the results.

You have been asked to analyze the test study's results and report your findings back to the Tailspin Toys' board of directors in a few days.

The test results figures consist of the following, as shown in Figure 4-16:

- The Category field contains a series of types of animals, such as Jungle, Cave, Forest, and Desert.

- Individual animals such as Alligator, Dolphin, Gorilla, and Panda are listed in the Animal field.

- The Gender field represents both boys and girls.

- The Age field groups boys and girls into age ranges, such as 3 to 5, 6 to 8, and so on.

- The Rating field contains the number 1 through 10 for the combination of each gender, age range, and animal.

- The Interviewer field specifies which survey taker, Joe or Mary, conducted the test for the combination of each gender, age range, and animal.

	A	B	C	D	E	F
1	Category	Animal	Gender	Age	Rating	Interviewer
2	Jungle	Alligator	Boy	3 to 5	6	Mary
3	Cave	Bat	Boy	3 to 5	4	Mary
4	Forest	Bear	Boy	3 to 5	6	Mary
5	Desert	Camel	Boy	3 to 5	6	Mary
6	House	Cat	Boy	3 to 5	5	Joe
7	Jungle	Chimpanzee	Boy	3 to 5	6	Joe
8	Sky	Condor	Boy	3 to 5	7	Mary
9	Ocean	Dolphin	Boy	3 to 5	6	Joe
10	Sky	Eagle	Boy	3 to 5	6	Joe
11	Desert	Elephant	Boy	3 to 5	6	Mary
12	House	Ferret	Boy	3 to 5	5	Joe
279	Forest	Porcupines	Girl	12 and up	10	Mary
280	Jungle	Python	Girl	12 and up	8	Joe
281	Forest	Raccoon	Girl	12 and up	8	Joe
282	Jungle	Rhinoceros	Girl	12 and up	8	Mary
283	Ocean	Sea Lion	Girl	12 and up	10	Joe
284	Ocean	Sea Otter	Girl	12 and up	8	Joe
285	Jungle	Tiger	Girl	12 and up	8	Joe
286	Pond	Turtle	Girl	12 and up	8	Mary
287	Ocean	Walrus	Girl	12 and up	8	Joe
288	Forest	Wolf	Girl	12 and up	10	Joe
289	Desert	Zebra	Girl	12 and up	10	Joe

FIGURE 4-16

Tailspin Toys test results figures to analyze (panes have been split for readability)

Create the PivotTable

Start by creating a PivotTable that connects to the test study's results:

1. Start Excel.

2. Open the TailspinToys.xls file.

3. Click File ➤ New.

4. In the New Workbook task pane, click Blank Workbook.

5. Click Data ➤ PivotTable and PivotChart.

6. Click Next.

7. Click Window ➤ TailspinToys.xls.

8. Select cells A1 through F289 on the Sheet1 worksheet tab.

9. Click Finish. Compare your work to Figure 4-17.

FIGURE 4-17

A PivotTable connected to the Tailspin Toys test study results

Now that you've connected the PivotTable to the test study results, let's add some data to the PivotTable and customize the PivotTable's initial results.

Add Fields to the PivotTable and Customize Data

Continue by adding fields to the PivotTable and customizing the initial results. First examine the average ratings by age group:

1. Drag the Age field from the field list to the column area.

2. Drag the Rating field from the field list to the data area.

3. Drag the Gender field from the field list to the page area.

4. Right click the Sum Of Rating area and click Field Settings.

5. In the Summarize By list, click Average.

6. Click Number.

7. In the Category list, click Number.

8. In the Decimal Places box, click or type the number **1**.

9. Click OK, and click OK again. Compare your results to Figure 4-18.

	A	B	C	D	E	F
1	Gender	(All) ▼				
2						
3	Average of Rating	Age ▼				
4		12 and up	3 to 5	6 to 8	9 to 11	Grand Total
5	Total	6.0	5.9	6.2	6.0	6.0

FIGURE 4-18

Initial layout for the PivotTable based on the Tailspin Toys workbook's data

Initially, the results don't reveal much. The average rating of 5.9 for children ages 3 to 5 rises slightly to 6.2 for children ages 6 to 8. It then drops slightly to 6.0 for children ages 9 and above, which is the average for all children surveyed.

Now that you've looked at the average ratings for all children together, let's look at the average ratings for boys and girls separately. As you'll practice in the next section, you can easily do this by showing one page for boys' average ratings and another page for girls' average ratings. You'll then show boys' and girls' average ratings side by side.

Create Multiple Pages from Page Field Values

Now determine whether any variations exist in the survey results based on the gender. To do this, you'll show the boys' and girls' values together in the original PivotTable. For additional analysis, you'll also create multiple worksheets based on the PivotTable's page field values. Each worksheet will contain its own PivotTable showing data with one worksheet per page field value.

Display one page worth of survey results per gender as follows:

1. Click the Gender field button.

2. On the PivotTable toolbar, click PivotTable ➤ Show Pages.

3. Click OK.

4. Click the Sheet1 worksheet tab.

5. Move the Gender field to the row area. Compare your results to Figures 4-19 through 4-21.

	A	B	C	D	E	F
1	Gender	Boy				
2						
3	Average of Rating	Age				
4		12 and up	3 to 5	6 to 8	9 to 11	Grand Total
5	Total	2.9	5.4	4.8	3.4	4.1

FIGURE 4-19

PivotTable based on boys' survey results (on the Boy worksheet tab)

	A	B	C	D	E	F
1	Gender	Girl				
2						
3	Average of Rating	Age				
4		12 and up	3 to 5	6 to 8	9 to 11	Grand Total
5	Total	9.2	6.4	7.6	8.5	7.9

FIGURE 4-20

PivotTable based on girls' survey results (on the Girl worksheet tab)

	A	B	C	D	E	F
1			Drop Page Fields Here			
2						
3	Average of Rating	Age				
4	Gender	12 and up	3 to 5	6 to 8	9 to 11	Grand Total
5	Boy	2.9	5.4	4.8	3.4	4.1
6	Girl	9.2	6.4	7.6	8.5	7.9
7	Grand Total	6.0	5.9	6.2	6.0	6.0

FIGURE 4-21

PivotTable showing both boys' and girls' survey results together (on the Sheet1 worksheet tab)

Now you can clearly see a trend between the girls' and boys' survey results. The girls' survey results start at 6.4 for ages 3 to 5, then go up to 7.6 for ages 6 to 8, then up to 8.5 for ages 9 to 11, and finally up to 9.2 for ages 12 and up. However, the boys' survey results go in the opposite direction: from 5.4 for ages 3 to 5 to 4.8 for ages 6 to 8, down to 3.4 for ages 9 to 11, and finally down to 2.9 for ages 12 and up.

In the next section, we'll focus on the gradually declining boys' survey results from one age group to the next by ordering and then sorting the boys' survey results in descending order.

Sort and Order Items

Focus on the PivotTable showing only boys' survey results to get more detail about the gradually lowering survey results from one age group to the next by first ordering and then sorting the PivotTable's items.

Start by ordering the column items by age group:

1. On the Boy worksheet tab, drag the Category field from the field list to the row area.

2. Right-click the 12 and Up Age item, and then click Order ➤ Move To End.

Next, sort the categories in descending order, with the highest average ratings at the top of the list:

1. Right-click the Category field button, and then click Field Settings.

2. Click Advanced.

3. Click Descending.

4. In the Using Field list, click Average Of Rating.

5. Click OK, and then click OK again. Compare your results to Figure 4-22.

	A	B	C	D	E	F
1	Gender	Boy				
2						
3	Average of Rating	Age				
4	Category	3 to 5	6 to 8	9 to 11	12 and up	Grand Total
5	Sky	5.7	4.3	4.0	4.3	4.6
6	House	5.7	5.0	4.3	2.7	4.4
7	Cave	4.0	6.0	2.0	5.0	4.3
8	Forest	4.8	5.2	4.2	2.7	4.2
9	Jungle	5.3	5.0	3.0	3.1	4.1
10	Pond	5.7	4.7	3.0	3.0	4.1
11	Desert	5.8	4.8	3.2	1.8	3.9
12	Ocean	5.5	3.8	3.3	2.5	3.8
13	Grand Total	5.4	4.8	3.4	2.9	4.1

FIGURE 4-22

Categories listed in descending order with the highest average ratings at the top of the list

The Sky Category item has the highest average with 4.6. Four categories are above the average of 4.1, two categories are at the average level, and two categories are below the average. Animals in the Sky, House, Cave, and Forest categories might be good sellers.

You now know the average survey results of each category. What about the highest-surveyed animal in each category? Let's find out in the next section.

AutoShow Inner Row Field Top Items

Now find the highest-surveyed Animal item for each category:

1. Click the Category field button.

2. On the PivotTable toolbar, click Show Detail.

3. Click Animal, and then click OK.

4. Right-click the Animal field button, and then click Field Settings.

5. Click Advanced.

6. Click On.

7. In the box next to the Show Top list, type or click the number **1**.

8. Click OK, and then click OK again. Compare your results to Figure 4-23.

	A	B	C	D	E	F	G
1	Gender	Boy ▼					
2							
3	Average of Rating		Age ▼				
4	Category ▼	Animal ▼	3 to 5	6 to 8	9 to 11	12 and up	Grand Total
5	Sky	Condor	7.0	6.0	5.0	5.0	5.8
6	Sky Total		7.0	6.0	5.0	5.0	5.8
7	Jungle	Lemur	6.0	6.0	3.0	5.0	5.0
8	Jungle Total		6.0	6.0	3.0	5.0	5.0
9	Forest	Bear	6.0	6.0	4.0	4.0	5.0
10	Forest Total		6.0	6.0	4.0	4.0	5.0
11	Pond	Turtle	7.0	3.0	5.0	4.0	4.8
12	Pond Total		7.0	3.0	5.0	4.0	4.8
13	Ocean	Walrus	5.0	4.0	5.0	5.0	4.8
14	Ocean Total		5.0	4.0	5.0	5.0	4.8
15	House	Cat	5.0	5.0	4.0	4.0	4.5
16		Fish	7.0	4.0	5.0	2.0	4.5
17	House Total		6.0	4.5	4.5	3.0	4.5
18	Cave	Bat	4.0	6.0	2.0	5.0	4.3
19	Cave Total		4.0	6.0	2.0	5.0	4.3
20	Desert	Elephant	6.0	6.0	4.0	1.0	4.3
21		Lion	6.0	6.0	4.0	1.0	4.3
22	Desert Total		6.0	6.0	4.0	1.0	4.3
23	Grand Total		5.9	5.2	4.1	3.6	4.7

FIGURE 4-23

The highest-surveyed Animal items for each category

The Condor Animal item has the highest average with 5.8. Five animals are above the average of 4.7 and five animals are below the average. Specifically, the Condor, Lemur, Bear, Turtle, and Walrus animals might be good sellers.

You might be able to better sell your animal toys by grouping them into product lines. Let's see in the next section what the results might look like.

Group Items

Perform additional data analysis by grouping similar categories together into ad hoc product lines:

1. Holding the Ctrl key down, click the Jungle, Forest, House, Cave, and Desert Category items. After you have clicked all of these items, release the Ctrl key.

2. Right-click the Desert item and click Group and Show Detail ➤ Group.

3. Click Group1.

4. Press the F2 key.

5. Delete the text Group1.

6. Type **Land**, and press the Enter key. Compare your results to Figure 4-24.

	A	B	C	D	E	F	G	H
1	Gender	Boy ▼						
2								
3	Average of Rating			Age ▼				
4	Category2 ▼	Category ▼	Animal ▼	3 to 5	6 to 8	9 to 11	12 and up	Grand Total
5	Land	Jungle	Lemur	6.0	6.0	3.0	5.0	5.0
6		Jungle Total		6.0	6.0	3.0	5.0	5.0
7		Forest	Bear	6.0	6.0	4.0	4.0	5.0
8		Forest Total		6.0	6.0	4.0	4.0	5.0
9		House	Cat	5.0	5.0	4.0	4.0	4.5
10			Fish	7.0	4.0	5.0	2.0	4.5
11		House Total		6.0	4.5	4.5	3.0	4.5
12		Cave	Bat	4.0	6.0	2.0	5.0	4.3
13		Cave Total		4.0	6.0	2.0	5.0	4.3
14		Desert	Elephant	6.0	6.0	4.0	1.0	4.3
15			Lion	6.0	6.0	4.0	1.0	4.3
16		Desert Total		6.0	6.0	4.0	1.0	4.3
17	Ocean	Ocean	Walrus	5.0	4.0	5.0	5.0	4.8
18		Ocean Total		5.0	4.0	5.0	5.0	4.8
21	Sky	Sky	Condor	7.0	6.0	5.0	5.0	5.8
22		Sky Total		7.0	6.0	5.0	5.0	5.8
23	Grand Total			5.9	5.2	4.1	3.6	4.7

FIGURE 4-24

Results of grouping the land animals together (panes have been split for readability)

7. Holding the Ctrl key down, click the Ocean and Pond Category2 items. After you have clicked these items, release the Ctrl key.

8. Right-click the Pond item and click Group and Show Detail ➤ Group.

9. Click Group2.

10. Press the F2 key.

11. Delete the text Group2.

12. Type **Water**, and press the Enter key.

13. Click the Category2 field button.

14. On the PivotTable toolbar, click Hide Detail.

15. Right-click the Category2 field button, and then click Field Settings.

16. Click Advanced.

17. Click Descending.

18. In the Using Field list, click Average Of Rating.

19. Click OK, and then click OK again. Compare your results to Figure 4-25.

	A	B	C	D	E	F	G	H
1	Gender	Boy ▼						
2								
3	Average of Rating			Age ▼				
4	Category2 ▼	Categor ▼	Animal ▼	3 to 5	6 to 8	9 to 11	12 and up	Grand Total
5	Sky			5.7	4.3	4.0	4.3	4.6
6	Land			5.3	5.0	3.5	2.8	4.1
7	Water			5.6	4.1	3.2	2.7	3.9
8	Grand Total			5.4	4.8	3.4	2.9	4.1

FIGURE 4-25

Similar categories grouped into product lines

You can see that the Sky product line had the highest survey average with 4.6, followed by the Land product line with an average of 4.1, and the Water product line with and average of 3.9. You can also clearly see that selling the products to boys ages 3 to 8 might be more profitable than selling to boys ages 9 and higher.

In the next section, you'll look for variations in survey results as compared to the overall average survey results.

Calculating Standard Deviation and Comparing to the Average

As a final analysis, were any of the groups of average survey results by age range widely higher or lower than the total average survey results? Also, were any of the average scores recorded by the survey takers way above or below the total average survey results? Calculating the standard deviation (the measure of how widely values are dispersed from a set average value) and comparing it to the average baseline survey results should help determine this:

1. On the Sheet1 worksheet, drag the Interviewer field from the field list to the PivotTable as an outer row field. Compare your results to Figure 4-26.

	A	B	C	D	E	F	G
1			Drop Page Fields Here				
2							
3	Average of Rating		Age ▾				
4	Interviewer ▾	Gender ▾	12 and up	3 to 5	6 to 8	9 to 11	Grand Total
5	Joe	Boy	2.7	5.5	4.9	3.3	4.1
6		Girl	9.2	6.4	7.5	8.6	7.9
7	Joe Total		6.5	6.0	6.4	6.4	6.3
8	Mary	Boy	3.0	5.3	4.7	3.5	4.2
9		Girl	9.2	6.4	7.7	8.4	7.9
10	Mary Total		5.4	5.8	5.9	5.6	5.7
11	Grand Total		6.0	5.9	6.2	6.0	6.0

FIGURE 4-26

Interviewer field as an outer row field

2. Hide the Gender details for now by right-clicking the Gender field button and clicking Group and Show Detail ➤ Hide Detail.

3. Right-click the Average Of Rating field and click Field Settings.

4. In the Summarize By List, click StdDevp.

5. Click Number.

6. In the Category list, click Number.

7. In the Decimal Places list, type or click the number **1**.

8. Click OK, and then click OK again. Compare your results to Figure 4-27.

	A	B	C	D	E	F	G
1			Drop Page Fields Here				
2							
3	StdDevp of Rating		Age				
4	Interviewer	Gender	12 and up 3 to 5		6 to 8	9 to 11	Grand Total
5	Joe		3.4	0.9	1.8	2.8	2.5
6	Mary		3.2	1.3	1.8	2.7	2.3
7	Grand Total		3.3	1.1	1.8	2.8	2.4

FIGURE 4-27

Calculating the StdDevp function for survey results

9. Drag the Rating field from the field list to the Data area.

10. Right-click the Sum Of Rating field and click Field Settings.

11. In the Summarize By list, click Average.

12. Click Number.

13. In the Category list, click Number.

14. In the Decimal Places list, type or click the number **1**.

15. Click OK, and then click OK again. Compare your results with Figure 4-28.

	A	B	C	D	E	F	G	H
1			Drop Page Fields Here					
2								
3				Age				
4	Interviewer	Gender	Data	12 and up 3 to 5		6 to 8	9 to 11	Grand Total
5	Joe		StdDevp of Rating	3.4	0.9	1.8	2.8	2.5
6			Average of Rating	6.5	6.0	6.4	6.4	6.3
7	Mary		StdDevp of Rating	3.2	1.3	1.8	2.7	2.3
8			Average of Rating	5.4	5.8	5.9	5.6	5.7
9	Total StdDevp of Rating			3.3	1.1	1.8	2.8	2.4
10	Total Average of Rating			6.0	5.9	6.2	6.0	6.0

FIGURE 4-28

Standard deviation by interviewer name and childrens' age group, compared to the baseline average values

Analyzing these figures doesn't reveal any odd-looking numbers. For each age range and for each interviewer, the average values and standard deviation values appear to be consistent. Therefore, you can theorize that the survey results were not unduly influenced by either of the survey takers.

Conclusions

Now that you've analyzed survey results for both boys and girls by sorting, ordering, grouping, and calculating averages and standard deviation, here are a few of the final conclusions that you can present to the Tailspin Toys board of directors:

- The overall average survey results didn't seem to favor one set of overall age ranges over another.

- Comparing average survey results for boys versus girls, however, provides some insights. Girls' average survey results go from about 6.5 to more than 9 from the lower to higher age ranges. Boys' average survey results go in the opposite direction, from about 5.5 to less than 3 from the lower to higher age ranges. In each age range, girls' average survey results were clearly higher than boys' average survey results, anywhere from 1 to 6 points.

- Drilling into the boys' overall average survey results, animals in the Sky, House, Cave, and Forest categories might be good sellers. More specifically, the Condor, Lemur, Bear, Turtle, and Walrus animals might be good sellers.

- Selling these toys to boys ages 3 to 8 might be more profitable than selling to boys ages 9 and higher.

Case Study 3: Contoso Publishing Ltd.

Contoso Publishing Limited is an academic book wholesaler that caters to several senior high schools and two-year community colleges across Contoso's home city. The vice president of Contoso's marketing department wants to investigate fluctuating book sales over the past three years. Sales in the year 2002 were 10% higher than in 2001, but sales dropped about 3% from 2002 to 2003.

The vice president has given you, Contoso's product manager, a list of book sales over the past three years and has asked you to report your analysis back to him at tomorrow morning's extended staff meeting.

The sales figures consist of the following, as shown in Figure 4-29:

	A	B	C	D
1	Category	Subcategory	Sales Year	Titles Sold
2	Agriculture	Dictionary	2001	3
3	Agriculture	General	2001	209
4	Animals	General	2001	418
5	Animals	Horses	2001	234
6	Anthropology	Archeology	2001	128
7	Anthropology	General	2001	105
8	Anthropology	Native American	2001	284
9	Architecture	Dictionary	2001	4
10	Architecture	General	2001	223
11	Architecture	House Plans	2001	52
12	Art	Calligraphy	2001	26
789	Sports	Yoga	2003	15
790	Sports	Youth	2003	8
791	Teen Reader	General	2003	161
792	Transportation	Automotive	2003	162
793	Transportation	Aviation	2003	173
794	Transportation	Boats	2003	148
795	Transportation	General	2003	197
796	Transportation	Trains	2003	121
797	Young Adult	General	2003	1021
798	Young Adult	Nonfiction	2003	240
799	Young Adult	Teen Reader	2003	168

FIGURE 4-29

Contoso Publishing Ltd. sales figures to analyze (panes have been split for readability)

- The Category field contains a list of book categories such as Art, Business, and Engineering.

- Book subcategories such as Calligraphy, Management, and Home Electronics are listed in the Subcategory field.

- The Sales Year field categorizes sales by the years 2001, 2002, and 2003.

- The Titles Sold field contains the number of books sold per year per subcategory.

Create the PivotTable

Start by creating a PivotTable that connects to the book sales figures:

1. Start Excel.

2. Open the ContosoPublishing.xls file.

3. Click File ➤ New.

4. In the New Workbook task pane, click Blank Workbook.

5. Click Data ➤ PivotTable And PivotChart.

6. Click Next.

7. Click Window ➤ ContosoPublishing.xls.

8. Select cells A1 through D799 on the Sheet1 worksheet tab.

9. Click Finish. Compare your results to Figure 4-30.

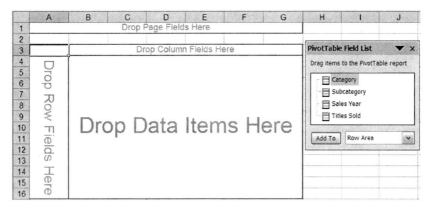

FIGURE 4-30
A PivotTable connected to the Contoso Publishing Ltd. sales figures

Now that you've connected the PivotTable to the sales figures, let's add some facts and figures to the PivotTable.

Add Fields to the PivotTable

Continue by adding fields to the PivotTable:

1. Drag the Category field from the field list to the PivotTable's row area.

2. Drag the Sales Year field from the field list to the column area.

3. Drag the Titles Sold field from the field list to the data area. Compare your results to Figure 4-31.

	A	B	C	D	E
1		Drop Page Fields Here			
2					
3	Sum of Titles Sold	Sales Year ▼			
4	Category ▼	2001	2002	2003	Grand Total
5	Agriculture	212	386	508	1106
6	Animals	652	753	929	2334
7	Anthropology	517	602	846	1965
8	Architecture	279	445	631	1355
9	Art	1112	1564	1921	4597
10	Beverage	44	126	216	386
11	Biography	1511	1824	2194	5529
12	Biology	902	1046	1442	3390
56	Sewing & Needle	526	601	692	1819
57	Sports	1418	1105	257	2780
58	Teen Reader	152	155	161	468
59	Transportation	247	538	801	1586
60	Young Adult	1349	1379	1429	4157
61	Grand Total	53129	58834	57197	169160

FIGURE 4-31

Initial layout for the PivotTable based on the Contoso Publishing Ltd. Book sales data (panes have been split for readability)

Although you can see a bunch of data in the PivotTable, it would be easier to analyze the data if it were sorted somehow. You'll practice doing that in the next section.

Sort and Order Items

Look at top-selling categories first by sorting the category items:

1. Right-click the Category field, and then click Field Settings.

2. Click Advanced.

3. Click Descending.

4. In the Using Field list, click Sum Of Titles Sold.

5. Click OK, and then click OK again. Compare your results to Figure 4-32.

	A	B	C	D	E
1		Drop Page Fields Here			
2					
3	Sum of Titles Sold	Sales Year ▾			
4	Category ▾	2001	2002	2003	Grand Total
5	Children	15131	13609	2390	31130
6	Literature	5492	5872	6525	17889
7	Business	1468	2476	3218	7162
8	Science Fiction	1944	2376	2754	7074
9	Calendars	3664	2230	924	6818
10	Nature	1515	2146	2901	6562
11	Biography	1511	1824	2194	5529
12	Art	1112	1564	1921	4597
56	Dance	39	122	165	326
57	Globes	39	90	105	234
58	Postcard	8	29	90	127
59	Politics	3	16	92	111
60	Faculty Authors	4	18	77	99
61	Grand Total	53129	58834	57197	169160

FIGURE 4-32

Book categories sorted by top-selling categories at the head of the list
(panes have been split for readability)

You can now see the top selling book categories by number of books sold.
Now look at the percentage of books sold as compared to all of the book sold.

Changing How the Data Format Is Displayed

Of the more than 169,000 books sold in the three years, Children and Literature
Category items seem to have sold the most. Uncover the percentage of the total
book sales by titles belonging to the Children and Literature Category items by
following these steps:

1. Right-click the Sum Of Titles Sold field button and click Field Settings.

2. Click Options.

3. In the Show Data As list, click % Of Column.

4. Click Number.

5. In the Decimal Places box, type or click **0**.

6. Click OK, and then click OK again. Compare your results to Figure 4-33.

	A	B	C	D	E
1		Drop Page Fields Here			
2					
3	Sum of Titles Sold	Sales Year ▼			
4	Category ▼	2001	2002	2003	Grand Total
5	Children	28%	23%	4%	18%
6	Literature	10%	10%	11%	11%
7	Business	3%	4%	6%	4%
8	Science Fiction	4%	4%	5%	4%
9	Calendars	7%	4%	2%	4%
10	Nature	3%	4%	5%	4%
11	Biography	3%	3%	4%	3%
12	Art	2%	3%	3%	3%
56	Dance	0%	0%	0%	0%
57	Globes	0%	0%	0%	0%
58	Postcard	0%	0%	0%	0%
59	Politics	0%	0%	0%	0%
60	Faculty Authors	0%	0%	0%	0%
61	Grand Total	100%	100%	100%	100%

FIGURE 4-33

Percentage of overall books sold by category

The Children category contributed 18% of total book sales, and Literature contributed 11% of total book sales. The next-highest contributing categories are a distant 4%.

Now revert the data back to the sum of books sold:

1. Right-click the Sum Of Titles Sold field button and click Field Settings.

2. If the Show Data As list is not visible, click Options.

3. In the Show Data As list, click Normal.

4. Click OK. Your PivotTable should now look similar to Figure 4-31.

Now that you've looked at sales percentages of individual book categories compared to all book categories, in the next section you'll look at sales percentages of individual book categories compared to the first year's sales.

Comparison of Sales as Percent Difference from Base Data

Now look at the change in sales for each year as a difference from the first year that sales were reported:

1. Right-click the Sum Of Titles Sold field button and click Field Settings.

2. Click Options.

3. In the Show Data As list, click % Difference From.

4. In the Base Field list, click Sales Year.

5. In the Base Item list, click 2001.

6. Click Number.

7. In the Decimal Places box, type or click the number **0**.

8. Click OK, and click OK again. Compare your results to Figure 4-34.

	A	B	C	D	E
1		Drop Page Fields Here			
2					
3	Sum of Titles Sold	Sales Year ⏷			
4	Category ⏷	2001	2002	2003	Grand Total
5	Children		-10%	-84%	
6	Literature		7%	19%	
7	Business		69%	119%	
8	Science Fiction		22%	42%	
9	Calendars		-39%	-75%	
10	Nature		42%	91%	
11	Biography		21%	45%	
12	Art		41%	73%	
53	Teen Reader		2%	6%	
54	K-12		414%	1181%	
55	Beverage		186%	391%	
56	Dance		213%	323%	
57	Globes		131%	169%	
58	Postcard		263%	1025%	
59	Politics		433%	2967%	
60	Faculty Authors		350%	1825%	
61	Grand Total		11%	8%	

FIGURE 4-34

Percentage difference of book sales by category in 2002 and 2003 compared to 2001 book sales (panes have been split for readability)

9. Drag the Titles Sold field from the field list to the data area.

10. Right-click the Sum Of Titles Sold Data item and click Field Settings.

11. In the Name box, type **Running Year Sales Change**, and then click OK.

12. Right-click the Sum Of Titles Sold2 Data item and click Field Settings.

13. In the Name box, type **Sum Of Titles Sold**, and then click OK. Compare your results to Figure 4-35.

	A	B	C	D	E	F
1			Drop Page Fields Here			
2						
3			Sales Year			
4	Category	Data	2001	2002	2003	Grand Total
5	Children	Running Year Sales Change		-10%	-84%	
6		Sum of Titles Sold	15131	13609	2390	31130
7	Literature	Running Year Sales Change		7%	19%	
8		Sum of Titles Sold	5492	5872	6525	17889
9	Business	Running Year Sales Change		69%	119%	
10		Sum of Titles Sold	1468	2476	3218	7162
11	Science Fiction	Running Year Sales Change		22%	42%	
12		Sum of Titles Sold	1944	2376	2754	7074
109	Globes	Running Year Sales Change		131%	169%	
110		Sum of Titles Sold	39	90	105	234
111	Postcard	Running Year Sales Change		263%	1025%	
112		Sum of Titles Sold	8	29	90	127
113	Politics	Running Year Sales Change		433%	2967%	
114		Sum of Titles Sold	3	16	92	111
115	Faculty Authors	Running Year Sales Change		350%	1825%	
116		Sum of Titles Sold	4	18	77	99
117	Total Running Year Sales Change			11%	8%	
118	Total Sum of Titles Sold		53129	58834	57197	169160

FIGURE 4-35

Change in sales for each year as a difference from the first year that sales were reported

The first category, Children, shows a 10% decrease in sales from 2001 to 2002, and a whopping 84% sales decrease from 2002 to 2003. This looks like a big decrease, but was it the biggest decrease for a book category? Let's find out in the next section.

Conditional Formatting

Did the Children category lose the most sales year-over-year? Use conditional formatting to highlight other categories that seem to be the biggest year-over-year sales losers:

1. Select cells D5 through E116.

2. Click Format ➤ Conditional Formatting.

3. In the list next to the Cell Value Is list, click Less Than.

4. In the box next to the Less Than list, type the number **0**.

5. Click Format.

6. On the Patterns tab, click a red square.

7. Click OK, and then click OK again.

Group Items

Now that you can see the categories in red that you're interested in, group those categories together and then remove the conditional formatting:

1. Holding down the Ctrl key, click each Category item—Children, Calendars, Sports, Gardening, and Family–with red cells on the same row. After you select each item, release the Ctrl key.

2. Right-click the Family item and click Group and Show Detail ➤ Group.

3. Click the arrow in the Category2 button, clear the (Show All) check box, select the Group1 check box, and click OK.

4. Click Edit ➤ Go To.

5. Click Special.

6. Click Conditional Formats, and then click OK.

7. Click Format ➤ Conditional Formatting.

8. Click Delete.

9. Select the Condition 1 check box.

10. Click OK, and then click OK again. Compare your results to Figure 4-36.

	A	B	C	D	E	F	G
1			Drop Page Fields Here				
2							
3				Sales Year ▾			
4	Category2 ▾	Category ▾	Data ▾	2001	2002	2003	Grand Total
5	Group1	Children	Running Year Sales Change		-10%	-84%	
6			Sum of Titles Sold	15131	13609	2390	31130
7		Calendars	Running Year Sales Change		-39%	-75%	
8			Sum of Titles Sold	3664	2230	924	6818
9		Sports	Running Year Sales Change		-22%	-82%	
10			Sum of Titles Sold	1418	1105	257	2780
11		Gardening	Running Year Sales Change		-63%	-57%	
12			Sum of Titles Sold	1493	559	645	2697
13		Family	Running Year Sales Change		-21%	-31%	
14			Sum of Titles Sold	692	549	480	1721
15	Total Running Year Sales Change				-19%	-79%	
16	Total Sum of Titles Sold			22398	18052	4696	45146

FIGURE 4-36

Categories losing the most book sales year–over–year

Conclusions

Now that you've grouped the book categories together that have lost the most sales, the analysis is becoming much clearer.

The Children category is most likely the cause of the sales problem. Book sales in this category went from more than 15,000 titles in 2001 (28% of that year's total book sales), down slightly to more than 13,500 titles in 2002 (23% of that year's total book sales), and then sharply down to less than 2,500 titles in 2003 (only 4% of that year's total book sales). The next-highest selling category, Literature, didn't have this problem. Book sales in this category were at a steady 10% to 11% of each year's total book sales, with decent year-over-year sale gains. Other book categories to keep an eye on include Calendars, Sports, Gardening, and perhaps Family.

Next Steps

In this chapter, you analyzed data for a furniture manufacturer, a toy distributor, and a book wholesaler. You used your skills with the PivotTable and PivotChart Wizard, the PivotTable Field dialog box, the PivotTable toolbar, and the PivotTable menu to draw conclusions and make recommendations for others to take well-informed business actions.

In this chapter, you learned how to

- Format data to display percentages of running changes over time or to show ratios.

- Group items for ad hoc categorization of results.

- Look at multiple PivotTables side by side or on different worksheets for easier data visualization.

- Sort, order, and filter items and data to quickly display the most important values.

- Create custom calculated fields and items to add depth and insight to your data.

- Use conditional formatting to visually highlight key data.

As you apply these exercises to your own data, you now have some techniques to try out and some approaches to consider for getting better insights that can turn into quicker and better decision-making based on what the PivotTables reveal to you.

5

Working with
PivotCharts

Until now, you've been working with PivotTables. In this chapter, you'll learn how to enhance your data analysis by using PivotCharts. PivotCharts can provide you with additional data analysis insights that you can't get from looking at facts and figures alone.

By the end of this chapter, you'll learn how to create and use both two-dimensional and three-dimensional PivotCharts to add life to your PivotTables. You'll not only add visual depth to your PivotCharts, but you'll also learn how to customize the visual appearance of your PivotCharts by adding color, text, and numbers to make your data analysis tasks even easier than before.

What Are PivotCharts?

As the name implies, you can use PivotCharts to provide a more graphically oriented representation of PivotTables. In previous chapters, you used PivotTables to organize and analyze facts and figures in a nongraphical format. However, you already know that presenting facts and figures graphically helps you spot trends, comparisons, contrasts, and anomalies more quickly. A PivotChart, like a picture in that old saying, can be worth a thousand facts and figures from a PivotTable. Think about your own experiences in dealing with facts and figures. Whether you're looking at how a particular stock price, local weather conditions, or sports statistics are trending over time, it can be much easier to see the numbers represented in a chart.

The sample data in Figure 5-1 shows an example of the various PivotChart types you can create.

	A	B	C
1	Month	Fish Type	Count
2	January	Chinook	0
3	February	Chinook	503
4	March	Chinook	593
5	April	Chinook	4240
6	May	Chinook	5494
7	June	Chinook	6579
8	January	Coho	0
9	February	Coho	300
10	March	Coho	500
11	April	Coho	1027
12	May	Coho	1670
13	June	Coho	2751
14	January	Steelhead	236
15	February	Steelhead	646
16	March	Steelhead	1799
17	April	Steelhead	1815
18	May	Steelhead	2947
19	June	Steelhead	8133
20	January	Sockeye	0
21	February	Sockeye	0
22	March	Sockeye	0
23	April	Sockeye	0
24	May	Sockeye	131
25	June	Sockeye	1070

FIGURE 5-1

Sample data on which to base your PivotCharts

Now create a PivotChart out of this data. From there, we'll explore other standard PivotCharts.

1. Start Excel. A new blank worksheet appears.

2. Type the data in Figure 5-1 into the worksheet.

3. Click Data ➤ PivotTable and PivotChart Report.

4. Click PivotChart Report (With PivotTable Report), and then click Next.

5. Select cells A1 through C25, and then click Finish. Compare your results to Figure 5-2.

FIGURE 5-2
A blank PivotChart

6. Drag the Month field from the PivotTable Field List dialog box to the PivotChart's Drop Category Fields Here area, as shown in Figure 5-3.

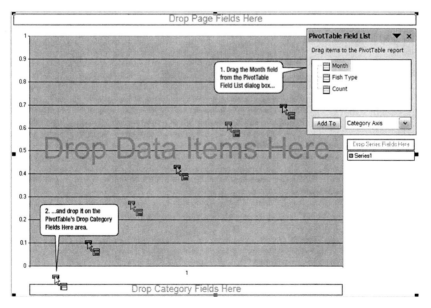

FIGURE 5-3.
Adding fields to the PivotChart's layout

7. Drag the Fish Type field from the PivotTable Field List dialog box to the PivotChart's Drop Series Fields Here area.

8. Drag the Count field from the PivotTable Field List dialog box to the PivotChart's Drop Data Items Here area. Compare your results to Figure 5-4.

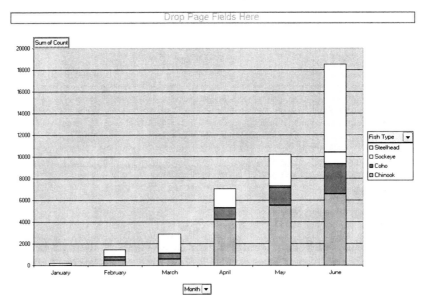

FIGURE 5-4

The finished PivotChart

Area charts represent data as a filled proportion of the entire plot area. You can display either a two-dimensional or three-dimensional area (as shown in Figure 5-5) chart.

9. To create this area chart, right-click a blank area of the PivotChart and click Chart Type.

10. On the Standard Types tab, click Area in the Chart Type list.

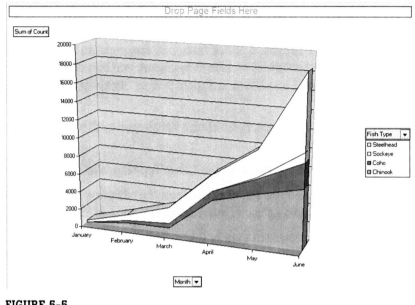

FIGURE 5-5

An area chart

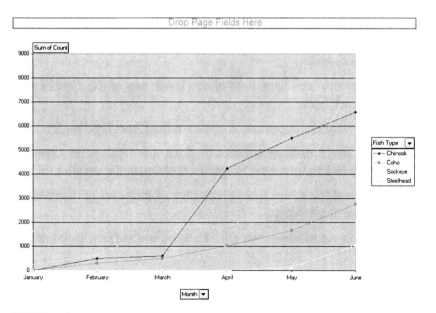

FIGURE 5-6

A line chart

11. In the Chart Sub-Type list, click the icon that displays the Stacked Area With A 3-D Visual Effect caption, and then click OK.

    Line charts are similar to area charts, but they represent data as a line and not a filled proportion. Like area charts, you can display either a two-dimensional (as shown in Figure 5-6) or three-dimensional line chart.

12. To create this line chart, right-click a blank area of the PivotChart and click Chart Type.

13. On the Standard Types tab, in the Chart Type list, click Line.

14. In the Chart Sub-Type list, click the icon that displays the Line With Markers Displayed At Each Data Value caption, and then click OK.

    Surface charts represent data in three dimensions using a textured plot area, similar to a geographical relief map. Surface charts are good for displaying data along three axes.

    Radar charts are similar to surface charts, but they do not use a textured plot area. Like surface charts, radar charts are good for displaying data along three axes.

    Bar charts (as shown in Figure 5-7) and column charts allow you to represent data in rectangular horizontal (left-to-right) bars or rectangular vertical (top-to-bottom) columns (as shown in Figure 5-8). You can display two-dimensional and three-dimensional bar and column charts.

15. To create this bar chart, right-click a blank area of the PivotChart and click Chart Type.

16. On the Standard Types tab, click Bar in the Chart Type list.

17. In the Chart Sub-Type list, click the icon that displays the Clustered Bar. Compares Values Across Categories caption, and then click OK.

18. To create this column chart, right-click a blank area of the PivotChart and click Chart Type.

19. On the Standard Types tab, click Column in the Chart Type list.

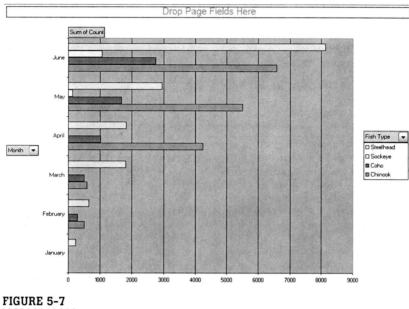

FIGURE 5-7

A bar chart

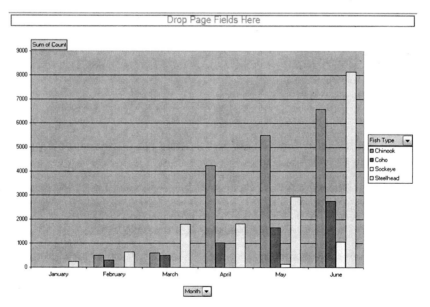

FIGURE 5-8

A column chart

20. In the Chart Sub-Type list, click the icon that displays the Clustered Column. Compares Values Across Categories caption, and then click OK.

Cylinder charts (as shown in Figure 5-9), *cone charts*, and *pyramid charts* are similar to bar and column charts, but they represent their bars and columns in different shapes.

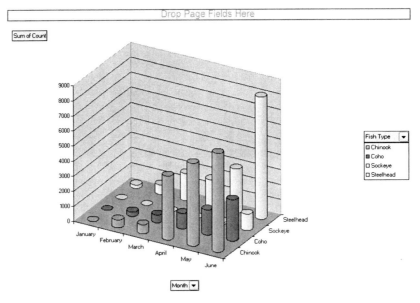

FIGURE 5-9
A cylinder chart

21. To create this cylinder chart, right-click a blank area of the PivotChart and click Chart Type.

22. On the Standard Types tab, click Cylinder in the Chart Type list.

23. In the Chart Sub-Type list, click the icon that displays the 3-D Column With A Cylindrical Shape caption, and then click OK.

Pie charts represent data as proportions of a circular pie shape, as shown in Figure 5-10. You can display either a two-dimensional or three-dimensional pie chart.

24. To create this pie chart, right-click a blank area of the PivotChart and click Chart Type.

25. On the Standard Types tab, click Pie in the Chart Type list.

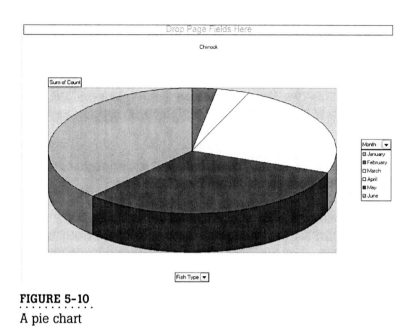

FIGURE 5-10
A pie chart

26. In the Chart Sub-Type list, click the icon that displays the Pie With A 3-D Visual Effect caption, and then click OK.

Doughnut charts are similar to pie charts, but they have the added capability to represent multiple data series as a set of nested rings, as shown in Figure 5-11.

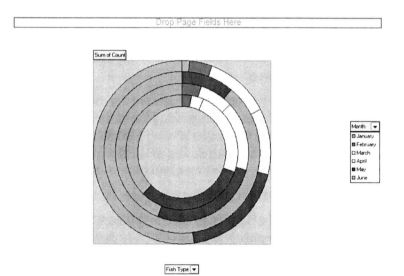

FIGURE 5-11
A doughnut chart

27. To create this doughnut chart, right-click a blank area of the PivotChart and click Chart Type.

28. On the Standard Types tab, click Doughnut in the Chart Type list.

29. In the Chart Sub-Type list, click the icon that displays the Doughnut Like A Pie Chart, But Can Contain Multiple Series caption, and then click OK.

You cannot use an *XY (scatter) chart*, *bubble chart*, or *stock chart* type with a PivotChart that has been created from PivotTable data.

NOTE Additional custom PivotChart formats are available, but aren't discussed in this chapter. You can explore these additional formats by clicking the Custom Types tab of the Chart Wizard, as discussed in the upcoming "Creating Pivot Charts" section.

PivotChart Terms

As with PivotTables, several terms are used to describe PivotChart components. It's important that you understand these terms when you work with PivotCharts. Use Figure 5-12 as a visual reference to help you understand the following PivotChart terms:

- The *category axis* in this case is the axis with the months January through December. The Month field in this case was dropped into the PivotChart's *category area*.

- The *chart area* is the entire PivotChart, including axes, the plot area, the legend, and field buttons.

- *Corners* on three-dimensional PivotCharts are the intersection points of the three-dimensional area encompassing the entire PivotChart. In this case, the corners include the points labeled 1800, 0, January, December, Chocolate, Vanilla, and their correlating unlabelled points at the top-right front, top-right rear, top-left rear, and bottom-left rear.

- The *data table* is the table containing the figures below each column.

- The *field buttons* are the buttons labeled in this case Sales Rep (*page field* dropped onto the *page area*), Sum Of Cases Sold (*data field* dropped onto the *data area*), Month (*category field*), and Flavor (*series field*).

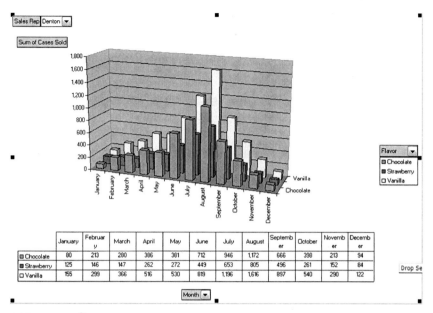

The chart and its data table:

	January	February	March	April	May	June	July	August	September	October	November	December
⊠ Chocolate	80	213	280	386	381	712	946	1,172	666	398	213	94
⊠ Strawberry	125	146	147	262	272	449	653	805	496	261	152	84
□ Vanilla	155	299	366	516	530	819	1,196	1,616	897	540	290	122

FIGURE 5-12

A sample PivotChart

NOTE In this instance, the PivotChart category field corresponds to the PivotTable row field, while the PivotChart series field corresponds to the PivotTable column field. This is the default layout when you use the Chart Wizard or PivotTable and PivotChart Wizard. This layout can be changed later by manually rearranging the fields on the PivotChart.

- The *floor* is the bottom-most plane of a three-dimensional PivotChart. In this case, the floor touches the points labeled January, 0, December, Chocolate, Vanilla, and the correlating unlabelled point in the bottom-left rear.

- *Items* include field items such as January (*category item*), Chocolate (*series item*), and Denton (*page item*).

- The *legend* is the box labeled Flavor.

- The *plot area* includes everything on the PivotChart except for the field buttons, the legend, and the data table.

- The *series axis* in this case is the axis with the flavors Chocolate, Strawberry, and Vanilla. Each of these items on a two-dimensional PivotChart is known as a *series*. The Flavor field was dropped onto the PivotChart's *series area*. Series are best represented by row field items and column field items.

- The *value axis* in this case is the axis with the values 0 through 1,800.

- The *value axis major gridlines* are the lines starting at the values 0 through 1,800 that proceed to the back and then along to the far right of the PivotChart.

- The *walls* are the planes along the left and rear sides of the PivotChart with the value axis major gridlines on them.

Now let's explore how to create and customize PivotCharts.

Creating PivotCharts

You can quickly create a PivotChart and a PivotTable at the same time by using the PivotTable and PivotChart Wizard. You can also create a PivotChart based on an existing PivotTable by using the Chart Wizard. You can then customize the PivotTable from there.

Let's try creating a PivotChart using the sample data as shown in Figure 5-13.

	A	B	C	D
1	Make	Model	Color	Quantity
2	Acme	A100	Red	100
3	Acme	A100	Blue	50
4	Acme	A100	White	90
5	Acme	A100	Black	80
6	Acme	B200	Red	90
7	Acme	B200	Blue	40
8	Acme	B200	White	80
9	Acme	B200	Black	90
10	Acme	C300	Red	120
11	Acme	C300	Blue	130
12	Acme	C300	White	150
13	Acme	C300	Black	140
14	Newco	X7	Red	80
15	Newco	X7	Blue	30
16	Newco	X7	White	70
17	Newco	X7	Black	90
18	Newco	X8	Red	50
19	Newco	X8	Blue	40
20	Newco	X8	White	30
21	Newco	X8	Black	20
22	Newco	X9	Red	60
23	Newco	X9	Blue	100
24	Newco	X9	White	90
25	Newco	X9	Black	80

FIGURE 5-13

Sample data for creating and customizing a PivotChart

Because every PivotChart relies on an associated PivotTable as its under-lying data source, if you don't have an existing PivotTable, you can create a PivotChart and an associated PivotTable at the same time using the PivotTable and PivotChart Wizard:

1. Type the data in Figure 5-13 into a blank Excel worksheet.

2. Click Data ➤ PivotTable and PivotChart Report.

3. Click PivotChart Report (With PivotTable Report), and click Next.

4. Select cells A1 through D25, and then click Finish. A PivotTable and PivotChart are created, as shown in Figures 5-14 and 5-15.

FIGURE 5-14
PivotTable based on the data in Figure 5-13

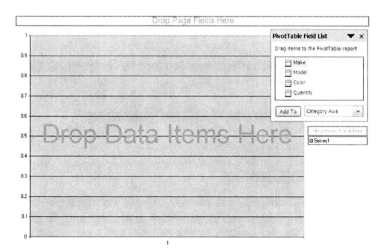

FIGURE 5-15
PivotChart based on the PivotTable in Figure 5-14

Now create a PivotChart based on an existing PivotTable:

1. Click a cell outside and not adjacent to the PivotTable report you created in Figure 5-14.

2. On the Standard toolbar, click Chart Wizard.

3. On the Chart Type tab, click the icon with the 3-D Column Compares Values Across Categories And Across Series caption.

4. Click Next.

5. Click anywhere inside the PivotTable, so that the reference in the Data Range box expands to include the entire PivotTable.

6. Click Finish. Your PivotChart is ready to be customized, as shown in Figure 5-16.

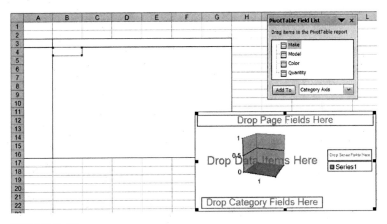

FIGURE 5-16

A new PivotTable and PivotChart, waiting for you to customize them

Next, experiment with your new PivotChart's formatting.

Formatting PivotCharts

After you create a PivotChart, you can format it to get just the right look to convey the insights or messages you want others to understand. In this section, we'll briefly cover the PivotTable toolbar and then how to use the PivotChart context menus to customize the chart area, fields, data series, axes, legend, data table, walls, plot area, gridlines, and floor.

PivotTable Toolbar

One of the ways you can format a PivotChart is by using the PivotTable toolbar. When you create a PivotChart, the PivotTable toolbar changes to display actions more suited to PivotCharts. The toolbar buttons are the same for PivotTables and PivotCharts; however, the PivotTable button title changes to PivotChart. The PivotChart menu includes actions such as Field Settings, Options, Refresh Data, Hide PivotChart Field Buttons, Formulas (which contains the Calculated Field, Calculated Item, Solve Order, and List Formulas commands), and Remove Field commands. These commands should be familiar or self-explanatory to you. For more details on most of these menu commands, see the "Working with the PivotTable Toolbar" and "Working with the PivotTable Menu" sections of Chapter 3.

Before moving on to customizing the PivotChart, let's define the PivotChart's layout:

1. With the PivotChart visible as shown earlier in Figure 5-15, drag the Quantity field from the field list to the data area.

2. Drag the Make field to the page area.

3. Drag the Color field to the category area.

4. Drag the Model field to the series area. Compare your results to Figure 5-17.

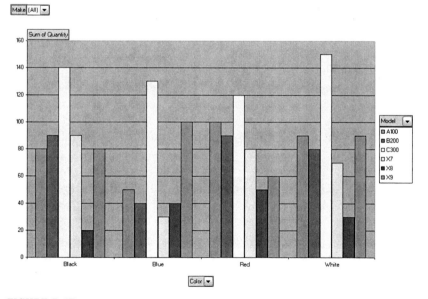

FIGURE 5-17

Customized PivotChart based on the PivotChart from Figure 5-15

Let's make this a three-dimensional PivotChart.

1. Right-click a blank area of the PivotChart and click Chart Type.

2. On the Standard Types tab, click Column in the Chart Type list.

3. In the Chart Sub-Type list, click the icon that displays the 3-D Column Compares Values Across Categories and Across Series caption, and then click OK. Compare your results to Figure 5-18.

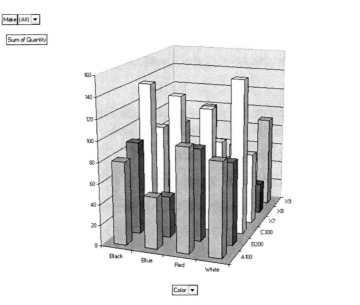

FIGURE 5-18

Three-dimensional version of the PivotChart from Figure 5-17

Next, you'll customize this PivotChart's visual display even further.

Chart Area

When you right-click the chart area, the following menu commands are available:

- Format Chart Area, which allows you to change the border, the chart background color and area/fill format, the chart's overall text font, and additional properties if the PivotChart is on a worksheet as shown in Figures 5-19 through 5-21.

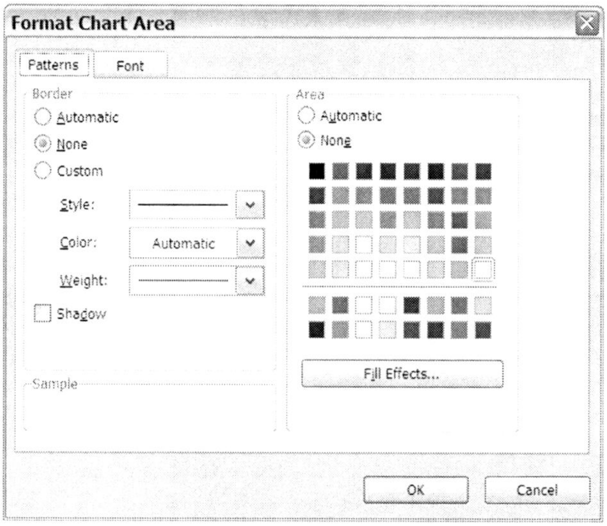

FIGURE 5-19
The Format Chart Area dialog box's Patterns tab

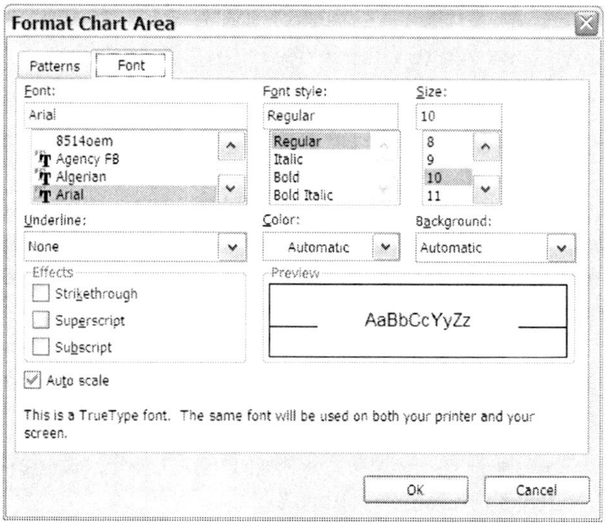

FIGURE 5-20
The Format Chart Area dialog box's Font tab

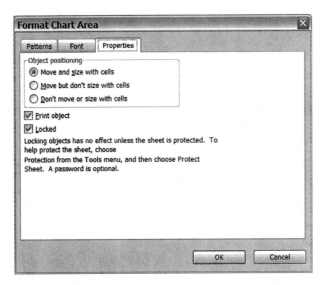

FIGURE 5-21

The Format Chart Area dialog box's Properties tab (only available if the PivotChart is on a worksheet)

- Chart Type, which allows you to change the type of PivotChart.

  NOTE The Source Data command is not enabled for PivotCharts. In a regular, noninteractive chart, you can use the Source Data command when you want to change the position of your series or category data or redefine the source data to be included. To complete these tasks with a PivotChart, you can either rearrange the fields on your PivotChart, or use the PivotTable and PivotChart Wizard to redefine the source data.

- Chart Options, which display the Chart Options dialog box. The tabs in this dialog box are described in the following list:

  - The Titles tab allows you to modify the PivotChart's title, category, and value axis titles, as shown in Figure 5-22.

  - The Axes tab allows you to specify whether item and value labels appear on the category and series axes, as shown in Figure 5-23.

    NOTE The Value (Z) Axis check box only appears for three-dimensional PivotChart types. Also, this tab does not appear for pie and doughnut PivotChart types.

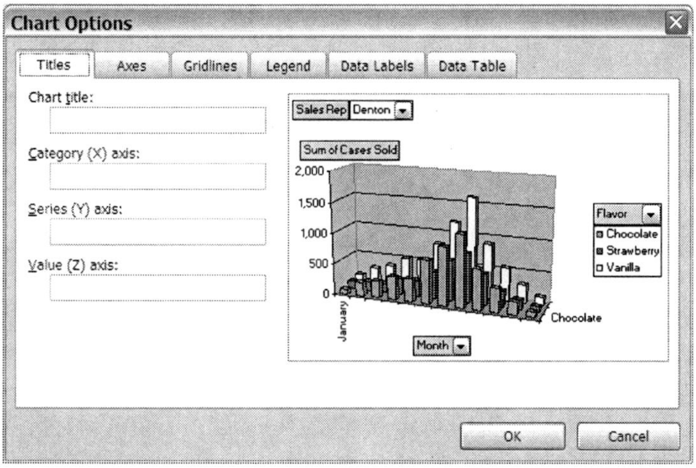

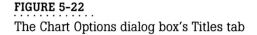

FIGURE 5-22
The Chart Options dialog box's Titles tab

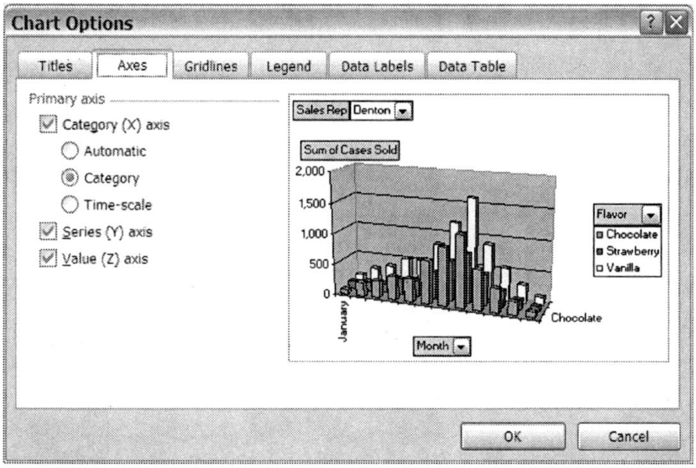

FIGURE 5-23
The Chart Options dialog box's Axes tab

- The Gridlines tab allows you to specify whether major or minor gridlines (or both) appear on the category and value axes, as shown in Figure 5-24.

NOTE The Value (Z) Axis area only appears for three-dimensional PivotChart types. Also, this tab does not appear for pie and doughnut PivotChart types.

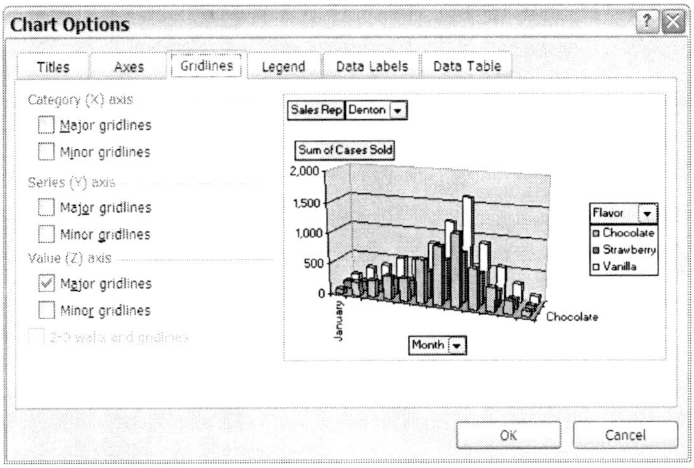

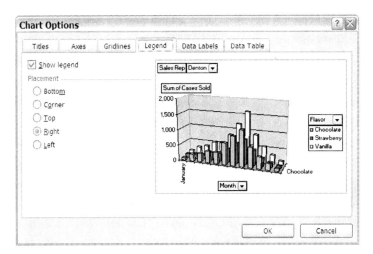

FIGURE 5-24

The Chart Options dialog box's Gridlines tab

- The Legend tab allows you to specify whether a legend appears, and if so, where it appears on the PivotChart, as shown in Figure 5-25.

FIGURE 5-25

The Chart Options dialog box's Legend tab

- The Data Labels tab allows you to specify whether data labels contain the series name, the category name, the value, the percentage, the separator character (if any) used to separate these names, as shown in Figure 5-26.

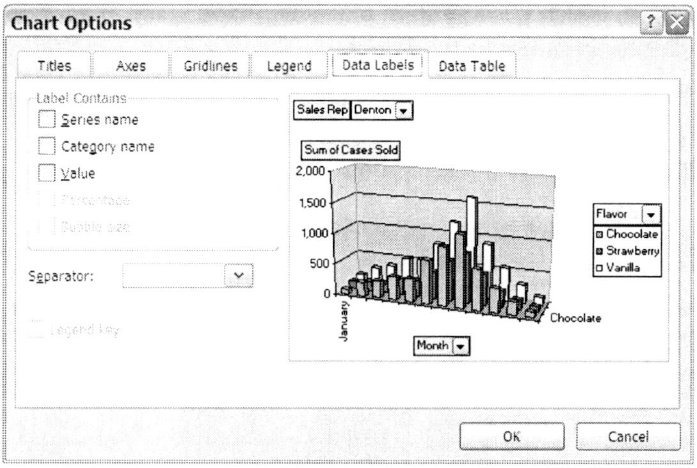

FIGURE 5-26
The Chart Options dialog box's Data Labels tab

- The Data Table tab allows you to specify whether a data table and legend keys are displayed, as shown in Figure 5-27.

NOTE The Data Table tab does not appear for pie, doughnut, and radar PivotChart types.

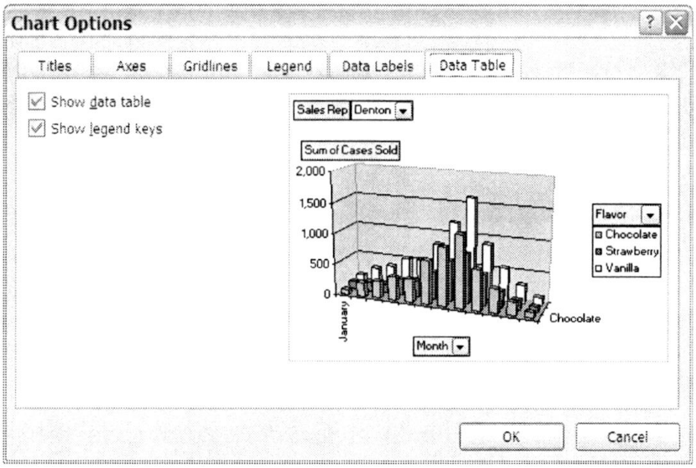

FIGURE 5-27
The Chart Options dialog box's Data Table tab

- Location, which allows you to place the PivotChart on another worksheet in the same workbook.

- 3-D View, for three-dimensional chart types, which allows you to change the elevation, rotation, perspective, and height of the PivotChart's dimensions, as shown in Figure 5-28.

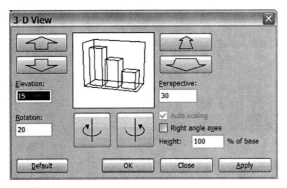

FIGURE 5-28

The 3-D View dialog box

- Chart Window, which is not available for PivotCharts on their own chart sheet, but is available to PivotCharts embedded on other worksheets.

- Clear, which clears the PivotChart from the worksheet.

NOTE If the PivotChart is on a worksheet, additional commands appear, such as Cut, Copy, Paste, Send To Back, and Assign Macro, which are fairly self explanatory.

Now, practice customizing the PivotChart's chart area by following these steps:

1. With the PivotChart from Figure 5-18 visible, right-click the PivotChart's chart area (for example, the blank space near the upper-right corner of the PivotChart) and click Format Chart Area.

2. On the Patterns tab, in the Border area, click Automatic, and then click OK.

3. Right-click the PivotChart's chart area and click Chart Options.

4. On the Titles tab, type **Products Shipped** in the Chart Title box.

5. In the Category (X) Axis box, type **Color**.

6. In the Series (Y) Axis box, type **Model**.

7. In the Value (Z) Axis box, type **Units**. Compare your results to Figure 5-29.

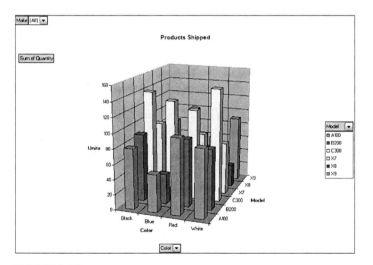

FIGURE 5-29
Customizing the PivotChart using the Chart Options dialog box's Titles tab

8. On the Gridlines tab, in the Category (X) Axis area, select the Major Gridlines check box.

9. In the Series (Y) Axis area, select the Major Gridlines check box. Click OK, and then compare your results to Figure 5-30.

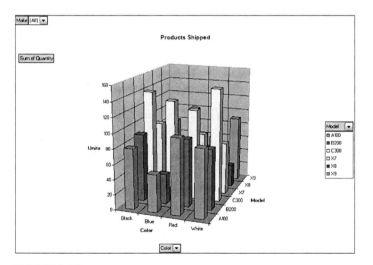

FIGURE 5-30
The layout shows major gridlines have been added to the category and series axes of the PivotChart after using the Chart Options dialog box.

Now you can customize the PivotChart's field buttons.

Field Buttons

When you right-click a field button, the following menu commands are available:

- Format PivotChart Field, which displays the Field Options dialog box. For more information, see the "Understanding the PivotTable Field Dialog Box" section of Chapter 3.

- PivotChart Options, which displays the PivotTable Options dialog box. For more information, see the "Setting PivotTable Report Formatting and Data Presentation Options" section of Chapter 2.

- Refresh Data, which refreshes the data in the underlying PivotTable with its source data and reflects any changes to the PivotChart.

- Hide PivotChart Field Buttons, which, as its name implies, hides the PivotChart's field buttons from display. To show the PivotChart field buttons again, click PivotChart ➤ Hide PivotChart Field Buttons on the PivotTable toolbar.

- Group and Show Detail (including Hide Detail, Show Detail, Group, and Ungroup actions), which groups and shows items. For more information, see Chapter 3.

- Remove Field, which removes the field from the PivotChart (but not from the field list).

Now practice removing and then redisplaying the PivotChart's field buttons by following these steps:

1. Right-click the Sum Of Quantity field on the PivotChart shown previously in Figure 5-30, and then click Hide PivotChart Field Buttons.

2. On the PivotChart toolbar, click PivotChart ➤ Hide PivotChart Field Buttons. The field buttons reappear.

Next, you'll customize the PivotChart's data series.

Data Series

When you right-click a data series (except for surface PivotChart types), the following menu commands are available:

- Format Data Series, which displays the Format Data Series dialog box. The tabs in this dialog box are described in the following list:

  - The Patterns tab allows you to change the border and area/fill color **and** pattern of the data series. This tab behaves similar to the Patterns tab in the Format Chart Area dialog box shown earlier in Figure 5-19.

  - **The** Shape tab allows you to change the series geometric shape for **three-**dimensional bar and column charts, as shown in Figure 5-31.

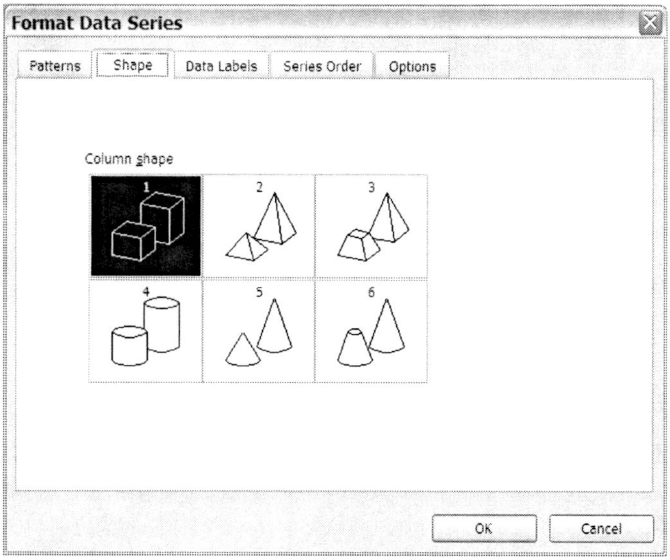

FIGURE 5-31
The Format Data Series dialog box's Shape tab

- The Axis tab (available for two-dimensional PivotCharts) allows you to specify whether you want to plot the series on a primary or secondary axis, as shown in Figure 5-32.

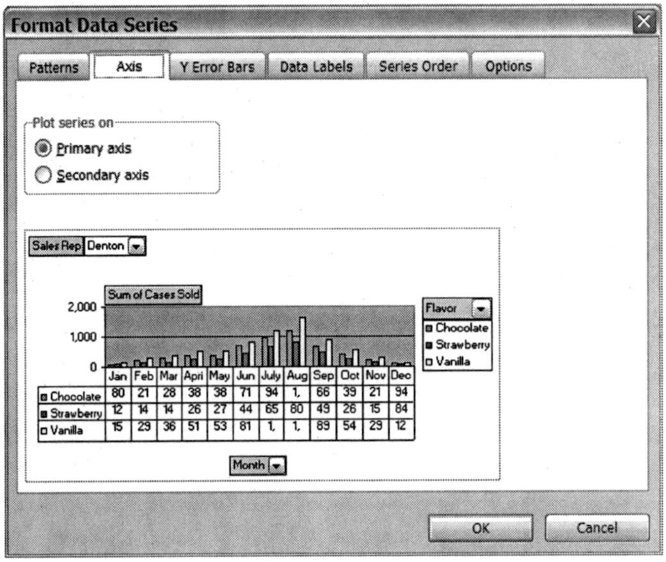

FIGURE 5-32

The Format Data Series dialog box's Axis tab

- The Y Error Bars tab allows you to specify whether you want to show Y error bars for two-dimensional bar, column, line, and area PivotChart types. If so, you also can determine what the error amount is, as shown in Figure 5-33.

- The Data Labels tab allows you to specify whether data labels contain the series name, the category name, the value, the percentage, and the separator character (if any) used to separate these names, as well as whether a legend key is displayed. This tab behaves similar to the Data Labels tab in the Chart Options dialog box shown earlier in Figure 5-26.

- The Series Order tab allows you to reposition series up or down on the PivotChart (except for pie PivotChart types), as shown in Figure 5-34.

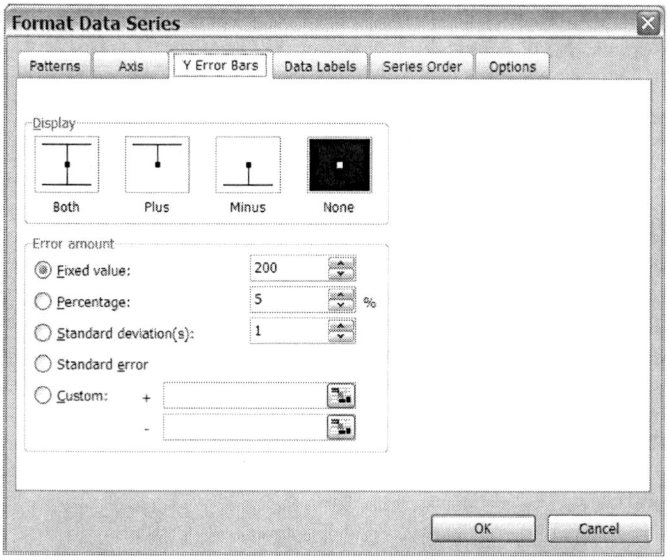

FIGURE 5-33

The Format Data Series dialog box's Y Error Bars tab

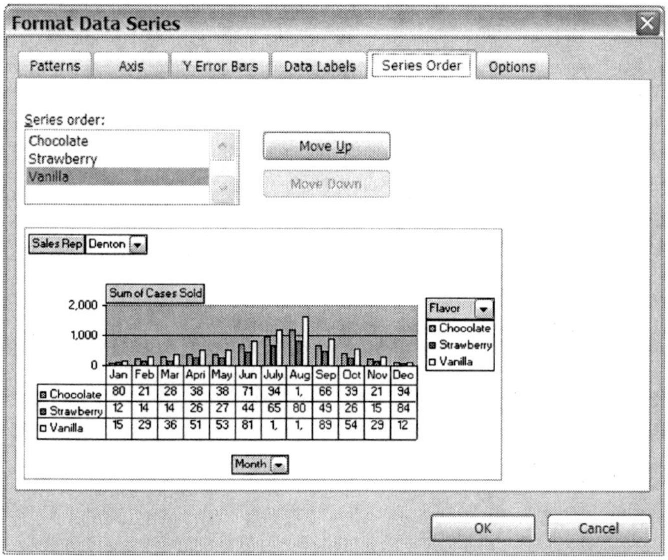

FIGURE 5-34

The Format Data Series dialog box's Series Order tab

- The Options tab differs by PivotChart type. Options concern overlap between series, gap between series, lines connecting series between gaps, and varying series colors by point. An example of the Options tab for a bar PivotChart type is shown in Figure 5-35.

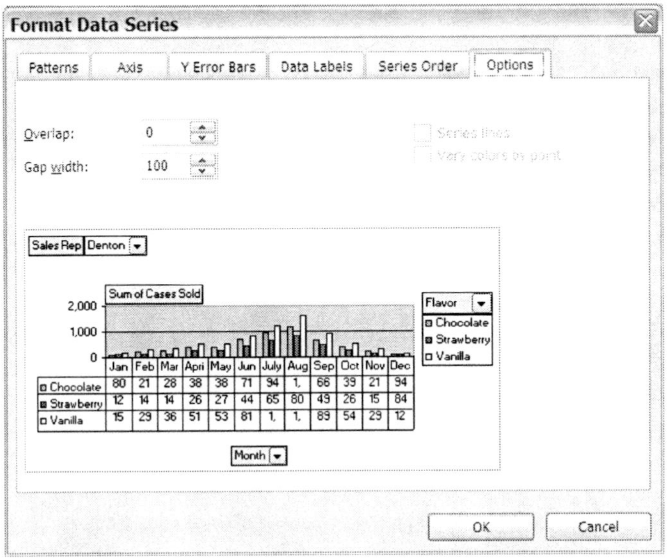

FIGURE 5-35

The Format Data Series dialog box's Options tab for a bar PivotChart type

- Chart Type, which allows you to change the PivotChart type.

- Add Trendline, which allows you to add a trendline to the series.

- Hide Detail, which allows you to hide series details, if they are showing.

- Show Detail, which allows you to show series details, if they are not already showing.

Now practice customizing the PivotChart's data series:

1. With the PivotChart from Figure 5-30 visible, right-click the PivotChart's A100 data series (for example, one of the dark blue three dimensional columns) and click Format Data Series.

2. On the Shape tab, click the Column Shape icon with the number 2 in it.

3. On the Options tab, in the Gap Depth box, type the number zero (**0**).

4. Click OK. Compare your results to Figure 5-36.

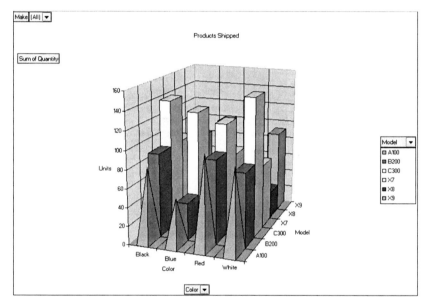

FIGURE 5-36

The layout shows the bars in the A100 data series changed to pyramids and the gaps between the bars eliminated in the PivotChart layout after using the Format Data Series dialog box.

Next, you'll customize the PivotChart's axes.

Axes

When you right-click an axis, the following menu commands are available:

- Format Axis, which displays the Format Axis dialog box. The tabs in this dialog box are described in the following list:

  - The Patterns tab allows you to specify patterns for axes lines, the tick mark type, and the tick mark label type, as shown in Figure 5-37.

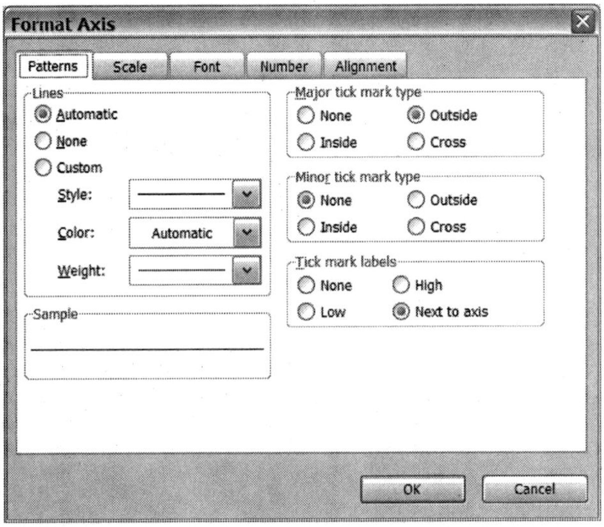

FIGURE 5-37

The Format Axis dialog box's Patterns tab

- The Scale tab allows you to change the axis' scale, as shown in Figures 5-38 and 5-39.

  NOTE The appearance of this tab varies based on PivotChart type. The following figures are for a two-dimensional bar PivotChart type.

- The Font tab allows you to specify the tick mark label text and number formatting. The appearance of this tab is similar to the Font tab in the Format Chart Area dialog box shown earlier in Figure 5-20.

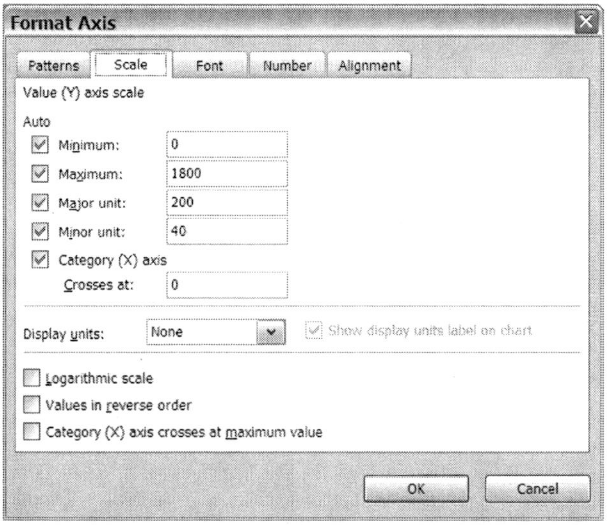

FIGURE 5-38

The Format Axis dialog box's Scale tab for the value (Y) axis of a two-dimensional bar PivotChart type

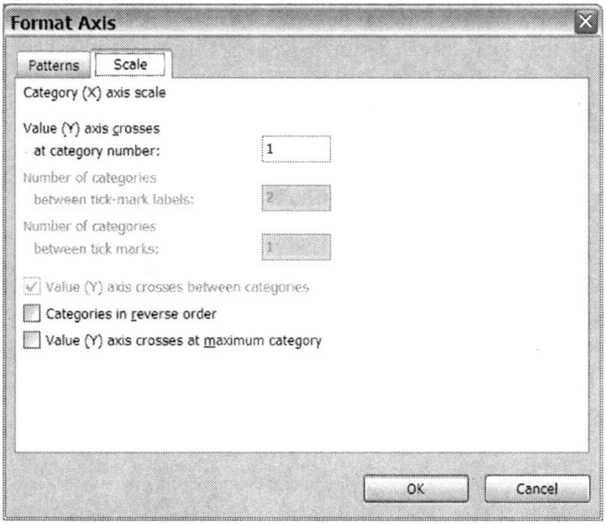

FIGURE 5-39

The Format Axis dialog box's Scale tab for the category (X) axis of a two-dimensional bar PivotChart type

- The Number tab allows you to change the text formatting of axis' items. For more information, see Chapter 3.

- The Alignment tab allows you to specify the tick mark label text alignment, as shown in Figure 5-40.

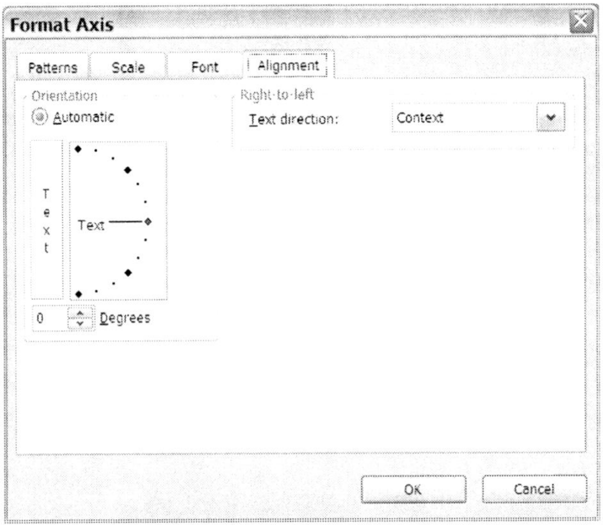

FIGURE 5-40

The Format Axis dialog box's Alignment tab

- Clear, which removes the axis from the PivotChart.

NOTE The Category axis also displays Hide Detail and Show Detail commands on this menu if lower levels of data are available on the category axis. As their names imply, these commands allow you to hide or show lower levels of data detail for the category axis.

Now practice customizing the PivotChart's category axis:

1. With the PivotChart from Figure 5-36 visible, right-click the PivotChart's category axis (the Color axis with the values Black, Blue, Red, and White) and click Format Axis.

2. On the Alignment tab, in the Degrees box, type **90**.

3. Click OK. Compare your results to Figure 5-41.

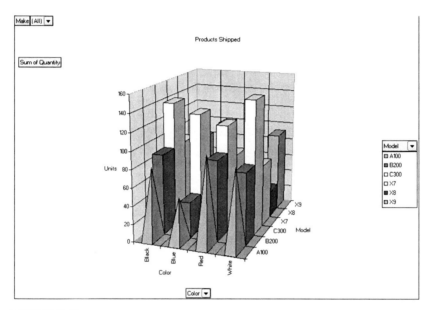

FIGURE 5-41

The layout shows the category axis (the Color axis with the values Black, Blue, Red, and White) changing from horizontal to vertical in the PivotChart after using the Format Axis dialog box.

Next, you'll customize the PivotChart's legend.

Legend

When you right-click the legend, the following menu commands are available:

- Format Legend, which displays the Format Legend dialog box. The tabs in this dialog box are described in the following list:

  - The Patterns tab allows you to change the border and fill color and pattern of the legend. This tab behaves similar to the Patterns tab in the Format Chart Area dialog box shown earlier in Figure 5-19.

  - The Font tab allows you to change the legend's font style. The appearance of this tab is similar to the Font tab in the Format Chart Area dialog box shown earlier in Figure 5-20.

  - The Placement tab allows you to specify where the legend appears on the PivotChart report, as shown in Figure 5-42.

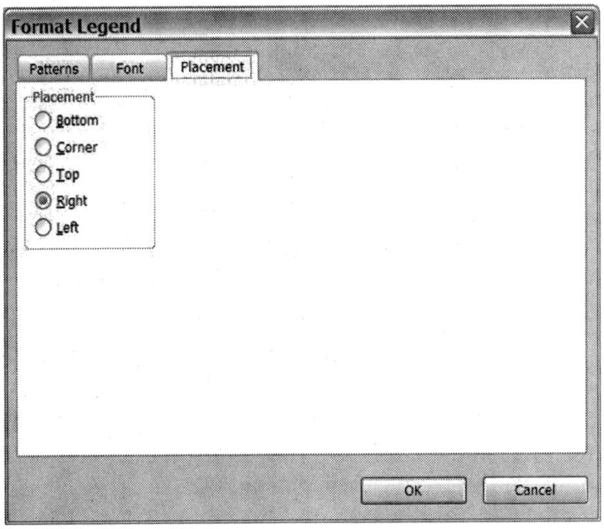

FIGURE 5-42

The Format Legend dialog box's Placement tab

- Clear, which removes the legend from the PivotChart.

Now practice customizing the PivotChart's legend:

1. With the PivotChart from Figure 5-41 visible, right-click the PivotChart's legend (the box underneath the field button labeled Model) and click Format Legend.

2. On the Placement tab, click the Left option.

3. Click OK. Compare your results to Figure 5-43.

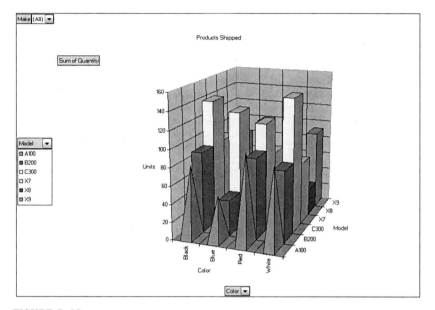

FIGURE 5-43

The layout shows the legend on the left side of the PivotChart after using the Format Legend dialog box.

Next, you'll customize the PivotChart's data table.

Data Table

When you right-click the data table, the following menu commands are available:

- Format Data Table, which displays the Format Data Table dialog box. The tabs in this dialog box are described in the following list:

  - The Patterns tab allows you to change the border and fill color and pattern of the data table. The Patterns tab is shown in Figure 5-44.

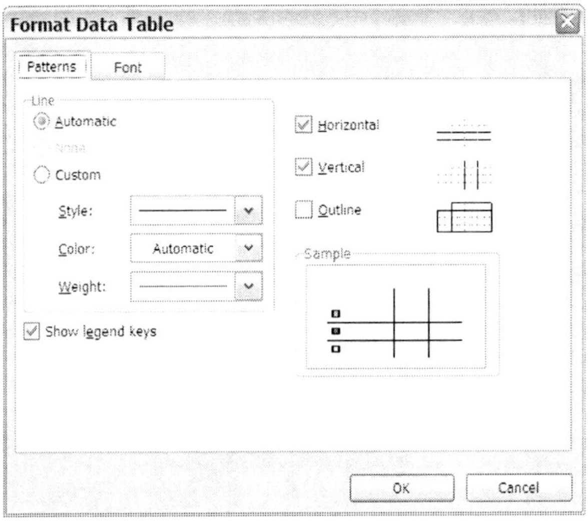

FIGURE 5-44

The Format Data Table dialog box's Patterns tab

  - The Font tab, which allows you to change the data table's font style. The appearance of this tab is similar to the Font tab in the Format Chart Area dialog box shown earlier in Figure 5-20.

- Clear, which removes the data table from the PivotChart.

Now practice customizing the PivotChart's data table:

1. With the PivotChart from Figure 5-43 visible, on the Chart menu, click Chart Options.

2. On the Data Table tab, select the Show Data Table check box, and then click OK.

3. Right-click the Data Table and click Format Data Table.

4. On the Patterns tab, clear the Outline check box, and then click OK. Compare your results to Figure 5-45.

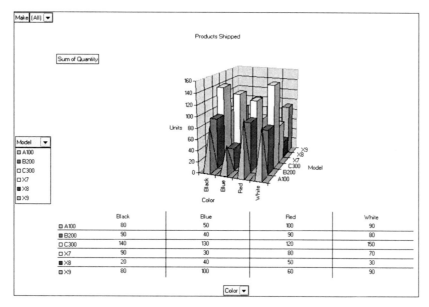

FIGURE 5-45

The layout shows a data table, minus the data table's outline, added to the PivotChart after using the Format Data Table dialog box.

Next, you'll customize the PivotChart's walls.

Walls

When you right-click a three-dimensional PivotChart's walls, the following menu commands appear:

- Format Walls, which displays the Format Walls dialog box. This dialog box has only one tab, Patterns, which changes the border and fill color and pattern of the walls. This tab behaves similar to the Patterns tab in the Format Chart Area dialog box shown earlier in Figure 5-19.

- 3-D View, for three-dimensional chart types, which allows you to change the elevation, rotation, perspective, and height of the PivotChart's dimensions, as shown in Figure 5-28.

- Clear, which clears the walls' visual formatting.

Now practice customizing the PivotChart's walls:

1. With the PivotChart from Figure 5-45 visible, right-click the PivotChart's walls (the gray walls in the PivotChart's plot area), and then click Format Walls.

2. In the Area area, click the None option, and then click OK. Compare your results to Figure 5-46.

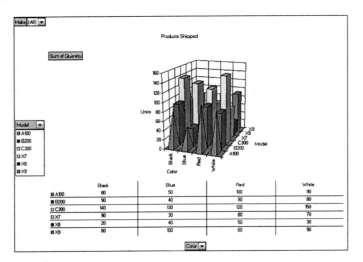

FIGURE 5-46
The layout shows the walls' background color removed from the PivotChart after using the Format Walls dialog box.

Next, you'll customize the PivotChart's plot area.

Plot Area

When you right-click the plot area, the following menu commands appear:

- Format Plot Area, which displays the Format Plot Area dialog box. This dialog box has only one tab, Patterns, which allows you to change the border and fill color and pattern of the plot table. This tab behaves similar to the Patterns tab in the Format Chart Area dialog box shown earlier in Figure 5-19.

- Chart Type, which allows you to change the type of PivotChart.

- Chart Options, which displays the Chart Options dialog box. The tabs on this dialog box are listed earlier in the "Chart Area" section.

- Location, which allows you to place the PivotChart on another worksheet in the same workbook.

- 3-D View, for three-dimensional chart types, allows you to change the elevation, rotation, perspective, and height of the PivotChart's dimensions, as shown earlier in Figure 5-28.

- Chart Window, not available for PivotCharts on their own chart sheet, but available to PivotCharts embedded on other worksheets.

    NOTE The Clear command is available on the plot area's right-click menu, but clicking on it appears to have no affect.

Now practice customizing the PivotChart's plot area:

1. With the PivotChart from Figure 5-46 visible, right-click the PivotChart's plot area (for example, the blank space immediately to the left of the PivotChart's value axis and immediately above the data table), and then click Format Plot Area.

2. In the Border area, click the Custom option, select the first dashed line entry in the Style list, and then click OK. Compare your results to Figure 5-47.

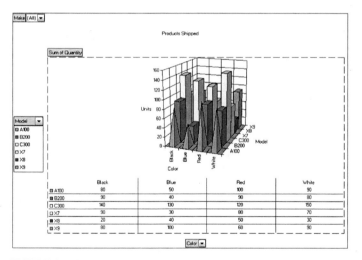

FIGURE 5-47

The layout shows a dashed line added to the plot area in the PivotChart after using the Format Plot Area dialog box.

Next you'll customize the PivotChart's gridlines.

Gridlines

When you right-click the gridlines, the following menu commands appear:

- Format Gridlines, which displays the Format Gridlines dialog box. The tabs in this dialog box are described in the following list:

  - Patterns allows you to change the border pattern of the gridlines. This tab behaves similar to the left side only of the Patterns tab in the Format Chart Area dialog box shown earlier in Figure 5-19.

  - Scale, which allows you to change the axis' scale, as shown earlier in Figures 5-38 and 5-39 of the Format Axis dialog box.

  NOTE The text of the Scale tab changes slightly for three-dimensional charts to reflect the Z-axis rather than the Y-axis.

- Clear, which clears the gridlines from the PivotChart.

Now practice customizing the PivotChart's gridlines:

1. With the PivotChart from Figure 5-47 visible, right-click the PivotChart's gridlines and then click Format Gridlines.

2. On the Scale tab, click Hundreds in the Display Units list and then click OK. Compare your results to Figure 5-48.

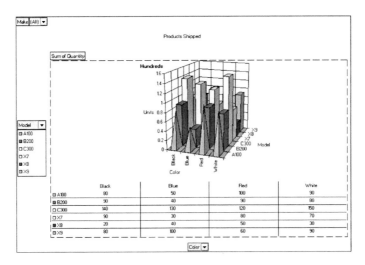

FIGURE 5-48

The layout shows the data axis' display units changed to hundreds in the PivotChart after using the Format Gridlines dialog box.

Finally, let's customize the PivotChart's floor.

Floor

When you right-click the floor on three-dimensional PivotCharts, the following menu commands become available:

- Format Floor, which displays the Format Floor dialog box. The only tab in this dialog box, Patterns, allows you to change the border and fill color and pattern of the plot table. This tab behaves similar to the Patterns tab in the Format Chart Area dialog box shown earlier in Figure 5-19.

- 3-D View, for three-dimensional chart types, allows you to change the elevation, rotation, perspective, and height of the PivotChart's dimensions, as shown earlier in Figure 5-28.

- Clear, which clears the walls' visual formatting.

Now practice customizing the PivotChart's floor:

1. With the PivotChart from Figure 5-48 visible, right-click the PivotChart's floor (the remaining gray area in the PivotChart's plot area), and then click Format Floor.

2. In the Area area, click None, and then click OK. Compare your results to Figure 5-49.

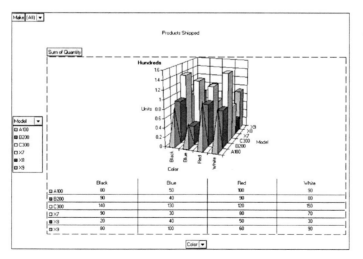

FIGURE 5-49

The layout shows the floor's background color removed from the PivotChart after using the Format Floor dialog box.

Now that you've created and customized a few PivotCharts, you might be wondering when you would not want to use a PivotChart? We'll answer that question in the next section.

Good Uses for PivotCharts

Although it might be tempting to create PivotCharts for all of your data, it's important to note that only certain types of data (and data analysis scenarios) lend themselves well to PivotCharts.

Good uses for PivotCharts include

- Data that is reflected over time

- Data analysis tasks involving ratios

- Large numbers of discrete data items (such as the 50 United States)

- Data analysis that uses a trendline

Poorer uses for PivotCharts include

- A very small number of data points

- PivotTables with only row fields, pages fields, or column fields. (however, because pie charts have only one data series, pie charts might still be useful for these types of PivotTables)

- For data that has very wide swings in relation to other similar data

- For data that lends itself well to an XY (Scatter), Bubble, or Stock chart type, as these types of PivotCharts cannot be created from PivotTable data

Lost Formatting in PivotCharts

It's important to note that when you make changes that affect what data is displayed in a PivotChart report or its associated PivotTable report, Excel discards any formatting you've applied to data labels, data points, and data series, including any trendlines and error bars you've added.

Changes that result in lost formatting include

- Changing the layout

- Adding or removing fields

- Displaying or hiding items

- Displaying a different page in a page field

- Grouping or ungrouping items

- Displaying or hiding detail

- Sorting

- Changing the summary function for a field

- Changing the display of subtotals

- Specifying different source data, including changing the query for external data

- Refreshing the report

Be sure that you are satisfied with the layout and data displayed in the PivotChart report before you make formatting changes.

Finally, in a PivotChart report, you can't move or resize the legend, titles, or plot area as you would in a regular, noninteractive chart. Excel automatically resizes the plot area to accommodate changes to the report.

Try It! Create and Customize a PivotChart

In this exercise, you'll create and customize a PivotChart based on sales data from an ice cream manufacturer/distributor. The source data for this set of exercises is available in an Excel workbook named IceCreamShipments.xls. This workbook is available from the Apress Web site Downloads section at http://www.apress.com.

Create the PivotChart

Start by creating the PivotTable that connects to the ice cream shipment data. At the same time, you'll create a PivotChart and connect it to the PivotTable.

1. Start Excel.

2. Open the IceCreamShipments.xls file.

3. Click File ➤ New.

4. In the New Workbook task pane, click Blank Workbook.

5. Click Data ➤ PivotTable and PivotChart.

6. Click PivotChart Report (With PivotTable Report).

7. Click Next.

8. Click Window ➤ IceCreamShipments.xls.

9. Select cells A1 through E433 on the Sheet1 worksheet tab.

10. Click Finish. A PivotTable and a PivotChart of the area type are created by default, as shown in Figures 5-50 and 5-51.

FIGURE 5-50

A PivotTable based on the ice cream manfacturer/distributor's data

FIGURE 5-51

A PivotChart based on the PivotTable in Figure 5-50

Now that you've created the initial PivotTable and PivotChart, you can add some fields and data to them.

Design the PivotChart by Modifying the PivotTable

Let's continue by designing the initial layout of the PivotChart. To do this, drop some fields onto the PivotTable and see how it affects the PivotChart:

1. On the Sheet1 worksheet, drag the Month field from the field list to the PivotTable's row area. This creates a category axis on the PivotChart for the months January through December.

2. Drag the Flavor field from the field list to the PivotTable's column area. This creates three series on the PivotChart, one series each for the flavors Chocolate, Strawberry, and Vanilla.

3. Drag the Cases Sold field from the field list to the PivotTable's data area. This creates a value axis with the values 0 through 10,000. Compare your PivotTable and PivotChart results to Figures 5-52 and 5-53.

	A	B	C	D	E
1					
2					
3	Sum of Cases Sold	Flavor			
4	Month	Chocolate	Strawberry	Vanilla	Grand Total
5	January	297	257	361	915
6	February	450	306	704	1460
7	March	684	389	869	1942
8	April	948	576	1187	2711
9	May	1008	668	1409	3085
10	June	1740	1053	2196	4989
11	July	2423	1613	3119	7155
12	August	2976	2012	3978	8966
13	September	1625	1072	2245	4942
14	October	956	640	1363	2959
15	November	499	385	713	1597
16	December	240	186	313	739
17	Grand Total	13846	9157	18457	41460

FIGURE 5-52
Initial PivotTable layout

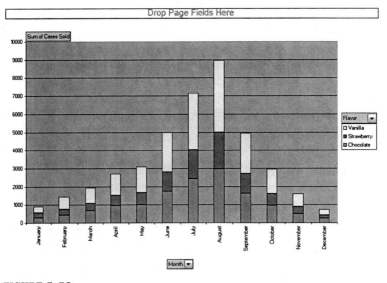

FIGURE 5-53
Initial PivotChart layout

As you've noticed, when you change the PivotTable's layout, the PivotChart's layout changes to match the PivotTable's layout. As you'll see in the next section, you can do the reverse of this as well.

Design the PivotTable by Modifying the PivotChart

Now change the PivotChart and see how it affects the PivotTable:

1. On the Chart1 worksheet, right-click the Month field button and click Remove Field.

2. Right-click the Flavor field button and click Remove Field.

3. Drag the Region field from the field list to the PivotChart's category area.

4. Drag the Sales Rep field from the field list to the series area. Compare your PivotTable and PivotChart results to Figures 5-54 and 5-55.

	A	B	C	D	E
1					
2					
3	Sum of Cases Sold	Sales Rep ▾			
4	Region ▾	Baker	Denton	Williams	Grand Total
5	East	2765	3384	2249	8398
6	North	4637	5662	3843	14142
7	South	3493	4355	2801	10649
8	West	2684	3338	2249	8271
9	Grand Total	13579	16739	11142	41460

FIGURE 5-54

PivotTable with rearranged field layout

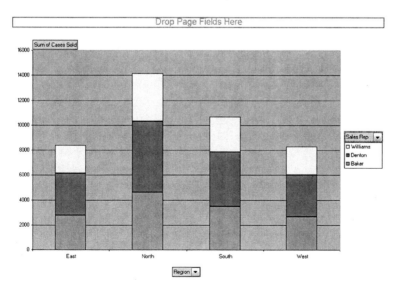

FIGURE 5-55

PivotChart with rearranged field layout

Next you'll change the PivotChart's layout by changing its layout type.

Change the PivotChart Type

Change the PivotChart type from stacked column to clustered column:

1. Right-click a blank area of the PivotChart and click Chart Type.

2. Click the picture with the Clustered Column Compares Values Across Categories label, and then click OK. Compare your results with Figure 5-56.

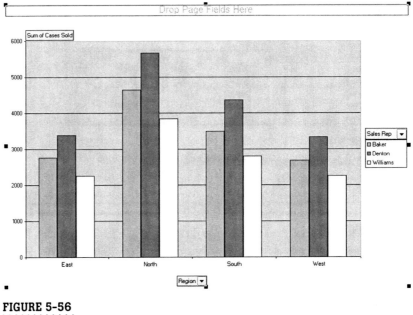

FIGURE 5-56
Clustered column PivotChart

You've changed the PivotChart's layout and layout type. Next, you'll change the PivotChart's visual display.

Change the PivotChart's Formatting

Finally, you'll change several aspects of the PivotChart's visual formatting.

First, order the columns by total sales in each region and then by salesperson in each region, from lowest on the left to highest on the right:

1. Right-click the Region field button, and click Format PivotChart Field.

2. Click Advanced.

3. Click Ascending.

4. In the Using Field list, click Sum Of Cases Sold. Compare your results to Figure 5-57.

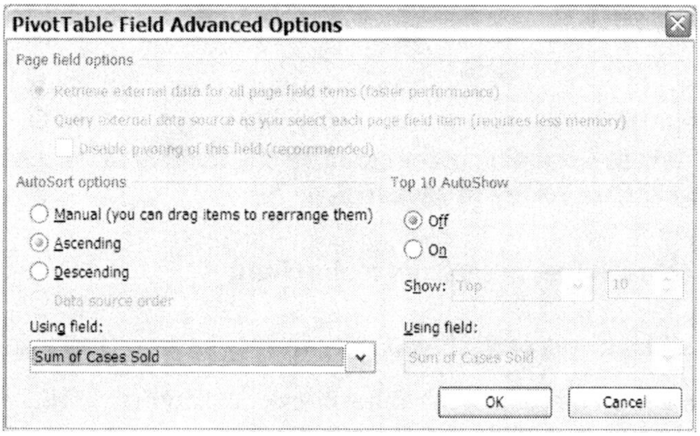

FIGURE 5-57

Using the PivotTable Field Advanced Options dialog box to sort data in ascending order based on the sum of ice cream cases sold

5. Click OK, and click OK again.

6. Repeat with the Sales Rep field: right-click the Sales Rep field button, and click Format PivotChart Field.

7. Click Advanced.

8. Click Ascending.

9. In the Using Field list, click Sum Of Cases Sold.

10. Click OK, and click OK again. Compare your results to Figure 5-58.

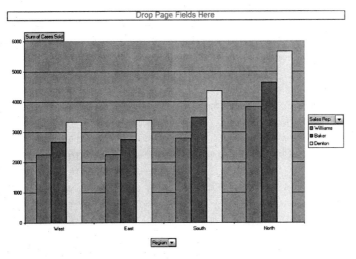

FIGURE 5-58

Sorting the data in ascending order based on the number of ice cream cases sold by each sales rep in each region

Now add the actual values in each bar to the chart:

1. Right-click a blank area of the PivotChart and click Chart Options.

2. On the Data Labels tab, select the Value check box, and click OK. Compare your results to Figure 5-59.

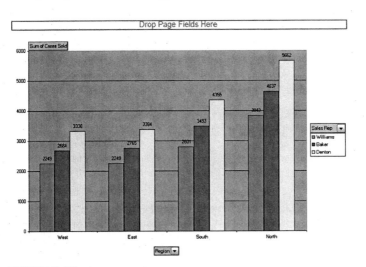

FIGURE 5-59

Adding data labels to the PivotChart from Figure 5-58

Better yet, now display a data table:

1. Right-click a blank area of the PivotChart and click Chart Options.

2. On the Data Labels tab, clear the Value check box.

3. On the Data Table tab, select the Show Data Table check box, and click OK. Compare your results to Figure 5-60.

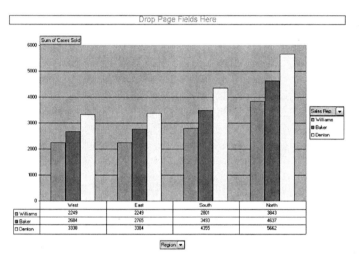

FIGURE 5-60

Removing data labels from the PivotChart in Figure 5-59 and adding a data table

Now change the value axis to display the thousands separator character:

1. Right-click the Sum Of Cases Sold field button, and click Format PivotChart Field.

2. Click Number.

3. In the Category list, click Number.

4. In the Decimal Places box, type or select the number **0**.

5. Select the Use 1000 Separator check box.

6. Click OK, and click OK again. Compare your results to Figure 5-61.

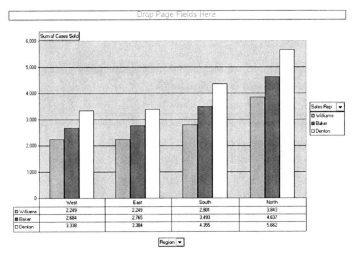

FIGURE 5-61

Adding the thousands separator to the data in the PivotChart in
Figure 5-60

Next, strip the thousands digits from the display:

1. Right-click the value axis, and click Format Axis.

2. On the Scale tab, select Thousands in the Display Units list.

3. Click OK. Compare your results to Figure 5-62.

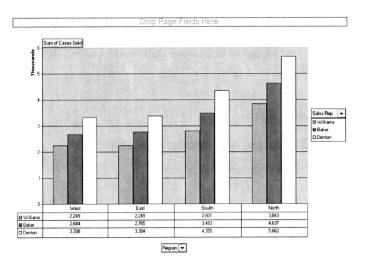

FIGURE 5-62

Changing the scale on the value axis from Figure 5-61 to thousands

Now finish the PivotChart by providing a title and axis titles, adding a trendline, and hiding the field buttons for printing purposes:

1. Right-click a blank area of the PivotChart and click Chart Options.

2. On the Titles tab, type **Ice Cream Shipments** in the Chart Title box.

3. In the Category (X) Axis box, type **Sales Region**.

4. In the Value (Y) Axis, type **Cases Sold**, and click OK.

5. Right-click any of the series bars, and click Add Trendline.

6. In the Based On Series list, click Baker, and click OK.

7. On the PivotTable toolbar, click PivotChart ➤ Hide PivotChart Field Buttons. Compare your results to Figure 5-63.

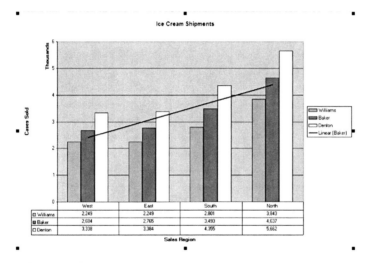

FIGURE 5-63

Captions for the category and value axes, as well as the overall title, have been added to the PivotChart. A trendline has also been added, and the field buttons have been removed.

Next Steps

In this chapter, you learned how to add visual depth and enhance your data analysis tasks by creating PivotCharts. Specifically, you learned how to create and format PivotCharts using the PivotTable and PivotChart Wizard, along with the PivotTable toolbar.

Now that you've used PivotTables on your own source data, you can try analyzing your data with PivotCharts. As you add PivotCharts to your PivotTables, you should be able to make more informed decisions based on what both the PivotCharts and PivotTables reveal to you, than if you tried to make the same decisions with PivotTables alone.

6

Analyzing Multidimensional Data with PivotTables

Until this point, you have been working with PivotTables connected to relatively small, simple collections of source data in Excel comprising a few hundred rows (also known as *records*) of facts and figures. However, most mission-critical data sources consist of more than a few hundred rows, unlike the sample source data that you've worked with in earlier chapters. Although it might be tempting to store all of your source data in Excel, you'll soon discover that Excel isn't designed to handle very large sets of data. When source data gets really large, even PivotTables have trouble summarizing information. Specifically, Excel and PivotTables have the following limitations:

- 65,536 rows (records) by 256 columns (fields) of data in a worksheet

- 32,500 unique items in a PivotTable field

- 256 page fields in a PivotTable or PivotChart

- 256 data fields in a PivotTable or PivotChart

- 255 data series in a PivotChart

- 4,000 data points in a data series on a three-dimensional PivotChart or 32,000 data points in a data series on a two-dimensional PivotChart

Before you think that these limitations are practically unreachable, consider the vast amounts of data in medium-size or large-size organizations. For example, imagine the complete set of stock market data for just one stock exchange for one year. Or consider the weather records for every city in a country for that same year. Going further for that same year, envision all teller transaction records for a major bank, sales slips for a chain of retail clothing stores, mortgage payment histories for all of a financial institution's customers, vital patient statistics for a hospital, and so on.

Performing analyses on all of these types of data can be cumbersome, stretching not only the limits of Excel, but also your computer's processing power limits as well. Answering data analysis questions such as what top selling items did your ten largest customers purchase over the past ten years can result in a complex query pulling data from several data sources that can take several hours or longer. Furthermore, performing a deeper investigation into the geographic regions and quarterly time periods within the returned data can greatly increase the time and computing processing needed. A field of data management and data analysis called *Online Analytical Processing (OLAP)* is designed to respond to these technical challenges. OLAP is well-suited to deal with hierarchical source data, a type of data that organizes and summarizes very large amounts of facts and figures into related hierarchies. Excel contains OLAP-specific features, including features specific to PivotTables, to work with summarized hierarchical data.

In short, OLAP is designed to take very large data sources and summarize their facts and figures in a format that is more compact and puts less stress on computing resources. PivotTables take advantage of this summarized information, presenting it in a way that makes data analysis tasks faster and simpler.

In this chapter, you will learn

- A definition of multidimensional data

- Multidimensional data terminology

- Contrasting differences between multidimensional data and other source data types

- Guidelines for using PivotTables to analyze multidimensional data

- How to create a multidimensional data source

- How to connect to and analyze multidimensional source data with PivotTables and PivotCharts

The sample data in this chapter exists in several files available from the Apress Web site Downloads section at http://www.apress.com. The files, which we'll examine throughout the chapter, include

- *NonRelationalData.xls*: An Excel workbook containing nonrelational data for illustrative purposes.

- *RelationalData.mdb*: An Access database containing relational data for illustrative purposes.

- *MultidimensionalData.mdb*: An Access database containing multidimensional data for illustrative purposes.

- *Prescriptions.cub*: An offline cube file summarizing the data in the MultidimensionalData.mdb database.

- *ClothesSales.xls*: An Excel workbook containing multidimensional data.

- *ClothesSales.cub*: An offline cube file summarizing the data in the ClothesSales.xls workbook.

To open the .mdb files, you must use Access 2003. You can use Excel for the other files.

What Is Multidimensional Data?

As its name implies, multidimensional data is data that consists of one or more dimensions. But what does that really mean, and why is multidimensional data architecture and terminology important, especially regarding PivotTables?

To help you understand what multidimensional data is, let's look at three main types of data sources in turn: nonrelational data, relational data, and multidimensional data. As we move from one type of data to the next, you'll see increasing degrees of complexity in how data is organized and presented. However, with this complexity comes flexibility. You'll see by the end of this section that you can work with multidimensional data in PivotTables to analyze summarized facts and figures more easily than nonmultidimensional data. Later in this chapter, we'll contrast multidimensional data with other types of data to a more specific degree.

First, look at Figure 6-1, which represents nondimensional, nonrelational source data from a branch pharmacy.

	A	B	C
1	Season	Pharmacist	Prescriptions
2	Winter	Elkins	7150
3	Spring	Elkins	6775
4	Summer	Elkins	6225
5	Autumn	Elkins	7005
6	Winter	Simpson	7025
7	Spring	Simpson	6600
8	Summer	Simpson	6105
9	Autumn	Simpson	6975
10	Winter	Templeton	6995
11	Spring	Templeton	6665
12	Summer	Templeton	6175
13	Autumn	Templeton	7040
14	Winter	Valencia	7300
15	Spring	Valencia	7000
16	Summer	Valencia	6475
17	Autumn	Valencia	7205

FIGURE 6-1

Sample nonrelational, nonmultidimensional source data

You'll notice that the data is very simple to understand. The season, pharmacist, and number of prescriptions filled are clear and easy to interpret. The data is nonrelational because none of the records depend on any other data to make its results known and readable. The data is nondimensional because you can't go any deeper with, or *drill into*, the data as it's presented. As one example, you can't figure out how many prescriptions were filled in February versus January. Not only is the data not very interesting to look at, it's a very inefficient way to store and present facts and figures. Most importantly, several season and pharmacist cells are duplicated, which is especially worrisome from a data entry perspective, especially if you add hundreds or thousands of rows to the worksheet later. If you misspell one of the pharmacist's names, you could potentially miss out on some prescriptions if you subtotaled them by pharmacist name. If you wanted to replace one pharmacist's name with another name, you might forget to replace all of the names in the correct cells. If you wanted to delete a pharmacist and their associated prescriptions, you might miss deleting all of the information in all of the correct cells.

Now let's move to relational, yet still nondimensional data, representing the same source data from the branch pharmacy in a way that addresses these inefficiencies. See Figures 6-2 through 6-5 for the set of tables comprising the source data and a conceptual diagram showing how all of the data tables relate together.

Seasons : Table	
Season_ID	Season
1	Winter
2	Spring
3	Summer
4	Autumn

FIGURE 6-2

Seasons data table from the sample relational, nonmultidimensional source data. Each season is included and has a unique identification number.

Pharmacists : Table	
Pharmacist_ID	Pharmacist
1	Elkins
2	Simpson
3	Templeton
4	Valencia

FIGURE 6-3

Pharmacists data table from the sample relational, nonmultidimensional source data. Each pharmacist is included and has a unique identification number.

Prescription_ID	Season_ID	Pharmacist_ID	Prescriptions
1	1	1	7150
2	1	2	7025
3	1	3	6995
4	1	4	7300
5	2	1	6775
6	2	2	6600
7	2	3	6665
8	2	4	7000
9	3	1	6225
10	3	2	6105
11	3	3	6175
12	3	4	6475
13	4	1	7005
14	4	2	6975
15	4	3	7040
16	4	4	7205

FIGURE 6-4

Prescriptions data table from the sample relational, nonmultidimensional source data. Each prescription record has a unique identification number. Each prescription also includes an identification number corresponding to a specific season and pharmacist. The sum of prescriptions for each combination of seasons and pharmacists is also included.

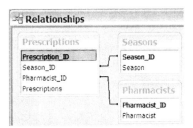

FIGURE 6-5

Conceptual diagram of how the three preceding data tables relate. If needed, the Prescriptions table can obtain the season names and pharmacist names by looking for matching unique identifiers in the Seasons and Pharmacists tables, following the lines between the related tables.

This data is fundamentally the same data that was presented earlier in Figure 6-1. However, the way this information has been restructured as relational source data can be more robust to work with than nonrelational data for two major reasons. First, it allows you to change the name of a pharmacist or the name of a season in just one place, leading to fewer data-entry errors. Second, depending on the relational data source's software application features, you can prevent a pharmacist's records from being accidentally deleted unless you first delete the pharmacist's name from the database (a feature known as *referential integrity*), leading to better overall data integrity.

Even though the data is relational, it hasn't been summarized. This data is better from a data integrity perspective, but it doesn't give you any better performance. This isn't much of a problem for relatively small data sources. For very large data sources, however, relational data sources can bring data analysis operations in PivotTables to a screeching halt. Also, the data isn't organized in a way that would allow you to drill into the data. In other words, you can't determine, for instance, how many prescriptions were filled in January versus February.

Now turn your attention to relational, multidimensional data, representing the same source data from the branch pharmacy, to see how you can make the data perform better and be more useful to drill into. See Figures 6-6 through 6-12 for the set of tables comprising the source data and a conceptual diagram showing how all of the data tables relate. (Note that the Seasons and Pharmacists data tables are the same in this database as the previous relational database and won't be shown again here.)

Years : Table

		Year_ID	Year
▶	+	1	2000
	+	2	2001
	+	3	2002
	+	4	2003

FIGURE 6-6

Years data table from the sample multidimensional source data. Adding this table to the relational data source allows you to drill into facts and figures by year.

Months : Table

		Month_ID	Months
▶	+	1	January
	+	2	February
	+	3	March
	+	4	April
	+	5	May
	+	6	June
	+	7	July
	+	8	August
	+	9	September
	+	10	October
	+	11	November
	+	12	December

FIGURE 6-7

Months data table from the sample multidimensional source data. Adding this table to the relational data source allows you to drill into facts and figures by month.

YearsSeasonsMonths : Table

		YearSeasonMonth_ID	Year_ID	Season_ID	Month_ID
▶	+	1	1	1	1
	+	2	1	1	2
	+	3	1	1	3
	+	4	1	2	4
	+	5	1	2	5
	+	6	1	2	6
	+	7	1	3	7
	+	8	1	3	8
	+	9	1	3	9
	+	10	1	4	10
	+	11	1	4	11
	+	12	1	4	12
	+	13	2	1	1
	+	14	2	1	2

FIGURE 6-8

YearsSeasonsMonths data table from the sample multidimensional source data (partial data shown). Adding this table to the relational data source allows you to categorize facts and figures by years, seasons, and months. This makes drilling into data by year, and then into data by season, and finally by month faster, easier, and more intuitive.

Customers : Table	
Customer_ID	Customer
1	Abercrombie
2	Baxter
3	Crighton
4	Delome
5	Eggers
6	Farsworth
7	Graebel
8	Hollingsworth

FIGURE 6-9

Customers data table from the sample multidimensional source data. Adding this table to the relational data source allows you to drill into facts and figures by customer name.

PharmacistsCustomers : Table		
PharmacistCustomer_ID	Pharmacist_ID	Customer_ID
1	1	1
2	1	2
3	1	3
4	1	4
5	1	5
6	1	6
7	1	7
8	1	8
9	2	1
10	2	2
11	2	3
12	2	4
13	2	5
14	2	6

FIGURE 6-10

PharmacistsCustomers data table from the sample multidimensional source data (partial data shown). Adding this table to the relational data source allows you to relate pharmacists to customers for more robust data analysis. Now you can analyze data not only by pharmacist, but also by their related customers as well.

Prescriptions : Table

Prescription_ID	YearSeasonMonth_ID	PharmacistCustomer_ID	Prescriptions
1	1	1	3
2	1	2	2
3	1	3	0
4	1	4	1
5	1	5	0
6	1	6	0
7	1	7	0
8	1	8	2
9	1	9	3
10	1	10	0
11	1	11	0
12	1	12	0
13	1	13	0
14	1	14	0
15	2	1	1
16	2	2	1

FIGURE 6-11

Prescriptions data table from the sample multidimensional source data (partial data shown). Prescriptions by time, pharmacist, and customer are brought together to enable data analysis from a time, pharmacist, or customer perspective.

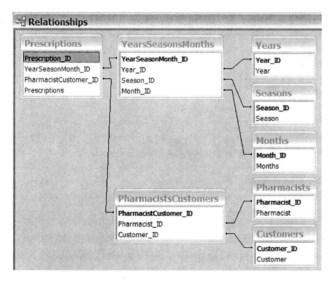

FIGURE 6-12

Conceptual diagram of how the preceding data tables relate. You can drill down from summarized information to more specific information by using matching unique identification numbers between any two related tables, as shown by the connecting lines.

This data begins with basically the same data that was presented in Figures 6-2 and 6-3. It builds on the data by providing additional data tables that bring together related data tables such as time periods and pharmacist/ customer relationships. This allows you to drill into the data if necessary, analyzing data by year, then by season, and then by month, for example.

Even this approach might not be totally sufficient. For several hundred or several thousand records, storing this data in Access might be enough to meet your needs; however, if the records grow to tens of thousands, hundreds of thousands, millions, or more, this type of relational, multidimensional data needs to be further organized and compacted in a way that won't strain all of your computer's memory.

OLAP experts recommend that you store and manage very large data sources in a *data warehouse*. A data warehouse is a computer software application such as Microsoft SQL Server 2000 Analysis Services or Oracle OLAP, specially designed to speed up data retrieval tasks, especially for very large data sources. Because the data warehouse calculates summarized values of large groups of records instead of Excel, fewer facts and figures need to be sent to Excel when you create or change a PivotTable or PivotChart. In fact, only summarized information about the data is sent to Excel. This approach lets you work with much larger amounts of source data than you could if the data were organized as presented previously, where Excel must get all of the individual facts and figures and then calculate the summarized values.

Understanding Multidimensional Data Terminology

Now that you've been introduced to some multidimensional data concepts, you need to learn some terms that Excel and PivotTables use when referring to various aspects of multidimensional data and OLAP. This will make it a lot easier to understand later how PivotTables and PivotCharts deal with multi-dimensional data.

NOTE As you research other OLAP resources, you might see the terms *multidimensional data*, *hierarchical data*, and *OLAP data* used interchangeably. For clarity and consistency, I use the term *multidimensional data* throughout this book because it best describes the types of data used in this chapter. This is because you can create or connect to source data that has multiple dimensions, but those dimensions don't necessarily contain hierarchies (although hierarchies allow for more robust data analysis). You can also create or connect to source data that has multiple dimensions, but does not reside in an OLAP data warehouse or an OLAP server computer (as I have done with the source data used in this chapter's last exercise).

To help you with multidimensional data terms, see Figures 6-13 and 6-14 for a hierarchical view of the data presented in the previous section.

FIGURE 6-13
Hierarchical view of the data in the MultidimensionalData.mdb file, as shown in the OLAP Cube Wizard

FIGURE 6-14
Hierarchical view of the data in the MultidimensionalData.mdb file, as shown in the PivotTable field list

Five basic components comprise multidimensional data: *dimensions, levels, members, measures,* and *cubes.*

Dimensions are categories or groupings of items into hierarchical, parent/child relationships called *levels.* Common hierarchical dimensions include time (with years, seasons, months, weeks, and days levels), geography (with continent, country or region, state or province, and county or city levels), products and services (with category, subcategory, department, and item levels), people (by employment organization or business relationship from seller to customer levels), and so on. In the preceding figures, People and Time are the dimensions, also as shown in Figure 6-15.

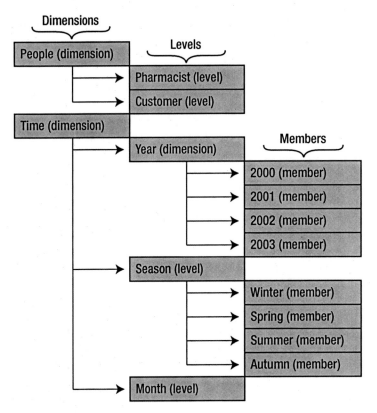

FIGURE 6-15

Conceptual view of the data in the MultidimensionalData.mdb file, as shown by dimension, level, and member (not all members are shown)

Members are a level's items. One way to think of it is members are to levels in multidimensional data as items are to fields in a PivotTable. Although not shown in Figures 6-13 and 6-14, the Year level's members could be 2000, 2001, 2002, and 2003; the Season level's members could be Winter, Spring, Summer, and Autumn; and so forth, as shown previously in Figure 6-15.

> **NOTE** Although not shown here, multidimensional data sources support the concept of *calculated members,* which are the equivalent of calculated fields for nonmultidimensional data.

Measures are the summarized data values. One way to think about measures is the individual cells in a PivotTable's data area. Measures could include the number of products sold, expenses, income, exam scores, survey results, and so on. These measures are summarized by dimension, level, and member. In the earlier Figure 6-14, the sole measure is Prescriptions, summarized using the Sum function.

Dimensions, levels, members, and measures are stored in files called *cubes.* Cubes get their name from a concept that is used to visually describe how the data is related and summarized. See Figure 6-16 as an example.

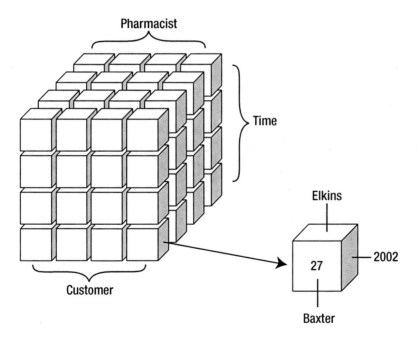

FIGURE 6-16

Conceptual representation of a data cube

In this figure, the Time, Pharmacist, and Customer dimensions are depicted as a set of three-dimensional smaller cubes that are part of a larger cube structure. Each cube is an intersection of a Time member, a Pharmacist member, and a Customer member. Inside the cube is a summarized data value for the number of prescriptions filled in 2002 by pharmacist Elkins for customer Baxter. Theoretically, if the cube supported it, you could drill further into the cube to determine how many of those prescriptions were filled in Winter and then in March by pharmacist Elkins for customer Baxter.

NOTE Cubes are not cubes in the strictly geometrical sense because they do not have equal sides. However, the term *cube* in this context is well understood and defined in this field of multidimensional data analysis.

Why is all this talk about dimensions, levels, members, measures, and cubes so important? Because the cube contains summarized data for the intersections of the measures for most or all of the various dimensions, levels, and members in advance, you can retrieve summarized data very quickly. Basically, all of the possible data summarizations are already sitting there waiting for you. For example, if a user asks for the number of prescriptions filled in April for each of the four years, by pharmacist and by customer, those summarized numbers are already available. If a user then asks for the number of prescriptions filled in August for just the years 2001 and 2002 for the first two pharmacists for all of the customers, those summarized numbers are already available as well.

If this concept is still a little fuzzy to you, think of cubes as little databases that already have the answers before you even ask the questions. When a PivotTable is connected to nonmultidimensional source data, the PivotTable has to take time to calculate summarized information each time you change the PivotTable's layout. This time is not so long for a relatively small group of records, but for hundreds of thousands or millions of records, PivotTable calculations can virtually grind to a halt. In short, cubes already contain the summarized calculations for each intersection of dimensions, levels, members, and measures.

NOTE Some data warehouses are so large that they don't actually contain the original data records! They perform calculations on the original data records and store only the summarized results of the calculations in cube files in the data warehouse.

One remaining term that isn't covered much in this chapter is the concept of a *property field*. For example, a Time dimension could have a field called Day Count, which would store the number of days for each month. Likewise, City members could have a Population property stored in the data warehouse, and the PivotTable could then display the size population of each city. You can display property fields in PivotTables, as discussed later in this chapter.

Let's now apply these concepts and terms to PivotTables and PivotCharts as we contrast multidimensional data sources to other types of data sources.

Contrasting Multidimensional Data and Other Types of Data in PivotTables and PivotCharts

As you work with PivotTables and PivotCharts based on multidimensional data sources, you'll notice some differences from when you base your Pivot-Tables and PivotCharts on nonmultidimensional data sources. After you understand these key differences, you'll be able to dive in and start using the OLAP features of PivotTables and PivotCharts.

If your data source is a data warehouse, the data warehouse server sends new data to Excel every time the layout of the report is changed. With other types of source data, you get all of the data at once. Obviously, sending all of the data in a data warehouse directly to Excel can be detrimental to PivotTable performance.

> **NOTE** PivotTables query for multidimensional data on an as-needed basis, so they don't need this option.

In the field list, dimensions have an icon like this: and can only be dropped into the row area, column area, or page area of a PivotTable.

Measures have an icon like this: and can only be dropped into the data area of a PivotTable.

If you rename a dimension or member, hide the dimension or member, and then show it again, the dimension or member displays its original name.

NOTE For nonmultidimensional source data, renamed fields and items retain their new names.

When displayed, dimensions' members first appear in the order in which they are stored in the cube. You can then rearrange or sort the members from there.

NOTE For nondimensional source data, fields' items first appear sorted in ascending order by item name.

Because summarized data is already provided in a cube's measures, you can't change measures' summarized data.

NOTE For nonmultidimensional source data, you can change data fields' summary functions, and you can also use multiple summary functions for a single data field.

You can't create calculated fields or calculated items in PivotTables based on multidimensional data. You can, however, include *calculated members*, which are basically calculated fields in a multidimensional data source, if the source data has any calculated members..
You can't show subtotals for inner row or column members.

NOTE For nondimensional source data, you can show and hide subtotals for both outer and inner row and column fields.

You can include or not include hidden items when you calculate subtotals.

NOTE For nondimensional source data, you can include hidden page field items in subtotals, but hidden items in row and column fields are initially not included.

Let's leverage these concepts to begin working with PivotTables, especially using the PivotTable menu and field settings.

Using PivotTables to Work with Multidimensional Data

Working with multidimensional data in PivotTables is not much different from working with nonmultidimensional data. Other than changes to the field list layout and its icons, the only major differences are the toolbar and menu commands. In this section, you'll learn the PivotTable toolbar and menu commands that are specific to working with multidimensional data, as well as how to use them.

On the PivotTable toolbar's PivotTable menu, the following menu commands have special significance when applied to hierarchical source data:

- The Refresh Data command refreshes and rebuilds an offline cube file from data in the associated data warehouse if the PivotTable is based on one.

- The Offline OLAP command, as described in the next section, allows you to connect to the data warehouse containing the source data or to connect to an offline copy of the data from the data warehouse, if available in either case.

- The Hide Levels command allows you to hide upper levels of detail on the PivotTable. To use this command, right-click the level field button for the lowest level that you want to hide, and then click Hide Levels. The level that you click and all the higher levels in the dimension are hidden.

- The Hide Dimension command removes the dimension from the PivotTable (but not from the field list).

- The Property Fields command allows you to display property fields, as discussed earlier in this chapter, if they are available in your source data. For row fields, you can display property fields for all levels of detail. However, for column fields, you can display property fields only for the lowest level of detail.

NOTE The commands on the Formulas menu are not available because multidimensional data sources don't allow you to create formulas. Also, the Show Pages command is not available for page fields in PivotTables that connect to multidimensional data.

When you right-click a dimension or level field button, or you right-click a member, click Field Settings, and then click Advanced, you have the option to specify sort options and whether to use the Top 10 AutoShow feature, but nothing else (including the subtotal type), as shown in Figure 6-17.

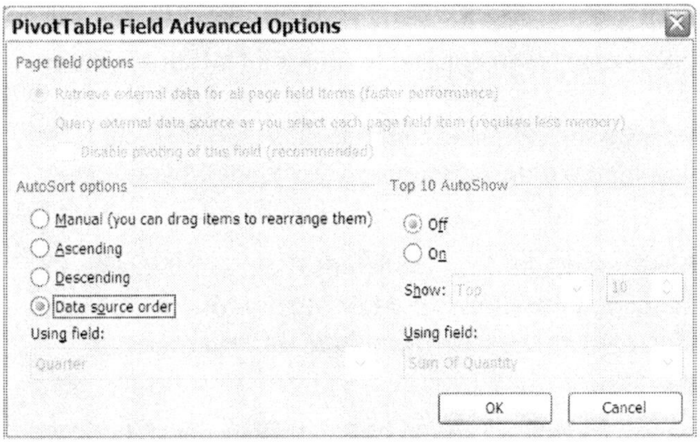

FIGURE 6-17

PivotTable Field Advanced Options dialog box for PivotTables connected to multidimensional data. Only the AutoSort Options and Top 10 AutoShow settings are available.

When you right-click a measure and then you click Field Settings, you can specify custom calculations such as Difference From and Running Total In, but you cannot specify the summary calculation, because it's already predetermined in the hierarchical source data, as shown in Figure 6-18.

For PivotTables that connect to multidimensional source data, you can select or hide a dimension's levels and members (if any exist) individually, as shown in Figure 6-19.

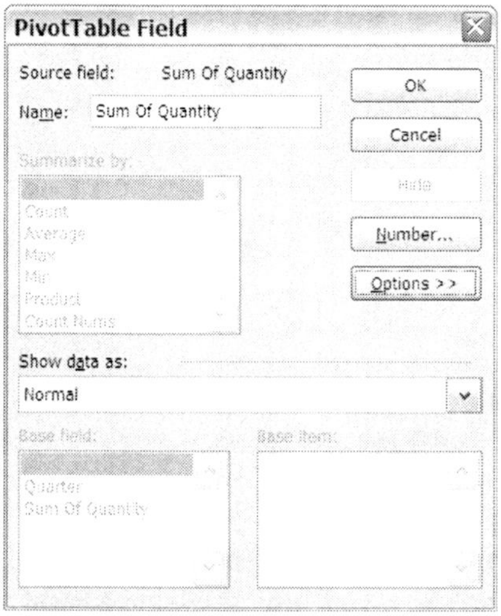

FIGURE 6-18

PivotTable Field Advanced Options dialog box for PivotTables connected to multidimensional data. Only the Show Data As setting is available.

FIGURE 6-19

The field drop-down list for row and column fields based on multidimensional source data allows you to select or hide a dimension's levels and members.

As you select or clear check boxes in this manner, a double check means that some or all of the lower levels and lower members are shown, a single check means that only the checked level or member is shown, and no check means that neither the lower levels nor lower members are displayed. Additionally, in page fields for multidimensional source data, after you click the arrow next to the page field button, you can select the Select Multiple Items check box to allow the selection of multiple levels and members, as shown in Figure 6-20.

FIGURE 6-20

The field drop-down list for a page field based on multidimensional source data allows you to select multiple page field items to display.

To practice these skills in a PivotTable, you need to connect to multidimensional source data. The next few sections show you how to create a local copy of some multidimensional source data that you can try out these PivotTable tools with.

Creating Offline Cube Files

If you want to or need to work with multidimensional data in PivotTables and PivotCharts when you're not connected to the network, you can create offline cube (.cub) files that store some or all of the data from the multidimensional data source, whether it's stored in a data warehouse or elsewhere. Even if you're connected to the network, offline cube files can help improve overall PivotTable and PivotChart performance, as shown in Figure 6-21.

> **NOTE** Because offline cube files can store large amounts of data, you should allow for enough disk space to store offline cube files on your computer. You should also allow enough time if you're creating and saving large offline cube files, especially if you're trying to create an offline cube file while hurrying out the door for a business trip!

Excel provides two tools to help you create offline cube files. The Offline Cube Wizard allows you to copy some of the data from a data warehouse into an offline cube file. The OLAP Cube Wizard allows you to create an offline cube wizard from multidimensional data retrieved by a data query using Microsoft Query.

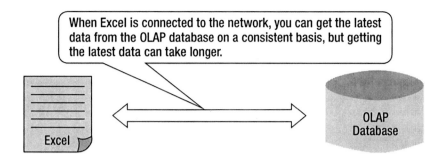

FIGURE 6-21
Offline cube files help ensure that you have access to data if your computer can't connect to a network-based database. Offline cube files also help improve your computer's performance.

In general, to use the Offline Cube Wizard from a PivotTable or PivotChart connected to data in a data warehouse:

1. Create a PivotTable or PivotChart that's based on data in a data warehouse.

2. On the PivotTable toolbar, click PivotTable ➤ Offline OLAP.

3. Follow the onscreen instructions to select the dimensions, levels, and measures that you want to include in the offline cube file.

   NOTE Not all data warehouses support the Offline Cube Wizard. For more information, contact the manufacturer of your data warehouse software.

TIP You can switch between using the data in the data warehouse (if you're connected to the network) and using the data in the offline cube file by clicking Offline OLAP in the PivotTable menu on the PivotTable toolbar. You can refresh the data in the offline cube file from the data in the data warehouse by clicking Refresh Data on the PivotTable menu.

In general, to use the OLAP Cube Wizard without an available PivotTable or PivotChart:

1. Click Data ➤ Import External Data ➤ New Database Query.

2. Create a connection to the data source using either the Choose Data Source dialog box's Databases or OLAP Cubes tab.

3. Click OK to start the Query Wizard.

4. In the last step of the Query Wizard, click Create An OLAP Cube From This Query, and click Finish.

5. Follow the onscreen instructions to select or create the dimensions, levels, and measures that you want to include in the offline cube file.

Let's practice using the OLAP Cube Wizard in the following exercise.

Try It! Create a Multidimensional Data Source

In this exercise, you'll create an offline cube file from a data source that can be expressed in a hierarchical format. The offline cube file represents sales for a chain of retail clothing stores. You will then create a PivotTable and a PivotChart that uses this offline cube file as a multidimensional data source.

1. Start Excel.

2. Click Data ➤ Import External Data ➤ New Database Query.

3. On the Databases tab, click Excel Files. Make sure the Use The Query Wizard To Create/Edit Queries check box is selected, and then click OK.

4. Browse to and select the ClothesSales.xls file that you downloaded from the Apress Web site Downloads section, and then click OK.

5. Click the right arrow to move all of fields in the Available Tables And Columns list to the Columns In Your Query list.

6. Click Next three more times.

7. In the What Would You Like To Do Next area, click Create An OLAP Cube From This Query, and then click Finish.

8. If the Welcome To The OLAP Cube Wizard page appears, click Next.

9. Clear the check box next to the Quarter field. Compare your results to Figure 6-22.

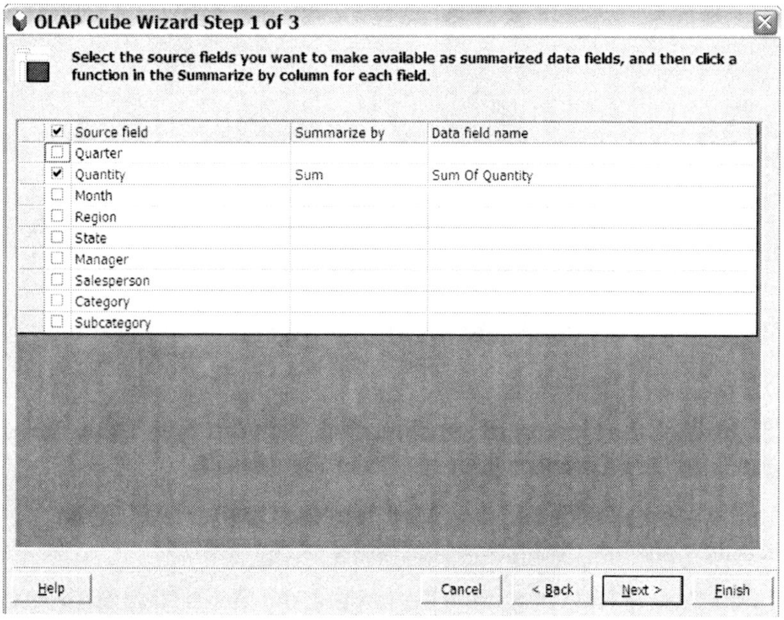

FIGURE 6-22

The OLAP Cube Wizard, Step 1 of 3

10. Click Next.

11. In the Source Fields list, drag Quarter to Drop Fields Here To Create A Dimension in the Dimensions list. Compare your results to Figure 6-23.

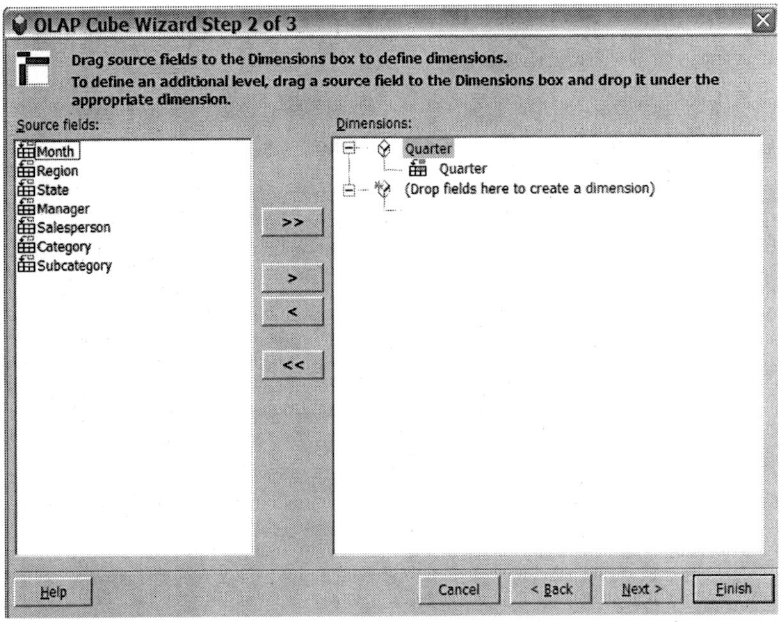

FIGURE 6-23
Beginning of the OLAP Cube Wizard, Step 2 of 3

12. Right-click the Quarter dimension, click Rename, type **Time**, and press the Enter key. Compare your results to Figure 6-24.

13. In the Source Fields list, drag Month to the Quarter level in the Dimensions list. Compare your results to Figure 6-25.

14. In the Source Fields list, drag Region to Drop Fields Here To Create A Dimension in the Dimensions list.

15. Right-click the Region dimension, click Rename, type **Location**, and press the Enter key.

16. From the Source Fields list, drag State to the Region level in the Dimensions list.

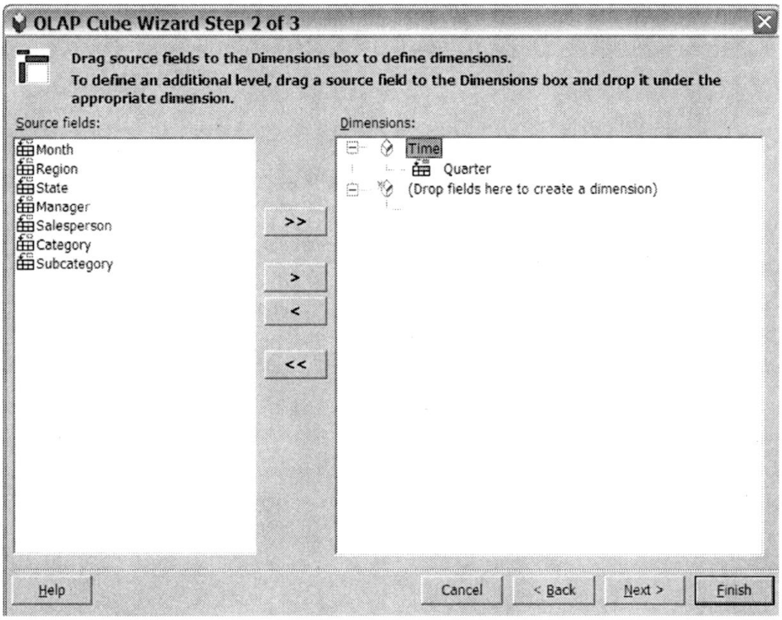

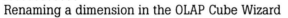

FIGURE 6-24
Renaming a dimension in the OLAP Cube Wizard

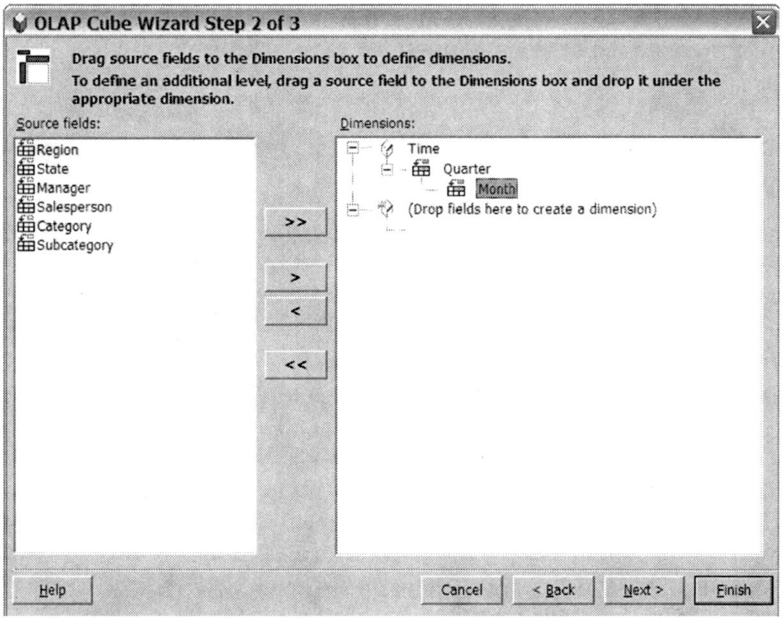

FIGURE 6-25
Adding a level to an existing level in the OLAP Cube Wizard

17. From the Source Fields list, drag Manager to Drop Fields Here To Create A Dimension in the Dimensions list. Compare your results to Figure 6-26.

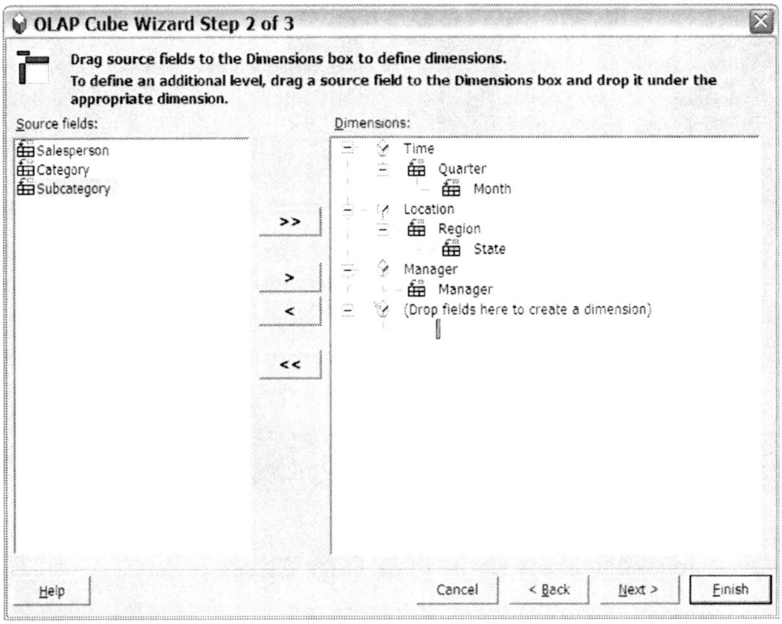

FIGURE 6-26

Adding more dimensions in the OLAP Cube Wizard

18. Right-click the Manager dimension, click Rename, type **Employees**, and press the Enter key.

19. From the Source Fields list, drag Salesperson to the Manager level in the Dimensions list.

20. From the Source Fields list, drag Category to Drop Fields Here To Create A Dimension in the Dimensions list.

21. Right-click the Category dimension, click Rename, and type **Products**.

22. From the Source Fields list, drag Subcategory to the Category level in the Dimensions list. Compare your results to Figure 6-27.

23. Click Next.

24. Save the cube file to a convenient location, naming the file ClothesSales.cub. Click Finish.

25. Click Save.

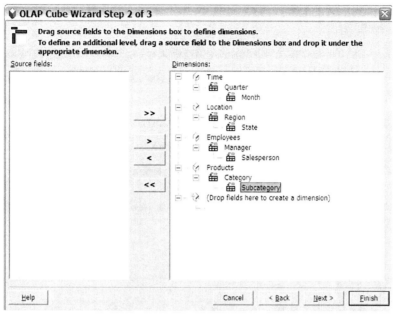

FIGURE 6-27
Finishing the OLAP Cube Wizard, Step 2 of 3

26. Click Finish again. An offline cube file is created, and a PivotTable is created to enable you to view the offline cube file's contents, as shown in Figure 6-28.

FIGURE 6-28
A PivotTable for viewing the offline cube file's contents

27. Expand the Employees dimension to see the Manager and Salesperson levels.

28. Expand the Location dimension to see the Region and State levels.

29. Expand the Products dimension to see the Category and Subcategory levels.

30. Expand the Time dimension to see the Quarter and Month levels.

Notice that the Sum Of Quantity measure is also visible.

31. Close the workbook, and do not save the changes.

In the next exercise, you'll analyze the data in this offline cube file using a PivotTable and a PivotChart.

Try It! Analyze Multidimensional Data with a PivotTable and a PivotChart

Now let's create a PivotTable and a PivotChart based on the cube file that you created in the previous exercise. Following that, you'll use the PivotTable and PivotChart to explore the multidimensional data in the cube file.

Create a PivotTable and PivotChart and Connect Them to the Cube File

First, you'll create a PivotTable and PivotChart. You'll use the cube file as the source data for the PivotTable and PivotChart.

1. Start Excel if it isn't already running.

2. Create a new, blank workbook if one isn't already available.

3. Click Data ➤ PivotTable and PivotChart Report.

4. Click External Data Source.

5. Click PivotChart Report (With PivotTable Report), and click Next.

6. Click Get Data.

7. Click the OLAP Cubes tab.

8. Click ClothesSales, and click OK.

9. Click Finish. Compare your results to Figure 6-29.

FIGURE 6-29

A PivotChart for viewing the offline cube file's contents. The PivotChart is connected to a PivotTable on the Sheet1 worksheet.

Now let's customize the PivotTable's and PivotChart's visual layout.

Add Dimensions and Measures to the PivotTable and PivotChart

Next, you'll drag dimensions and measures to the PivotTable layout. Remember from the previous chapter that the PivotChart will synchronize its layout to match the PivotTable layout. You can click the Chart1 worksheet tab at any time to see the visual results of what you're doing to the PivotTable layout on the Sheet1 worksheet.

1. On the Sheet1 worksheet, drag the Employees dimension from the field list to the PivotTable's row area.

2. Drag the Time dimension from the field list to the column area.

   NOTE Notice that the row field name changes to Manager, and the column field name changes to Quarter. This is because Manager is the top-most level in the Employees dimension, and Quarter is the top-most level in the Time dimension.

3. Drag the Sum Of Quantity measure from the field list to the PivotTable's data area. Compare your results with Figure 6-30. Also, notice the PivotChart layout, as shown in Figure 6-31.

	A	B	C	D	E	F
1	Drop Page Fields Here					
2						
3	Sum Of Quantity	Quarter ▾				
4	Manager ▾	1	2	3	4	Grand Total
5	Andersen	4737	5087	5231	5878	20933
6	Bailey	4602	5055	5328	5836	20821
7	Collins	3988	4251	4546	4985	17770
8	Donaldson	3923	4269	4494	5011	17697
9	Eddings	5234	5694	6101	6821	23850
10	Franks	5266	5821	6126	6836	24049
11	Gerry	3460	3783	3931	4404	15578
12	Hastings	3533	3792	3938	4544	15807
13	Grand Total	34743	37752	39695	44315	156505

FIGURE 6-30

Initial PivotTable layout

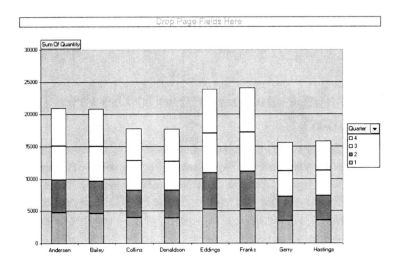

FIGURE 6-31

Initial PivotChart layout

Rearrange Dimensions in the PivotTable and PivotChart

Let's rearrange some of the dimensions in the PivotTable and see what happens:

1. On the Sheet1 worksheet, drag the Manager level to the PivotTable's page area.

   NOTE Notice that the Manager level reverts to the Employees dimension because you have the ability to filter the PivotTable by any combination of employees, not just managers.

2. Drag the Location dimension to the row area.

3. Drag the Products dimension to the row area as an inner row field.

   NOTE Notice that the outer row field name changes to Region, and the inner row field name changes to Category. This is because Region is the top-most level in the Location dimension, and Category is the top-most level in the Products dimension.

4. Compare your results with Figure 6-32. Also, notice the PivotChart layout, as shown in Figure 6-33.

	A	B	C	D	E	F	G
1	Employees	All					
2							
3	Sum Of Quantity		Quarter				
4	Region	Category	1	2	3	4	Grand Total
5	East	Business	5281	5783	6122	6865	24051
6		Casual	5219	5732	6105	6792	23848
7	East Total		10500	11515	12227	13657	47899
8	North	Business	4625	5112	5347	5826	20910
9		Casual	4714	5030	5212	5888	20844
10	North Total		9339	10142	10559	11714	41754
11	South	Business	3987	4248	4530	5015	17780
12		Casual	3924	4272	4510	4981	17687
13	South Total		7911	8520	9040	9996	35467
14	West	Business	3494	3798	3946	4527	15765
15		Casual	3499	3777	3923	4421	15620
16	West Total		6993	7575	7869	8948	31385
17	Grand Total		34743	37752	39695	44315	156505

FIGURE 6-32
Results of changing the initial PivotTable layout

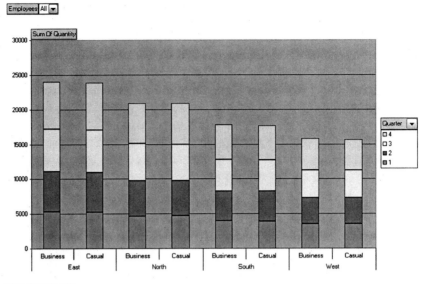

FIGURE 6-33

Results of changing the initial PivotChart layout

Filter Data in the PivotTable and PivotChart by Selecting a Combination of Members

Next, let's select a random combination of members in the Employees dimension and see how that affects our data:

1. On the Sheet1 worksheet, click the arrow in the cell next to the Employees field button.

2. Select the Select Multiple Items check box.

3. Expand All.

4. Clear the All check box.

5. Select the Andersen check box.

6. Expand Collins.

7. Select the Baker and Campo check boxes.

8. Select the Eddings check box, and click OK. Compare your results with Figure 6-34. Also, notice the PivotChart layout, as shown in Figure 6-35.

	A	B	C	D	E	F	G
1	Employees	(Multiple Items) ▼					
2							
3	Sum Of Quantity		Quarter ▼				
4	Region ▼	Category ▼	1	2	3	4	Grand Total
5	East	Business	2598	2858	3053	3436	11945
6		Casual	2636	2836	3048	3385	11905
7	East Total		5234	5694	6101	6821	23850
8	North	Business	2317	2561	2638	2928	10444
9		Casual	2420	2526	2593	2950	10489
10	North Total		4737	5087	5231	5878	20933
11	South	Business	976	1046	1149	1274	4445
12		Casual	996	1048	1145	1211	4400
13	South Total		1972	2094	2294	2485	8845
14	Grand Total		11943	12875	13626	15184	53628

FIGURE 6-34

Results of selecting a combination of members in the PivotTable

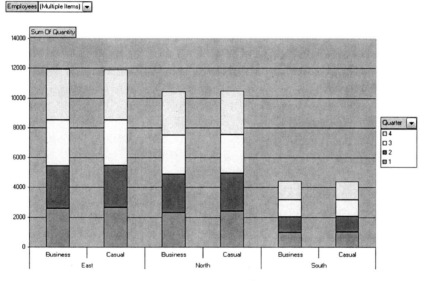

FIGURE 6-35

Results of selecting a combination of members in the PivotChart

9. Return the results to their original state by clicking the arrow in the cell next to the Employees field button.

10. Select the All check box, and click OK.

Show and Hide Levels in the PivotTable and PivotChart

Let's practice showing and hiding the dimensions' levels:

1. To show a lower level, on the Sheet1 worksheet, right-click the Category field button, and click Group And Show Detail ➤ Show Detail.

2. To hide an upper level, right-click the Category field button, and click Hide Levels. The Category level disappears from the PivotTable.

3. To show hidden upper levels, right-click the Subcategory field button, and click Show Levels. The Category level reappears on the PivotTable.

4. To hide a lower level, click the arrow in the Category field button.

5. Expand Business, and expand Casual.

6. Filter to only include the Business level by clearing the Business check box, and selecting the Business check box again.

7. Filter to only include the Casual level by clearing the Casual check box, and selecting the Casual check box again. Compare your results to Figure 6-36.

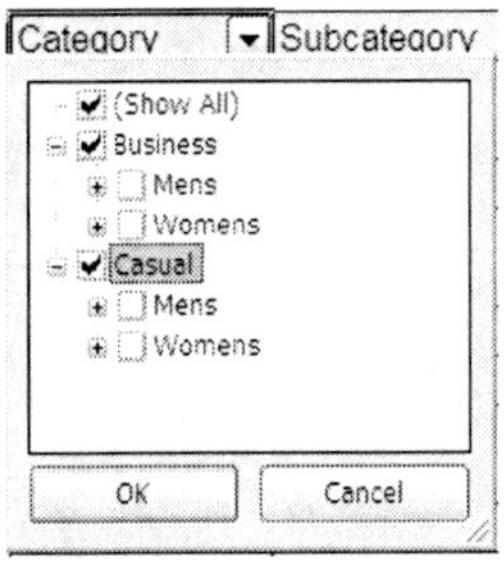

FIGURE 6-36

Modfying the check boxes to hide a lower level from the PivotTable

8. Click OK. The Subcategory level disappears from the PivotTable.

Grouping Members in Row, Column, and Page Fields

Now let's further organize members by grouping them in row, column, and page fields:

1. On the Sheet1 worksheet, in the Region column, click the North member, hold the Ctrl key, and click the West member.

2. Right-click the West member, and click Group And Show Detail ➤ Group. Compare your results with Figure 6-37. Also, notice the PivotChart layout, as shown in Figure 6-38.

	A	B	C	D	E	F	G	H
1	Employees	All ▾						
2								
3	Sum Of Quantity			Quarter ▾				
4	Location1 ▾	Region	Category ▾	1	2	3	4	Grand Total
5	Group1	North	Business	4625	5112	5347	5826	20910
6			Casual	4714	5030	5212	5888	20844
7		North Total		9339	10142	10559	11714	41754
8		West	Business	3494	3798	3946	4527	15765
9			Casual	3499	3777	3923	4421	15620
10		West Total		6993	7575	7869	8948	31385
11	Group1 Total			16332	17717	18428	20662	73139
12	Other	East	Business	5281	5783	6122	6865	24051
13			Casual	5219	5732	6105	6792	23848
14		East Total		10500	11515	12227	13657	47899
15		South	Business	3987	4248	4530	5015	17780
16			Casual	3924	4272	4510	4981	17687
17		South Total		7911	8520	9040	9996	35467
18	Other Total			18411	20035	21267	23653	83366
19	Grand Total			34743	37752	39695	44315	156505

FIGURE 6-37

Results of grouping members in a row field in a PivotTable

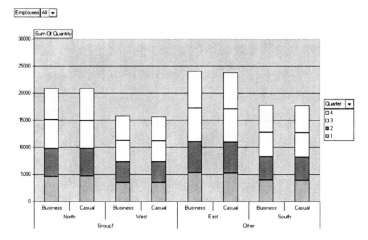

FIGURE 6-38

Results of grouping members in a row field in a PivotTable, as reflected in the accompanying PivotChart

3. In the row beneath the Quarter field, click the 1 member, hold the Ctrl key, and click the 4 member.

4. Right-click the 4 member, and click Group And Show Detail ➤ Group. Compare your results with Figure 6-39. Also, notice the PivotChart layout, as shown in Figure 6-40.

	A	B	C	D	E	F	G	H	I	J
1	Employees	All								
2										
3	Sum Of Quantity			Time1	Quarter					
4				Group1		Group1 Total	Other		Other Total	Grand Total
5	Location1	Region	Category	1	4		2	3		
6	Group1	North	Business	4625	5826	10451	5112	5347	10459	20910
7			Casual	4714	5888	10602	5030	5212	10242	20844
8		North Total		9339	11714	21053	10142	10559	20701	41754
9		West	Business	3494	4527	8021	3798	3946	7744	15765
10			Casual	3499	4421	7920	3777	3923	7700	15620
11		West Total		6993	8948	15941	7575	7869	15444	31385
12	Group1 Total			16332	20662	36994	17717	18428	36145	73139
13	Other	East	Business	5281	6865	12146	5783	6122	11905	24051
14			Casual	5219	6792	12011	5732	6105	11837	23848
15		East Total		10500	13657	24157	11515	12227	23742	47899
16		South	Business	3987	5015	9002	4248	4530	8778	17780
17			Casual	3924	4981	8905	4272	4510	8782	17687
18		South Total		7911	9996	17907	8520	9040	17560	35467
19	Other Total			18411	23653	42064	20035	21267	41302	83366
20	Grand Total			34743	44315	79058	37752	39695	77447	156505

FIGURE 6-39

Results of grouping members in a column field in a PivotTable

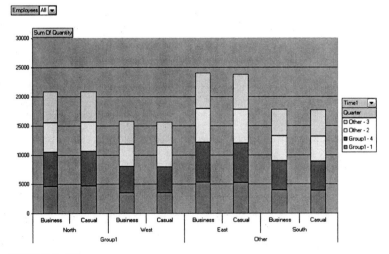

FIGURE 6-40

Results of grouping members in a column field in a PivotTable, as reflected in the accompanying PivotChart

5. On the Sheet1 worksheet, drag the Employees field from the page area to the row area as an outer row field.

6. In the row beneath the Manager field, click the Bailey member, hold the Ctrl key, and click the Donaldson member, the Eddings member, and the Gerry member.

7. Right-click the Gerry member, and click Group And Show Detail ➤ Group.

8. Drag the Employees1 field from the row area to the page area.

9. Click the arrow in the cell next to the Employees field button.

10. Expand All.

11. Expand Other and Group1.

12. Continue expanding levels and members until all of the levels and members are displayed, as shown in Figure 6-41.

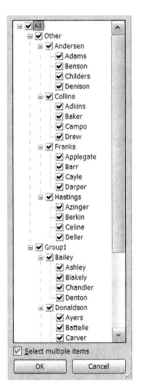

FIGURE 6-41

Expanding levels and members in the field drop-down list

13. With the Select Multiple Items check box selected, experiment with selecting and clearing the check boxes.

14. When you're done, click Cancel.

15. Now return the PivotTable to its original state by dragging the Employees field from the page area to the row area as an outer row field.

16. In the Employees1 column, right-click the Group1 item, and click Group And Show Detail ➤ Ungroup.

17. In the Location1 column, right-click the Group1 item, and click Group And Show Detail ➤ Ungroup.

18. In the row underneath the Time1 field button, right-click the Group1 item, and click Group And Show Detail ➤ Ungroup.

19. Move the Manager field from the row area to the page area. Compare your results with Figure 6-32 (shown earlier).

Sorting and Showing Top Members

Finally, let's sort some of the members, from highest to lowest in terms of the Sum Of Quantity field, on the PivotTable and PivotChart. From there, we'll show only the top two members for selected dimensions.

1. On the Sheet1 worksheet, right-click the Quarter field, and click Field Settings.

2. Click Advanced.

3. Click Descending.

4. In the Using Field list, click Sum Of Quantity.

5. Click OK, and click OK again.

6. Right-click the Region field, and click Field Settings.

7. Click Advanced.

8. Click Descending.

9. In the Using Field list, click Sum Of Quantity.

10. Click OK, and click OK again. Compare your results with Figure 6-42. Also, notice the PivotChart layout, as shown in Figure 6-43.

	A	B	C	D	E	F	G
1	Employees	All ▼					
2							
3	Sum Of Quantity		Quarter ▼				
4	Region ▼	Category ▼	4	3	2	1	Grand Total
5	East	Business	6865	6122	5783	5281	24051
6		Casual	6792	6105	5732	5219	23848
7	East Total		13657	12227	11515	10500	47899
8	North	Business	5826	5347	5112	4625	20910
9		Casual	5888	5212	5030	4714	20844
10	North Total		11714	10559	10142	9339	41754
11	South	Business	5015	4530	4248	3987	17780
12		Casual	4981	4510	4272	3924	17687
13	South Total		9996	9040	8520	7911	35467
14	West	Business	4527	3946	3798	3494	15765
15		Casual	4421	3923	3777	3499	15620
16	West Total		8948	7869	7575	6993	31385
17	Grand Total		44315	39695	37752	34743	156505

FIGURE 6-42

Results of sorting members in a PivotTable

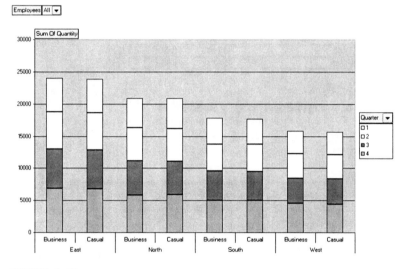

FIGURE 6-43

Results of sorting members in a PivotChart

11. On the Sheet1 worksheet, right-click the Quarter field, and click Field Settings.

12. Click Advanced.

13. Click On.

14. In the box next to the Show Top list, type or click **2**.

15. Click OK, and click OK again.

16. Right-click the Region field, and click Field Settings.

17. Click Advanced.

18. Click On.

19. In the box next to the Show Top list, type or click **2**.

20. Click OK, and click OK again. Compare your results with Figure 6-44. Also, notice the PivotChart layout, as shown in Figure 6-45.

	A	B	C	D	E
1	Employees	All			
2					
3	Sum Of Quantity		Quarter		
4	Region	Category	4	3	Grand Total
5	East	Business	6865	6122	12987
6		Casual	6792	6105	12897
7	East Total		13657	12227	25884
8	North	Business	5826	5347	11173
9		Casual	5888	5212	11100
10	North Total		11714	10559	22273
11	Grand Total		25371	22786	48157

FIGURE 6-44

Results of using AutoShow in a PivotTable

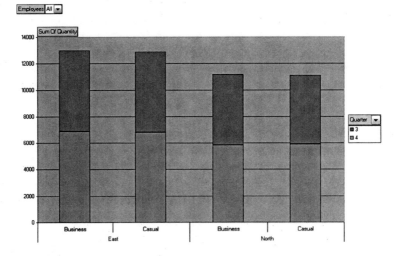

FIGURE 6-45

Results of using AutoShow in a PivotChart

21. Return the PivotTable and PivotChart to their original state: On the Sheet1 worksheet, right-click the Region field, and click Field Settings.

22. Click Advanced.

23. Click Data Source Order, and click Off.

24. Click OK, and click OK again.

25. Right-click the Quarter field, and click Field Settings.

26. Click Advanced.

27. Click Data Source Order, and click Off.

28. Click OK, and click OK again.

Next Steps

In this chapter, you learned the differences between nonrelational nonmulti-dimensional data, relational data, and multidimensional data. You learned key terms used in multidimensional data analysis such as *dimension*, *level*, *member*, *measure*, and *cube*. You practiced creating an offline cube file and then connecting to the cube file with both a PivotTable and a PivotChart.

Now that you've used a PivotTable and a PivotChart to analyze your own source data, you can try to create an offline cube file out of it and then analyze the offline cube file with a PivotTable and a PivotChart. Of course, your own source data needs to be presented in terms of dimensions, levels, members, and measures. Is it? If not, you might want to experiment with a copy of your data and create dimensions, levels, members, and measures for your data. Understanding and applying multidimensional data analysis will come in useful as your source data grows beyond the limits of Excel to display the source data in traditional row-and-column format.

7

Programming PivotTables

In this chapter, you'll bring together the skills you've learned in the first six chapters to automate the creation and display of PivotTables using Visual Basic for Applications (VBA) code in Excel. Not only will you learn about useful scenarios for programming PivotTables, but you will also learn about the PivotTable programmatic object model. You'll also learn how to programmatically

- Create a new PivotTable based on existing source data in an Excel workbook, an Access database file, an existing PivotTable, and an offline cube file.

- Create a PivotChart at the same time as, or based on an existing, PivotTable.

- Add fields to a PivotTable's visual layout.

- Change the placement and position of fields in a PivotTable.

- Set and remove a field's item filters to show and hide field items.

- Create calculated fields and calculated items.

- Use the AutoSort and AutoShow features to sort and show the most significant items for a field.

- Change the custom calculations and visual display formatting of fields.

NOTE The information in this chapter applies to Excel 2003. For information about what was added in Excel 2000 and Excel 2002, see the Appendix.

If you frequently lay out the same sets of fields in PivotTables or PivotCharts in a predictable sequence, select the same item filters in similar field sets again and again, set the same sort orders for fields' items repetitively, or change the same sets of custom calculations over and over, then automating these tasks with code is a good idea.

Before Getting Started

Before you start working your way through this chapter, I assume that you have intermediate-level experience with the following:

- The Visual Basic for Applications (VBA) programming language
- The Excel programmatic object model, including the Workbook and Worksheet programmatic objects
- The Visual Basic Editor (VBE) in Excel

An understanding of the Visual Basic .NET and C# programming languages is helpful, but not necessary.

For more information on these topics, see the following:

- *Definitive Guide to Excel VBA Second Edition* by Michael Kofler (Apress, 2003)
- *Microsoft Office Programming: A Guide for Experienced Developers* by Rod Stephens (Apress, 2003)
- *Moving to VB .NET: Strategies, Concepts, and Code Second Edition* by Dan Appleman (Apress, 2003)
- *A Programmer's Introduction to C# Second Edition* by Eric Gunnerson (Apress, 2001)

Understanding the PivotTable Object Model

To help you better understand how the PivotTable's programmatic objects and collections relate to each other, a visual representation of the PivotTable object model is shown in Figure 7-1. The main objects and collections of the PivotTable programmatic object model are listed in Table 7-1.

TABLE 7-1

The Main Objects and Collections in the PivotTable Programmatic Object Model

Object/Collection	Description
CalculatedFields collection	All of the calculated fields in the specified PivotTable
CalculatedItems collection	All of the calculated items in the specified PivotTable
CalculatedMember object	A calculated member or calculated measure in the specified PivotTable
CalculatedMembers collection	All of the calculated members and calculated measures in the specified PivotTable
Chart object	A PivotChart
CubeField object	A dimension or measure field in a PivotTable based on multidimensional source data
CubeFields collection	All of the dimension and measure fields in a PivotTable based on multidimensional source data
PivotCache object	The memory cache for a PivotTable
PivotCaches collection	All of the memory caches for all of the PivotTables in a workbook
PivotCell object	A cell in a PivotTable
PivotField object	A field in a PivotTable
PivotFields collection	All of the fields in a PivotTable
PivotFormula object	A calculated field or calculated item in a PivotTable
PivotFormulas collection	All of the calculated fields and calculated items in a PivotTable
PivotItem object	An item in a PivotTable field
PivotItemList object	All of the items in all of the fields in a PivotTable
PivotItems collection	All of the items in a PivotTable field
PivotLayout object	The placement of all of the fields in a PivotChart
PivotTable object	A PivotTable on a worksheet
PivotTables collection	All of the PivotTables on a worksheet
Range object	A cell, a row of cells, a column of cells, or a selection of cells in a PivotTable

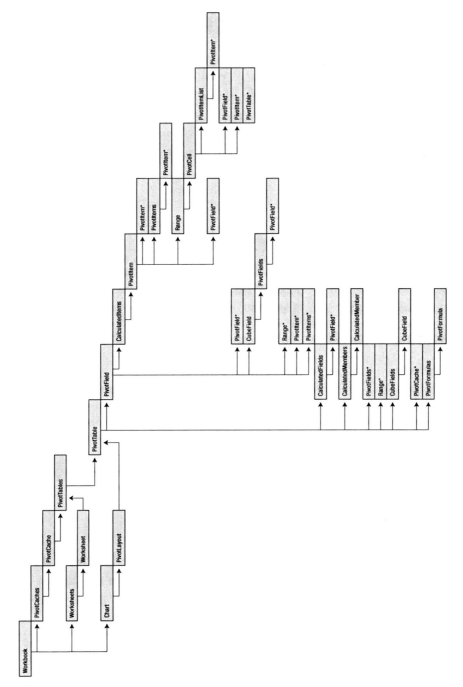

FIGURE 7-1

The PivotTable Programmatic Object Model (an asterisk (*) indicates child objects are repeated elsewhere in the model)

To create a new PivotTable or access an existing PivotTable, you must first access the Excel workbook that will contain or already contains the PivotTable. You can access the Excel Workbook object using VBA code using one of the following programmatic constructs.

The Application object's ActiveWorkbook property accesses the workbook in the active window (the window on top), for example:

```
Sub GetActiveWorkbook ()

    ' Purpose:
    ' Displays the active Excel workbook's name.

    ' Assumes:
    ' An Excel workbook is displayed in the top-most window.

    ' Notes:
    ' If an Excel workbook is already displayed in the
    ' top-most window, you can simply use the ActiveWorkbook
    ' property to refer to it, for example:
    ' MsgBox ActiveWorkbook.Name

    Dim xlApp As Excel.Application
    Dim objWorkbook As Workbook

    Set xlApp = Excel.Application
    Set objWorkbook = xlApp.ActiveWorkbook

    MsgBox objWorkbook.Name

    Set objWorkbook = Nothing
    Set xlApp = Nothing

End Sub
```

In the preceding code, the Excel Application object's ActiveWorkbook property returns a Workbook programmatic object representing the Excel workbook that is *active* or has the *focus*, which means the workbook waiting for action to be taken on it. After you have the Workbook object, you can access the workbook's properties programmatically; in this case, you return the workbook's file name.

NOTE It's a good practice to clean up all unused computer memory by setting all of your programmatic resources to Nothing when your VBA code stops running.

The Application object's ThisWorkbook property accesses the workbook where the current VBA code is running, for example:

```
Sub GetThisWorkbook ()

    ' Purpose:
    ' Displays the name of the Excel workbook in which
    ' this code example resides.

    ' Notes:
    ' You do not need to specify an Application object nor
    ' a Workbook object. You can simply use the following code:
    ' MsgBox ThisWorkbook.Name

    Dim xlApp As Excel.Application

    Set xlApp = Excel.Application

    MsgBox xlApp.ThisWorkbook.Name

    Set objWorkbook = Nothing
    Set xlApp = Nothing

End Sub
```

In contrast to the code preceding this code, the Application object's ThisWorkbook property does not necessarily return the workbook that has the focus. The ThisWorkbook property returns a Workbook object representing the Excel workbook that contains the currently running VBA code. After you have this Workbook object, you can access the workbook's properties just like the workbook returned as a result of accessing the ActiveWorkbook property.

The Application object's Workbooks collection represents all open workbooks. The Workbooks collection's Add method can be used to create a new workbook and access the new workbook at the same time. Similarly, the Workbooks collection's Open method can be used to open an existing workbook and access the workbook at the same time. Furthermore, the Workbooks collection's Item property can be used to access an individual workbook that is already open, for example:

```
Sub GetSpecifiedWorkbook ()

    ' Purpose:
    ' Accesses an Excel workbook.

    ' Assumes:
    ' An Excel workbook named SampleCode.xls is
    ' already open.

    On Error GoTo GetSpecifiedWorkbook_Err

    Dim xlApp As Excel.Application
    Dim objWorkbook As Workbook

    Set xlApp = Excel.Application
    Set objWorkbook = _
        xlApp.Workbooks.Item(Index:="SampleCode.xls")

    ' You can open an Excel workbook using code similar
    ' to the following:
    ' Set objWorkbook = xlApp.Workbooks.Open _
        ("C:\Program Files\Microsoft Office\" & _
        "OFFICE11\SAMPLES\SOLVSAMP.XLS")

    ' You can create a new Excel workbook using code similar
    ' to the following:
    ' Set objWorkbook = xlApp.Workbooks.Add

    MsgBox objWorkbook.Name

GetSpecifiedWorkbook_End:

    Set objWorkbook = Nothing
    Set xlApp = Nothing

    Exit Sub

GetSpecifiedWorkbook_Err:

    Select Case Err.Number
        Case 9
            MsgBox "Can't open file. Check the file name " & _
```

```
                    "and try opening the file again."
          Case Else
                MsgBox "Error " & Err.Number & ": " & Err.Description
      End Select

      Resume GetSpecifiedWorkbook_End

End Sub
```

In the preceding code, the Workbooks collection's Item property accesses an individual workbook that is already open. The workbook is identified by its ordinal index number relative to other open workbooks, or in this case, by the open workbook's name. The Open method, in contrast, opens and accesses a workbook that is not yet open. At a minimum, you must specific the workbook's file name (and path if you feel that Excel may have trouble finding the workbook). Finally, the Add method creates and accesses a new workbook (giving it a default file name) at the same time.

NOTE This is the first code example in this chapter that features error-handling code. As a general practice in VBA, you should add error-handling code when you know the circumstances in which a piece of code might fail and any of the errors that are returned might not be understandable by the user. In this case, the text for error number 9 is Subscript Out Of Range, which doesn't make any sense to the user. A more helpful message is coded to appear to the user instead. The other error that can occur when a file is misspelled is error number 1004, and the resulting default error message that Excel displays in this case is understandable to the user.

To access the Workbook object using Visual Basic .NET or C# code, you must use the Excel Application object. Here are two examples using a console application written using Microsoft Visual Studio .NET 2003:

```
' Visual Basic .NET
Imports Excel = Microsoft.Office.Interop.Excel

Module modGetWorkbookConsoleApp

    Sub Main()

        ' Non-standard References:
        '    Microsoft Excel 11.0 Object Library (COM)

        Try
```

```vbnet
        Dim xlApp As Excel.Application
        Dim objWorkbook As Excel.Workbook

        xlApp = CType(CreateObject(ProgId:="Excel.Application"), _
            Excel.Application)
        objWorkbook = xlApp.Workbooks.Open _
            (Filename:="C:\Program Files\Microsoft Office\OFFICE11\" & _
            "SAMPLES\SOLVSAMP.XLS")

        Console.WriteLine(value:=objWorkbook.Name)

    Catch ex As System.Runtime.InteropServices.COMException

        MsgBox("File cannot be opened. File name may be spelled " & _
            "incorrectly. Check the file name and try again.")

    Catch ex As Exception

        MsgBox(ex.Message)

    End Try
    End Sub

End Module
```

```csharp
// C#
using System;
using Excel = Microsoft.Office.Interop.Excel;

namespace GetWorkbookConsoleAppCS
{
    class GetWorkbookConsoleApp
    {
        static void Main(string[] args)
        {
            try
            {
                Excel.Application xlApp;
                Excel.Workbook objWorkbook;
                object missing = Type.Missing;

                xlApp = new Excel.ApplicationClass();
```

```
        objWorkbook = xlApp.Workbooks.Open(
            @"C:\Program Files\Microsoft Office\OFFICE11\" +
            @"SAMPLES\SOLVSAMP.XLS", missing, missing,
            missing, missing, missing, missing, missing,
            missing, missing, missing, missing, missing,
            missing, missing);
        Console.WriteLine(objWorkbook.Name);
    }
    catch(System.Runtime.InteropServices.COMException)
    {
        Console.WriteLine("File cannot be opened. File name may be" +
            "spelled incorrectly. Check the file name and try " +
            "again.");
    }
    catch(System.Exception ex)
    {
        Console.WriteLine(ex.Message);
    }
    }
  }
}
```

In the preceding Visual Basic .NET code, the Imports statement (the using statement in C#) is used to reduce the repetitive typing the coder must do to qualify the System and Excel programmatic namespaces in the code. The Module keyword is used to define a programmatic code module. Finally, the CType method is called to convert an object from one type (in this case, an Object) to another type (in this case, an Excel Application object).

In the preceding C# example, code resides in programmatic classes instead of modules, while the class's programmatic namespace must be explicitly called out in the code (in Visual Basic .NET, the namespace is hidden by default from the coder, but the coder can still modify it if desired.) Also, because C# does not accept optional parameters, all 14 optional parameters must be specified in the call to the Open method by indicating that they are intentionally missing, even though we're not interested in using any of them here.

In both of the preceding code snippets, because they are applications that are run from the command line, the Console object's WriteLine method is used to display the workbook's name, rather than using a message box.

NOTE In Visual Basic .NET and C# code, you don't need to programmatically clean up all of your system's unused computer memory by setting all of your programmatic resources to Nothing or null when your code stops running. This is because the underlying runtime engine automatically frees these resources for you at the appropriate time using a feature called *garbage collection*.

Furthermore, you can access the Workbook object using Microsoft Visual Studio Tools for the Microsoft Office System, Version 2003 (VSTO). VSTO provides a ThisWorkbook item representing the associated workbook that makes much of the preceding Visual Basic .NET and C# code unnecessary. For example, you can use Visual Basic .NET or C# code in a VSTO solution as follows to access the current workbook:

```
' Visual Basic .NET
Private Sub ThisWorkbook_Open() Handles ThisWorkbook.Open

    MsgBox(ThisWorkbook.Name)

End Sub

// C#
protected void ThisWorkbook_Open()
{
    MessageBox.Show(ThisWorkbook.Name);
}
```

In this section, you've learned the basic principles of how to get programmatic access to an Excel workbook. After you have access to the Workbook object representing the desired Excel workbook, you can create a new Pivot-Table or PivotChart or access an existing PivotTable or PivotChart, as shown in the next section.

Code Examples

The rest of this chapter provides you with a series of Excel VBA code examples that demonstrates how to create and format PivotTables. To run these code examples, you need the files named HouseSales.xls and ClothesSales.cub.

The VBA code examples are also available in a file named SampleCode.xls if you don't want to type them manually into the Visual Basic Editor. These three files are available at the Apress Web site's Downloads section at http://www.apress.com. To run one of the code examples, you also need the sample database file Northwind.mdb, included with Access 2003. After the Northwind.mdb file is installed, it can be found in a default Access 2003 installation at <Drive:>\Program Files\Microsoft Office\ OFFICE11\SAMPLES\Northwind.mdb.

> **NOTE** For more information about installing the Northwind.mdb sample database file, see the "Sample databases included with Access" and "What's installed with Access 2003" topics in Access 2003 Help.

These code examples can easily be adapted to run using Visual Basic .NET or C# using code similar to that presented in the previous section to access the workbook in which your new or existing PivotTables and PivotCharts reside.

Create PivotTables

This section demonstrates how to create a PivotTable from data in an Excel worksheet, an Access database file, and an offline cube file.

The following code example creates a PivotTable from data in the HouseSales.xls file. You would use code similar to the following when you want to create a PivotTable based on an existing range of Excel worksheet cells.

```
Sub CreatePivotTableFromRange ()

    ' Purpose:
    ' Creates a PivotTable in the activated workbook
    ' based on an Excel list.

    ' Assumes:
    ' 1. An open workbook named HouseSales.xls with data in
    ' the range A1 through E601 on the Sheet1 worksheet.
    ' 2. An open workbook named SampleCode.xls with a
    ' blank worksheet named Sheet1.

    ' Note:
    ' You could call the Open method of the Workbooks collection
    ' to open the workbook if it is not already open.
```

```
    On Error GoTo CreatePivotTableFromRange_Err

    Dim objPivotCache As PivotCache

    Application.Workbooks.Item(Index:="SampleCode.xls").Activate

    Set objPivotCache = ActiveWorkbook.PivotCaches.Add _
        (SourceType:=xlDatabase, _
        SourceData:="[HouseSales.xls]Sheet1!A1:E601")

    objPivotCache.CreatePivotTable _
        TableDestination:="[SampleCode.xls]Sheet1!R3C1", _
        TableName:="HouseSalesPivotTable"

CreatePivotTableFromRange_End:

    Set objPivotCache = Nothing

    Exit Sub

CreatePivotTableFromRange_Err:

    Select Case Err.Number
        Case 5, 9
            MsgBox "Can't open file. Check the file name " & _
                "and try opening the file again."
        Case 1004
            MsgBox "A PivotTable already exists at this location. " & _
                "Change the PivotTable location and try creating the " & _
                "PivotTable again."
        Case Else
            MsgBox "Error " & Err.Number & ": " & Err.Description
    End Select

    Resume CreatePivotTableFromRange_End

End Sub
```

In the preceding code, the SampleCode.xls is made the active workbook.
From there, a pivot cache is added to the SampleCode.xls workbook, based
on data in the HouseSales.xls workbook's Sheet1 worksheet, cells A1 through
E601. To display a PivotTable based on this data in the SampleCode.xls workbook's pivot cache, the CreatePivotTable method creates a PivotTable in the

SampleCode.xls workbook's Sheet worksheet, beginning in cell A3 (A3 is
R3C1, or Row 3, Column 1). The PivotTable is named HouseSalesPivotTable.
The results of running this code are shown in Figure 7-2.

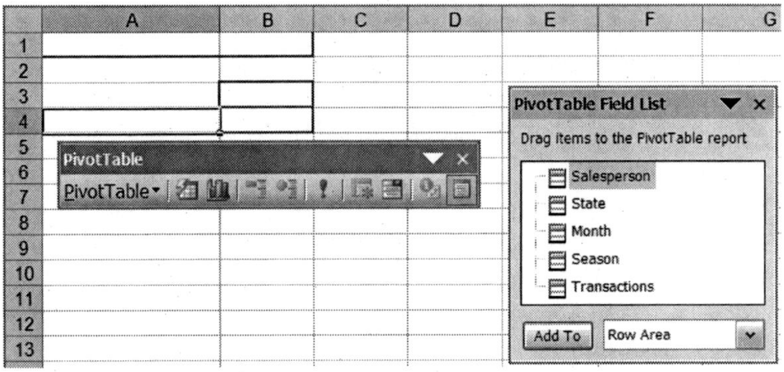

FIGURE 7-2

A PivotTable based on data in the HouseSales.xls workbook's Sheet1
worksheet, cells A1 through E601

The following code example creates a PivotTable from data in the
HouseSales.xls file; however, this code example uses the PivotTable and
PivotChart Wizard to create the PivotTable. You would use code similar to
the following when you want to more quickly create a PivotTable in an
already-active workbook.

```
Sub UsePivotTableWizard()

    ' Purpose:
    ' Creates a PivotTable in the active worksheet
    ' based on an Excel list.

    ' Assumes:
    ' An open workbook named HouseSales.xls with data in
    ' the range A1 through E601 on the Sheet1 worksheet.

    ' Note:
    ' You could call the Open method of the Workbooks collection
    ' to open the workbook if it is not already open.

    On Error GoTo UsePivotTableWizard_Err
```

```
    ActiveSheet.PivotTableWizard SourceType:=xlDatabase, _
        SourceData:="[HouseSales.xls]Sheet1!A1:E601", _
        TableName:="HouseSalesPivotTable"

UsePivotTableWizard_End:

    Exit Sub

UsePivotTableWizard_Err:

    Select Case Err.Number
        Case 1004
            MsgBox "Can't open file. Check the file name " & _
                "and try opening the file again."
        Case Else
            MsgBox "Error " & Err.Number & ": " & Err.Description
    End Select

    Resume UsePivotTableWizard_End

End Sub
```

The results of running this code are all but identical to the code immediately preceding this code.

The following code example creates a PivotTable based on the Customers table in the Northwind.mdb sample database file included with Access:

```
Sub CreatePivotTableFromExternalDatabase ()

    ' Purpose:
    ' Creates a PivotTable in the active workbook
    ' based on an external database.

    ' Assumes:
    ' 1.An Access database file named Northwind.mdb
    ' in the specified path.
    ' 2. An open workbook named SampleCode.xls with a
    ' worksheet named Sheet2.

    On Error GoTo CreatePivotTableFromExternalDatabase_Err

    Dim objPivotCache As PivotCache
```

```
        Dim objArray As Variant
        Dim objPivotTable As PivotTable

        Set objPivotCache = ActiveWorkbook.PivotCaches.Add _
            (SourceType:=xlExternal)

        With objPivotCache
            .Connection = Array(Array( _
                "ODBC;DSN=MS Access Database;DBQ=C:\" & _
                "Program Files\Microsoft Office\OFFICE11\" & _
                "SAMPLES\Northwind.mdb;DefaultDir=" & _
                "C:\Program Files\Microso" _
                ), Array( _
                "ft Office\OFFICE11\SAMPLES;DriverId=25;" & _
                "FIL=MS Access;MaxBufferSize=2048;PageTimeout=5;" _
                ))
            .CommandType = xlCmdSql
            .CommandText = Array( _
                "SELECT * FROM " & _
                "`C:\Program Files\Microsoft Office\OFFICE11\SAMPLES\" & _
                "Northwind`.Customers Customers" _
                )
        End With

        Set objPivotTable = objPivotCache.CreatePivotTable _
            (TableDestination:="[SampleCode.xls]Sheet2!R3C1", _
            TableName:="CustomersPivotTable")

    CreatePivotTableFromExternalDatabase_End:

        Set objPivotTable = Nothing
        Set objArray = Nothing
        Set objPivotCache = Nothing

        Exit Sub

    CreatePivotTableFromExternalDatabase_Err:

        Select Case Err.Number
            Case 5
                MsgBox "Connection string or file name could be incorrect. " & _
                    "Check the connection string or file name and try again."
```

```
      Case 1004
          MsgBox "Can't open file or a PivotTable already exists " & _
              "at this location. Check the file name or change the " & _
              "PivotTable location and try creating the " & _
              "PivotTable again."
      Case Else
          MsgBox "Error " & Err.Number & ": " & Err.Description
  End Select

  Resume CreatePivotTableFromExternalDatabase_End

End Sub
```

The preceding code is fairly complicated when it comes to specifying database connection and query strings in the calls to the Connection and CommandText properties. Otherwise, this code is similar to the code immediately preceding this code, in that when the connection is established, a simple call to the CreatePivotTable method is all that is needed to create the PivotTable.

> **TIP** For more information about specifying connection and query strings, see the "Connection Property" and "CommandText Property" topics in Excel Help. You can also search for files on your computer with the .odc, .oqy, and .dqy extensions and open them with a text editor (don't edit them) to familiarize yourself with connection and query string syntax.

The following code example creates a new PivotTable based on an existing PivotTable:

```
Sub CreatePivotTableFromExistingPivotTable()

  ' Purpose:
  ' Creates a PivotTable in the active workbook
  ' based on an existing PivotTable.

  ' Assumes:
  ' An open workbook named SampleCode.xls with a
  ' worksheet named Sheet1 containing a PivotTable
  ' named HouseSalesPivotTable, as well as a worksheet
  ' named Sheet2.

  On Error GoTo CreatePivotTableFromExistingPivotTable_Err
```

```
        Dim objPivotTable As PivotTable

        Set objPivotTable = _
            ActiveWorkbook.Sheets(Index:="Sheet1"). _
            PivotTables("HouseSalesPivotTable")

        objPivotTable.PivotCache.CreatePivotTable _
            TableDestination:="[SampleCode.xls]Sheet2!R3C1", _
            TableName:="DerivedHouseSalesPivotTable"

        CreatePivotTableFromExistingPivotTable_End:

        Set objPivotTable = Nothing

        Exit Sub

    CreatePivotTableFromExistingPivotTable_Err:

        Select Case Err.Number
            Case 5
                MsgBox "Can't open file. Check the file name " & _
                    "and try opening the file again."
            Case 1004
                MsgBox "PivotTable doesn't exist at this location. " & _
                    "Check the PivotTable name and location " & _
                    "and try again."
            Case Else
                MsgBox "Error " & Err.Number & ": " & Err.Description
        End Select

        Resume CreatePivotTableFromExistingPivotTable_End

    End Sub
```

The preceding code is straightforward. The existing PivotTable is identified using a call to the PivotTables collection. The CreatePivotTable method then creates a new PivotTable using the existing PivotTable as its data source.

The following code example creates a PivotTable based on an offline cube file:

```
Sub WorkWithCubeFile()

    ' Purpose:
    ' Opens the an offline cube file
    ' named ClothesSales.cub and creates a
    ' PivotTable based on the offline cube file's data.

    ' Assumes:
    ' 1. An offline cube file named ClothesSales.cub in
    ' the specified path.
    ' 2. The offline cube file contains dimensions named Time,
    ' Employees, and Location, and a measure named Sum of Quantity.

    On Error GoTo WorkWithCubeFile_Err

    Dim objPivotTable As PivotTable

    Workbooks.OpenDatabase Filename:= _
        "C:\ClothesSales.cub", _
        CommandText:=Array("OCWCube"), _
        CommandType:=xlCmdCube

    Set objPivotTable = ActiveSheet.PivotTables(1)

    With objPivotTable
        .CubeFields("[Time]").Orientation = xlRowField
        .CubeFields("[Employees]").Orientation = xlColumnField
        .CubeFields("[Location]").Orientation = xlPageField
        .AddDataField ActiveSheet.PivotTables(1).CubeFields _
            ("[Measures].[Sum Of Quantity]"), "Sum Of Quantity"
    End With

WorkWithCubeFile_End:

    Set objPivotTable = Nothing

    Exit Sub
```

```
WorkWithCubeFile_Err:

    Select Case Err.Number
        Case 9
            MsgBox "Can't add a field to the PivotTable. Check " & _
            "the field name spelling and try again."
        Case 1004
            MsgBox "Can't open file or reference PivotTable. " & _
            "Check the file name, connection string, and " & _
            "PivotTable reference and try again."
        Case Else
            MsgBox "Error " & Err.Number & ": " & Err.Description
    End Select

    Resume WorkWithCubeFile_End

End Sub
```

In the preceding code, a single call to the OpenDatabase method, passing in an offline cube file as a file name, automatically creates a PivotTable with the offline cube file as the PivotTable's data source. The CubeFields property returns a field corresponding to the specified field name. The Orientation property adds the field to the PivotTable as a row field, column field, or page field accordingly. The AddDataField method adds the specified data field as a data field. The results of running this code are shown in Figure 7-3.

	A	B	C	D	E	F	G	H	I	J
1	Location	All ▼								
2										
3	Sum Of Quantity	Manager ▼								
4	Quarter ▼	Andersen	Bailey	Collins	Donaldson	Eddings	Franks	Gerry	Hastings	Grand Total
5	1	4737	4602	3988	3923	5234	5266	3460	3533	34743
6	2	5087	5055	4251	4269	5694	5821	3783	3792	37752
7	3	5231	5328	4546	4494	6101	6126	3931	3938	39695
8	4	5878	5836	4985	5011	6821	6836	4404	4544	44315
9	Grand Total	20933	20821	17770	17697	23850	24049	15578	15807	156505

FIGURE 7-3

A PivotTable based on the ClothesSales.cub offline cube file's data

In this section, you've learned how to programmatically create PivotTables. Now, let's learn how to programmatically create PivotCharts.

Create a PivotChart

This section demonstrates how to create a PivotChart at the same time that you create a PivotTable, as well as how to create a PivotChart based on an existing PivotTable.

The following code example creates a PivotChart at the same time a PivotTable is created:

```
Sub CreatePivotTablePivotChartFromRange ()

    ' Purpose:
    ' Creates a PivotTable and a PivotChart in the
    ' active workbook based on an Excel list.

    ' Assumes:
    ' 1. An open workbook named HouseSales.xls with data in
    ' the range A1 through E601 on the Sheet1 worksheet.
    ' 2. An open workbook named SampleCode.xls with a
    ' blank worksheet named Sheet1.

    ' Note:
    ' You could call the Open method of the Workbooks collection
    ' to open the workbook if it is not already open.

    On Error GoTo CreatePivotTablePivotChartFromRange_Err

    Dim objPivotCache As PivotCache
    Dim objPivotTable As PivotTable

    Set objPivotCache = ActiveWorkbook.PivotCaches.Add _
        (SourceType:=xlDatabase, _
        SourceData:="[HouseSales.xls]Sheet1!A1:E601")
    Set objPivotTable = objPivotCache.CreatePivotTable _
        (TableDestination:="[SampleCode.xls]Sheet1!R3C1", _
        TableName:="HouseSalesPivotTable")

    Charts.Add

    With ActiveChart
        .Location Where:=xlLocationAsNewSheet
        .SetSourceData Source:=objPivotTable.TableRange1
    End With

CreatePivotTablePivotChartFromRange_End:

    Set objPivotTable = Nothing
    Set objPivotCache = Nothing
```

```
        Exit Sub

CreatePivotTablePivotChartFromRange_Err:

    Select Case Err.Number
        Case 5, 9
            MsgBox "Can't open file. Check the file name " & _
                "and try opening the file again."
        Case 1004
            MsgBox "A PivotTable cannot be created at this location. " & _
                "Check the data source and PivotTable location and " & _
                "try creating the PivotTable again."
        Case Else
            MsgBox "Error " & Err.Number & ": " & Err.Description
    End Select

    Resume CreatePivotTablePivotChartFromRange_End

End Sub
```

In the preceding code, the Charts collection's Add method adds a new chart sheet to the active workbook and then makes the new chart active. The chart's data source is the PivotTable. See Figure 7-4 for the results of running this code.

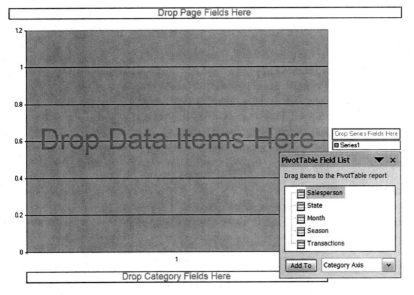

FIGURE 7-4

A PivotChart based on the HouseSales.xls file's data

The following code example creates a PivotChart based on an existing PivotTable. The results of running this code are fairly identical to the code in the preceding code example.

```
Sub CreatePivotChartFromPivotTable ()

    ' Purpose:
    ' Creates a PivotChart in the
    ' active workbook based on an existing
    ' PivotTable in the active workbook.

    ' Assumes:
    ' A worksheet named Sheet1 containing a PivotTable
    ' named HouseSalesPivotTable.

    On Error GoTo CreatePivotChartFromPivotTable_Err

    Dim objPivotTable As PivotTable
    Dim objChart As Chart

    Set objPivotTable = ActiveWorkbook.Worksheets. _
        Item(Index:="Sheet1").PivotTables. _
        Item(Index:="HouseSalesPivotTable")
    Set objChart = ActiveWorkbook.Charts.Add

    objChart.SetSourceData Source:=objPivotTable.TableRange1

CreatePivotChartFromPivotTable_End:

    Set objChart = Nothing
    Set objPivotTable = Nothing

    Exit Sub

CreatePivotChartFromPivotTable_Err:

    Select Case Err.Number
        Case 9
            MsgBox "Can't access worksheet. Check the worksheet name " & _
                "and try again."
        Case 438
            MsgBox "Can't set the PivotChart's source data. " & _
```

```
                          "Check the source data connection details and try again."
              Case 1004
                  MsgBox "Cannot access the PivotTable. " & _
                      "Check the PivotTable name and try again."
              Case Else
                  MsgBox "Error " & Err.Number & ": " & Err.Description
          End Select

          Resume CreatePivotChartFromPivotTable_End

  End Sub
```

The following code example creates a PivotChart based on an existing PivotTable. It also modifies the PivotChart's field layout:

```
Sub ModifyPivotChartLayout()

    ' Purpose:
    ' 1. Creates a PivotChart in the
    ' active workbook based on an existing
    ' PivotTable in the active workbook.
    ' 2. Modifies the PivotChart's field layout,
    ' which modifies the PivotTable's field layout
    ' at the same time.

    ' Assumes:
    ' 1. A worksheet named Sheet1 containing a PivotTable
    ' named HouseSalesPivotTable.
    ' 2. The field list contains fields named Salesperson,
    ' Season, and State.

    On Error GoTo ModifyPivotChartLayout_Err

    Dim objPivotTable As PivotTable
    Dim objChart As Chart

    Set objPivotTable = ActiveWorkbook.Worksheets. _
        Item(Index:="Sheet1").PivotTables. _
        Item(Index:="HouseSalesPivotTable")
    Set objChart = ActiveWorkbook.Charts.Add
```

```
        With objChart
            .SetSourceData Source:=objPivotTable.TableRange1
            .PivotLayout.PivotTable.AddFields _
                RowFields:="Salesperson", ColumnFields:="Season", _
                PageFields:="State"
        End With

ModifyPivotChartLayout_End:

        Set objChart = Nothing
        Set objPivotTable = Nothing

        Exit Sub

ModifyPivotChartLayout_Err:

        Select Case Err.Number
            Case 9
                MsgBox "Can't access worksheet. Check the worksheet name " & _
                    "and try again."
            Case 438
                MsgBox "Can't set the PivotChart's source data. " & _
                    "Check the source data connection details and try again."
            Case 1004
                MsgBox "Cannot access the PivotTable or " & _
                    "add a field to the PivotChart layout. " & _
                    "Check the PivotTable name or field name and try again."
            Case Else
                MsgBox "Error " & Err.Number & ": " & Err.Description
        End Select

        Resume ModifyPivotChartLayout_End

End Sub
```

The preceding code extends the code in the immediately preceding example by adding the Salesperson field to the PivotChart as a row field, the Season field as a column field, and the State field as a page field. The results of running this code are shown in Figure 7-5.

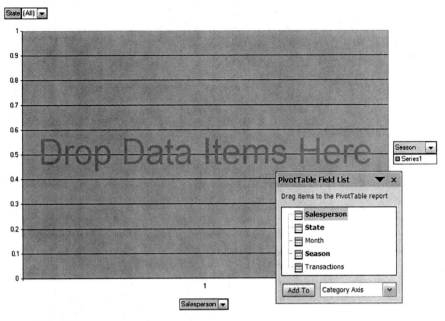

FIGURE 7-5
Adding fields to the PivotChart's layout

In this section, you've learned how to create PivotCharts. Now, let's turn our attention back to adding fields to PivotTables.

Add Fields to the PivotTable Visual Layout

The following code example adds fields from the field list to a PivotTable:

```
Sub AddFieldsToPivotTable()

    ' Purpose:
    ' Adds the Season (row), Month (row),
    ' State (page), Salesperson (column),
    ' and Sum of Transactions (data) fields from the field list
    ' to a PivotTable.

    ' Assumes:
    ' 1. A worksheet named Sheet1 containing a PivotTable
    ' named HouseSalesPivotTable.
```

```
' 2. The field list contains fields named Season,
' Month, State, and Transactions.

On Error GoTo AddFieldsToPivotTable_Err

Dim objPivotTable As PivotTable

Set objPivotTable = ActiveWorkbook.Worksheets. _
    Item(Index:="Sheet1").PivotTables. _
    Item(Index:="HouseSalesPivotTable")

With objPivotTable
    .AddFields RowFields:=Array("Season", "Month"), _
        ColumnFields:="Salesperson", PageFields:="State"
    .AddDataField _
        Field:=objPivotTable.PivotFields(Index:="Transactions"), _
        Function:=xlSum
End With

AddFieldsToPivotTable_End:

    Set objPivotTable = Nothing

    Exit Sub

AddFieldsToPivotTable_Err:

    Select Case Err.Number
        Case 9
            MsgBox "Can't access worksheet. Check the worksheet " & _
                "name and try again."
        Case 1004
            MsgBox "Can't access the PivotTable or a " & _
            "field. Check the PivotTable and field names " & _
            "and try again."
        Case Else
            MsgBox "Error " & Err.Number & ": " & Err.Description
    End Select

    Resume AddFieldsToPivotTable_End

End Sub
```

In the preceding code, the PivotTable object's AddFields method adds the Season and Month fields as row fields, the Salesperson field as a column field, the State field as a page field, and the Sum Of Transactions field as a data field. The results of running this code are shown in Figure 7-6.

	A	B	C	D	E	F	G	H	I	J
1	State	(All)								
2										
3	Sum of Transactions		Salesperson							
4	Season	Month	Crosby	Fisher	Johnson	Jones	Lundgren	McDonald	Smith	Grand Total
5	Autumn	September	11654	5268	7838	1398	6474	2168	600	35400
6		October	11634	5526	7878	1538	6500	2014	500	35590
7		November	11748	5752	7496	1458	6662	2072	594	35782
8	Autumn Total		35036	16546	23212	4394	19636	6254	1694	106772
9	Spring	March	11604	5722	7750	1312	6568	1754	544	35254
10		April	11566	5554	7778	1506	6444	1886	618	35352
11		May	11754	5644	7654	1422	6596	2062	534	35666
12	Spring Total		34924	16920	23182	4240	19608	5702	1696	106272
13	Summer	June	35232	17484	23022	4416	18876	6300	2010	107340
14		July	35274	16542	24264	4068	19674	6354	1818	107994
15		August	35034	16536	22866	4116	19698	6396	2280	106926
16	Summer Total		105540	50562	70152	12600	58248	19050	6108	322260
17	Winter	January	6058	2790	3910	710	3325	1001	238	18032
18		February	6036	2834	3850	721	3302	944	346	18033
19		December	5945	2627	3761	719	3219	1050	275	17596
20	Winter Total		18039	8251	11521	2150	9846	2995	859	53661
21	Grand Total		193539	92279	128067	23384	107338	34001	10357	588965

FIGURE 7-6

Adding fields to the PivotTable's layout

After adding fields to a PivotTable, you'll almost certainly want to change the placement of the fields in the PivotTable. Let's explore how to do this in the next section.

Change Field Placement

The following code example moves a field from one drop area to another drop area:

```
Sub ChangeFieldOrientation()

    ' Purpose:
    ' Changes the Season field's orientation in a
    ' PivotTable to the page area.
```

```
' Assumes:
' 1. A worksheet named Sheet1 containing a PivotTable
' named HouseSalesPivotTable.
' 2. The field list contains a field named Season.

On Error GoTo ChangeFieldOrientation_Err

Dim objPivotTable As PivotTable

Set objPivotTable = ActiveWorkbook.Worksheets. _
    Item(Index:="Sheet1").PivotTables. _
    Item(Index:="HouseSalesPivotTable")

objPivotTable.PivotFields(Index:="Season").Orientation = _
    xlPageField

ChangeFieldOrientation_End:

Set objPivotTable = Nothing

Exit Sub

ChangeFieldOrientation_Err:

Select Case Err.Number
    Case 9
        MsgBox "Can't access worksheet. Check the worksheet " & _
            "name and try again."
    Case 1004
        MsgBox "Can't access the PivotTable or a " & _
        "field. Check the PivotTable and field names " & _
        "and try again."
    Case Else
        MsgBox "Error " & Err.Number & ": " & Err.Description
End Select

Resume ChangeFieldOrientation_End

End Sub
```

In the preceding code, the Season field's orientation was changed to a page field. The results of running this code are shown in Figure 7-7. This figure is based on the assumption that you have already run the code in the previous section.

	A	B	C	D	E	F	G	H	I
1	Season	(All)							
2	State	(All)							
3									
4	Sum of Transactions	Salesperson							
5	Month	Crosby	Fisher	Johnson	Jones	Lundgren	McDonald	Smith	Grand Total
6	January	6058	2790	3910	710	3325	1001	238	18032
7	February	6036	2834	3850	721	3302	944	346	18033
8	March	11604	5722	7750	1312	6568	1754	544	35254
9	April	11566	5554	7778	1506	6444	1886	618	35352
10	May	11754	5644	7654	1422	6596	2062	534	35666
11	June	35232	17484	23022	4416	18876	6300	2010	107340
12	July	35274	16542	24264	4068	19674	6354	1818	107994
13	August	35034	16536	22866	4116	19698	6396	2280	106926
14	September	11654	5268	7838	1398	6474	2168	600	35400
15	October	11634	5526	7878	1538	6500	2014	500	35590
16	November	11748	5752	7496	1458	6662	2072	594	35782
17	December	5945	2627	3761	719	3219	1050	275	17596
18	Grand Total	193539	92279	128067	23384	107338	34001	10357	588965

FIGURE 7-7
Changing the Season field's layout in the PivotTable

Set and Remove Field Filters

The code examples in this section demonstrate how to set and remove field filters, hiding or showing specific field items.

The following code example filters a PivotTable to display only a certain set of field items:

```
Sub FilterFieldItems ()

    ' Purpose:
    ' 1. Filters the Salesperson field in a PivotTable
    ' to only display the Johnson and Lundgren items.
    ' 2. Filters the Season page field to only display the
    ' Winter item.

    ' Assumes:
    ' 1. A worksheet named Sheet1 containing a PivotTable
    ' named HouseSalesPivotTable.
```

```
' 2. The field list contains fields named Salesperson and Season.
' 3. The Salesperson field is not a page field and
' contains items named Johnson and Lundgren.
' 4. The Season field is a page field and contains
' an item named Winter.

On Error GoTo FilterFieldItems_Err

Dim objPivotTable As PivotTable
Dim objPivotItem As PivotItem

Set objPivotTable = ActiveWorkbook.Worksheets. _
    Item(Index:="Sheet1").PivotTables. _
    Item(Index:="HouseSalesPivotTable")

For Each objPivotItem In _
    objPivotTable.PivotFields(Index:="Salesperson").PivotItems

    If objPivotItem.Name = "Johnson" Or _
            objPivotItem.Name = "Lundgren" Then
        objPivotItem.Visible = True
    Else
        objPivotItem.Visible = False
    End If

Next objPivotItem

objPivotTable.PivotFields(Index:="Season").CurrentPage = "Winter"

FilterFieldItems_End:

    Set objPivotItem = Nothing
    Set objPivotTable = Nothing

    Exit Sub

FilterFieldItems_Err:

    Select Case Err.Number
        Case 9
            MsgBox "Can't access worksheet. Check the worksheet " & _
                "name and try again."
```

```
        Case 1004
            MsgBox "Can't access the PivotTable, " & _
                "field, or field item. Check the PivotTable, field, " & _
                "and item names and try again."
        Case Else
            MsgBox "Error " & Err.Number & ": " & Err.Description
    End Select

    Resume FilterFieldItems_End

End Sub
```

In the preceding code, only data for the Salesperson field's Johnson and Lundgren items are shown for only the Winter season. See Figure 7-8 for the results of running this code, based on code run in the previous section.

	A	B	C	D
1	Season	Winter ▼		
2	State	(All) ▼		
3				
4	Sum of Transactions	Salesperson ▼		
5	Month ▼	Johnson	Lundgren	Grand Total
6	January	3910	3325	7235
7	February	3850	3302	7152
8	December	3761	3219	6980
9	Grand Total	11521	9846	21367

FIGURE 7-8

Filtering the PivotTable's data to show only selected Salesperson and Season fields' items

The following code example removes a specific field's filter, displaying all of the field's items:

```
Sub RemoveFilterFromFieldItem ()

    ' Purpose:
    ' Removes the filter in the Salesperson field in a PivotTable field,
    ' showing all of the field's items.

    ' Assumes:
    ' 1. A worksheet named Sheet1 containing a PivotTable
    ' named HouseSalesPivotTable.
    ' 2. The field list contains a field named Salesperson.
```

```
    ' 3. The Salesperson field is not a page field.

    On Error GoTo RemoveFilterFromFieldItem_Err

    Dim objPivotTable As PivotTable
    Dim objPivotItem As PivotItem

    Set objPivotTable = ActiveWorkbook.Worksheets. _
        Item(Index:="Sheet1").PivotTables. _
        Item(Index:="HouseSalesPivotTable")

    For Each objPivotItem In _
        objPivotTable.PivotFields(Index:="Salesperson").PivotItems

        objPivotItem.Visible = True

    Next objPivotItem

RemoveFilterFromFieldItem_End:

    Set objPivotItem = Nothing
    Set objPivotTable = Nothing

    Exit Sub

RemoveFilterFromFieldItem_Err:

    Select Case Err.Number
        Case 9
            MsgBox "Can't access worksheet. Check the worksheet " & _
                "name and try again."
        Case 1004
            MsgBox "Can't access the PivotTable, " & _
            "field, or field item. Check the PivotTable, field, " & _
            "and item names and try again."
        Case Else
            MsgBox "Error " & Err.Number & ": " & Err.Description
    End Select

    Resume RemoveFilterFromFieldItem_End

End Sub
```

In the preceding code, all of the Salesperson field's items are displayed in the PivotTable. See Figure 7-9 for the results of running this code. This figure is based on the assumption that you have already run the code in the previous section.

	A	B	C	D	E	F	G	H	I
1	Season	Winter ▾							
2	State	(All) ▾							
3									
4	Sum of Transactions	Salesperson ▾							
5	Month ▾	Crosby	Fisher	Johnson	Jones	Lundgren	McDonald	Smith	Grand Total
6	January	6058	2790	3910	710	3325	1001	238	18032
7	February	6036	2834	3850	721	3302	944	346	18033
8	December	5945	2627	3761	719	3219	1050	275	17596
9	Grand Total	18039	8251	11521	2150	9846	2995	859	53661

FIGURE 7-9

Showing all of the Salesperson field's items

Move a Field's Position

The following code example moves a field's position in a specific PivotTable's drop area:

```
Sub MoveFieldPosition ()

    ' Purpose:
    ' Changes the Season field's position in a PivotTable to the
    ' first position.

    ' Assumes:
    ' 1. A worksheet named Sheet1 containing a PivotTable
    ' named HouseSalesPivotTable.
    ' 2. The field list contains a field named Season.

    On Error GoTo MoveFieldPosition_Err

    Dim objPivotTable As PivotTable
    Dim objPivotField As PivotField
```

```vba
    Set objPivotTable = ActiveWorkbook.Worksheets. _
        Item(Index:="Sheet1").PivotTables. _
        Item(Index:="HouseSalesPivotTable")
    Set objPivotField = objPivotTable.PivotFields(Index:="Season")

    With objPivotField
        .Orientation = xlRowField
        .Position = 1
    End With

MoveFieldPosition_End:

    Set objPivotField = Nothing
    Set objPivotTable = Nothing

    Exit Sub

MoveFieldPosition_Err:

    Select Case Err.Number
        Case 9
            MsgBox "Can't access worksheet. Check the worksheet " & _
                "name and try again."
        Case 1004
            MsgBox "Can't access the PivotTable, " & _
            "field, or field item. Check the PivotTable, field, " & _
            "and item names and try again."
        Case Else
            MsgBox "Error " & Err.Number & ": " & Err.Description
    End Select

    Resume MoveFieldPosition_End

End Sub
```

In the preceding code, the Season field is changed to a row field orientation and then moved to the left-most position in the row field list, also known as an *outer row field*. The results of running this code are shown in Figure 7-10. This figure assumes that you have already run the code in the previous section.

	A	B	C	D	E	F	G	H	I	J
1										
2	State	(All)								
3										
4	Sum of Transactions		Salesperson							
5	Season	Month	Crosby	Fisher	Johnson	Jones	Lundgren	McDonald	Smith	Grand Total
6	Autumn	September	11654	5268	7838	1398	6474	2168	600	35400
7		October	11634	5526	7878	1538	6500	2014	500	35590
8		November	11748	5752	7496	1458	6662	2072	594	35782
9	Autumn Total		35036	16546	23212	4394	19636	6254	1694	106772
10	Spring	March	11604	5722	7750	1312	6568	1754	544	35254
11		April	11566	5554	7778	1506	6444	1886	618	35352
12		May	11754	5644	7654	1422	6596	2062	534	35666
13	Spring Total		34924	16920	23182	4240	19608	5702	1696	106272
14	Summer	June	35232	17484	23022	4416	18876	6300	2010	107340
15		July	35274	16542	24264	4068	19674	6354	1818	107994
16		August	35034	16536	22866	4116	19698	6396	2280	106926
17	Summer Total		105540	50562	70152	12600	58248	19050	6108	322260
18	Winter	January	6058	2790	3910	710	3325	1001	238	18032
19		February	6036	2834	3850	721	3302	944	346	18033
20		December	5945	2627	3761	719	3219	1050	275	17596
21	Winter Total		18039	8251	11521	2150	9846	2995	859	53661
22	Grand Total		193539	92279	128067	23384	107338	34001	10357	588965

FIGURE 7-10

Moving the Season field to an outer row field orientation

Create a Calculated Field and a Calculated Item

The code examples in this section demonstrate how to create a calculated field and a calculated item in a PivotTable.

The following code example creates a calculated field based on an existing field's values:

```
Sub CreateCalculatedField ()

    ' Purpose:
    ' Creates a calculated field named Commission
    ' in a PivotTable.

    ' Assumes:
    ' 1. A worksheet named Sheet1 containing a PivotTable
    ' named HouseSalesPivotTable.
    ' 2. The field list contains a field named Transactions
    ' that contains numeric-based data.

    On Error GoTo CreateCalculatedField_Err

    Dim objPivotTable As PivotTable
    Dim objPivotField As PivotField
```

```
    Set objPivotTable = ActiveWorkbook.Worksheets. _
        Item(Index:="Sheet1").PivotTables. _
        Item(Index:="HouseSalesPivotTable")
    Set objPivotField = objPivotTable.CalculatedFields. _
        Add(Name:="Commission", Formula:="=Transactions*0.035")

    objPivotField.Orientation = xlDataField

CreateCalculatedField_End:

    Set objPivotField = Nothing
    Set objPivotTable = Nothing

    Exit Sub

CreateCalculatedField_Err:

    Select Case Err.Number
        Case 9
            MsgBox "Can't access worksheet. Check the worksheet " & _
                "name and try again."
        Case 1004
            MsgBox "Can't access the PivotTable, " & _
                "field, or field item. Check the PivotTable, field, " & _
                "and item names and try again."
        Case -2147024882
            MsgBox "Invalid calculated field formula. Check the " & _
                "formula and try again."
        Case Else
            MsgBox "Error " & Err.Number & ": " & Err.Description
    End Select

    Resume CreateCalculatedField_End

End Sub
```

In the preceding code, a calculated field named Commission is created. This calculated field reflects 3.5% of the Transactions field's value. The results of running this code are shown in Figure 7-11. This figure assumes that you have already run the code in the previous section.

	A	B	C	D	E	F	G	K
1								
2	State	(All)	▾					
3								
4				Salesperson ▾				
5	Season ▾	Month ▾	Data ▾	Crosby	Fisher	Johnson	Jones	Grand Total
6	Autumn	September	Sum of Transactions	11654	5268	7838	1398	35400
7			Sum of Commission	407.89	184.38	274.33	48.93	1239
8		October	Sum of Transactions	11634	5526	7878	1538	35590
9			Sum of Commission	407.19	193.41	275.73	53.83	1245.65
10		November	Sum of Transactions	11748	5752	7496	1458	35782
11			Sum of Commission	411.18	201.32	262.36	51.03	1252.37
12	Autumn Sum of Transactions			35036	16546	23212	4394	106772
13	Autumn Sum of Commission			1226.26	579.11	812.42	153.79	3737.02
30	Winter	January	Sum of Transactions	6058	2790	3910	710	18032
31			Sum of Commission	212.03	97.65	136.85	24.85	631.12
32		February	Sum of Transactions	6036	2834	3850	721	18033
33			Sum of Commission	211.26	99.19	134.75	25.235	631.155
34		December	Sum of Transactions	5945	2627	3761	719	17596
35			Sum of Commission	208.075	91.945	131.635	25.165	615.86
36	Winter Sum of Transactions			18039	8251	11521	2150	53661
37	Winter Sum of Commission			631.365	288.785	403.235	75.25	1878.135
38	Total Sum of Transactions			193539	92279	128067	23384	588965
39	Total Sum of Commission			6773.865	3229.765	4482.345	818.44	20613.775

FIGURE 7-11

Creating the Commission calculated field (panes have been split for readability)

The following code example creates a calculated item based on an existing field item:

```
Sub CreateCalculatedItem()

    ' Purpose:
    ' Creates a calculated item named Next Winter in
    ' the Season field in a PivotTable.

    ' Assumes:
    ' 1. A worksheet named Sheet1 containing a PivotTable
    ' named HouseSalesPivotTable.
    ' 2. The field list contains a field named Season.
    ' 3. The Season field contains an item named Winter.

    On Error GoTo CreateCalculatedItem_Err

    Dim objPivotTable As PivotTable
    Dim objPivotField As PivotField
```

```
    Set objPivotTable = ActiveWorkbook.Worksheets. _
        Item(Index:="Sheet1").PivotTables. _
        Item(Index:="HouseSalesPivotTable")
    Set objPivotField = objPivotTable.PivotFields(Index:="Season")

    objPivotField.CalculatedItems.Add Name:="Next Winter", _
        Formula:="=Winter*0.03"

CreateCalculatedItem_End:

    Set objPivotField = Nothing
    Set objPivotTable = Nothing

    Exit Sub

CreateCalculatedItem_Err:

    Select Case Err.Number
        Case 9
            MsgBox "Can't access worksheet. Check the worksheet " & _
                "name and try again."
        Case 1004
            MsgBox "Can't access the PivotTable, " & _
                "field, or field item. Check the PivotTable, field, " & _
                "and item names and try again."
        Case -2147024882
            MsgBox "Invalid calculated field formula. Check the " & _
                "formula and try again."
        Case Else
            MsgBox "Error " & Err.Number & ": " & Err.Description
    End Select

End Sub
```

In the preceding code, a calculated item named Winter is added to the existing Season field. The Next Winter calculated item reflects 3% of the Winter item's data. Figure 7-12 shows the results of running this code. This figure assumes that you have already run the code in the previous section.

	A	B	C	D	E	F	K
1							
2	State	(All) ▼					
3							
4				Salesperson ▼			
5	Season ▼	Month ▼	Data ▼	Crosby	Fisher	Johnson	Grand Total
30	Winter	January	Sum of Transactions	6058	2790	3910	18032
31			Sum of Commission	212.03	97.65	136.85	631.12
32		February	Sum of Transactions	6036	2834	3850	18033
33			Sum of Commission	211.26	99.19	134.75	631.155
34		December	Sum of Transactions	5945	2627	3761	17596
35			Sum of Commission	208.075	91.945	131.635	615.86
36	Winter Sum of Transactions			18039	8251	11521	53661
37	Winter Sum of Commission			631.365	288.785	403.235	1878.135
38	Next Winter	January	Sum of Transactions	181.74	83.7	117.3	540.96
39			Sum of Commission	6.3609	2.9295	4.1055	18.9336
40		February	Sum of Transactions	181.08	85.02	115.5	540.99
41			Sum of Commission	6.3378	2.9757	4.0425	18.93465
42		March	Sum of Transactions	0	0	0	0
43			Sum of Commission	0	0	0	0
44		April	Sum of Transactions	0	0	0	0
45			Sum of Commission	0	0	0	0

FIGURE 7-12

Creating the Next Winter calculated item (panes have been split for readability, and only partial results are displayed)

Show and Hide Field Items

The code examples in this section demonstrate how to show and hide all of a field's items.

The following code example shows all of a field's items in a PivotTable:

```
Sub ShowItemDetails ()

    ' Purpose:
    ' 1. Removes all row fields from a PivotTable.
    ' 2. Adds the Month and Season fields to the row area.
    ' 3. Adds the Sum of Transactions field to the data area.
    ' 4. Makes the Season field an outer row field.
    ' 5. Shows item details for the Month field.

    ' Assumes:
    ' 1. A worksheet named Sheet1 containing a PivotTable
    ' named HouseSalesPivotTable.
    ' 2. The field list contains fields named Season, Month,
    ' and Transactions.

    On Error GoTo ShowItemDetails_Err
```

```
        Dim objPivotTable As PivotTable
        Dim objPivotField As PivotField
        Dim objSeasonPivotField As PivotField
        Dim objMonthPivotField As PivotField
        Dim objSumOfTransactionsField As PivotField
        Dim objPivotItem As PivotItem
        Dim objChildItem As PivotItem

        Set objPivotTable = ActiveWorkbook.Worksheets. _
            Item(Index:="Sheet1").PivotTables. _
            Item(Index:="HouseSalesPivotTable")
        Set objSeasonPivotField = _
            objPivotTable.PivotFields(Index:="Season")
        Set objMonthPivotField = _
            objPivotTable.PivotFields(Index:="Month")
        Set objSumOfTransactionsField = _
            objPivotTable.PivotFields(Index:="Transactions")

        For Each objPivotField In objPivotTable.RowFields
                objPivotField.LabelRange.Select
                Selection.Delete
        Next objPivotField

        objMonthPivotField.Orientation = xlRowField
        objPivotTable.AddDataField Field:=objSumOfTransactionsField

        With objSeasonPivotField
            .Orientation = xlRowField
            .Position = 1
            .LabelRange.Select
        End With

        Selection.ShowDetail = True

ShowItemDetails_End:

    Set objChildItem = Nothing
    Set objPivotItem = Nothing
    Set objMonthPivotField = Nothing
    Set objSeasonPivotField = Nothing
    Set objSumOfTransactionsField = Nothing
    Set objPivotField = Nothing
```

```
        Set objPivotTable = Nothing

        Exit Sub

ShowItemDetails_Err:

    Select Case Err.Number
        Case 9
            MsgBox "Can't access worksheet. Check the worksheet " & _
                "name and try again."
        Case 1004
            MsgBox "Can't access PivotTable or field. Check " & _
                "the PivotTable or field name or field placement " & _
                "and try again."
        Case -2147024882
            MsgBox "Can't add data field. Remove existing data field or " & _
                "remove calculated items from existing fields " & _
                "and try again."
        Case Else
            MsgBox "Error " & Err.Number & ": " & Err.Description
    End Select

        Resume ShowItemDetails_End

End Sub
```

In the preceding code, each row field is represented by a PivotField object. Each PivotField object's LabelRange property returns a Range object representing each row field's corresponding field button. The Range object's Select method in turn returns a Selection object representing the field button selection. From there, the Selection object's Delete method is called to remove the field from the PivotTable. Similarly, the Season row field's LabelRange property returns a Range object representing the Season row field's field button. The Range object's Select method in turn returns a Selection object representing the field button selection. From there, the Selection object's ShowDetail property is set to True to display the row field's items. The result of running this code is shown in Figure 7-13.

	A	B	C
4	Sum of Transactions		
5	Season ▾	Month ▾	Total
6	Autumn	September	35400
7		October	35590
8		November	35782
9	Autumn Total		106772
21	Winter Total		53661
22	Next Winter	January	540.96
23		February	540.99
24		March	0
25		April	0
26		May	0
27		June	0
28		July	0
29		August	0
30		September	0
31		October	0
32		November	0
33		December	527.88
34	Next Winter Total		1609.83
35	Grand Total		590574.83

FIGURE 7-13

Displaying all of the Season field's items (panes have been split for readability)

The following code example hides all of a field's items in a PivotTable:

```
Sub HideItemDetails ()

    ' Purpose:
    ' 1. Removes all row fields from a PivotTable.
    ' 2. Adds the Month and Season fields to the row area.
    ' 3. Makes the Season field an outer row field.
    ' 4. Hides item details for the Month field.
    ' 5. Optionally removes the Month field from the row area.

    ' Assumes:
    ' 1. A worksheet named Sheet1 containing a PivotTable
    ' named HouseSalesPivotTable.
    ' 2. The field list contains fields named Season and Month.

    On Error GoTo HideItemDetails_Err

    Dim objPivotTable As PivotTable
    Dim objPivotField As PivotField
    Dim objSeasonPivotField As PivotField
```

```
    Dim objMonthPivotField As PivotField
    Dim objPivotItem As PivotItem
    Dim objChildItem As PivotItem

    Set objPivotTable = ActiveWorkbook.Worksheets. _
        Item(Index:="Sheet1").PivotTables. _
        Item(Index:="HouseSalesPivotTable")
    Set objSeasonPivotField = _
        objPivotTable.PivotFields(Index:="Season")
    Set objMonthPivotField = _
        objPivotTable.PivotFields(Index:="Month")

    For Each objPivotField In objPivotTable.RowFields
            objPivotField.LabelRange.Select
            Selection.Delete
    Next objPivotField

    objMonthPivotField.Orientation = xlRowField

    With objSeasonPivotField
        .Orientation = xlRowField
        .Position = 1
        .LabelRange.Select
    End With

    Selection.ShowDetail = False

    ' Uncomment the next two lines of code to remove
    ' the Month field from the row area.

    ' objMonthPivotField.LabelRange.Select
    ' Selection.Delete

HideItemDetails_End:

    Set objChildItem = Nothing
    Set objPivotItem = Nothing
    Set objMonthPivotField = Nothing
    Set objSeasonPivotField = Nothing
    Set objPivotField = Nothing
    Set objPivotTable = Nothing
```

```
        Exit Sub

HideItemDetails_Err:

    Select Case Err.Number
        Case 9
            MsgBox "Can't access worksheet. Check the worksheet " & _
                "name and try again."
        Case 1004
            MsgBox "Can't access PivotTable or field. Check " & _
                "the PivotTable or field name or field placement " & _
                "and try again."
        Case Else
            MsgBox "Error " & Err.Number & ": " & Err.Description
    End Select

    Resume HideItemDetails_End

End Sub
```

The preceding code is very similar to the code in the previous example in that instead of setting the Selection object's ShowDetail property to True to show the Month row field's items, it sets the Selection object's ShowDetail property to False to hide the Month row field's items. The results of running this code are shown in Figure 7-14. This figure assumes that you have already run the code in the previous section.

	A	B	C
4	Sum of Transactions		
5	Season ▼	Month ▼	Total
6	Autumn		106772
7	Spring		106272
8	Summer		322260
9	Winter		53661
10	Next Winter		1609.83
11	Grand Total		590574.83

FIGURE 7-14

Hiding all of the Month row field's items

In this section, you've learned how to show and hide field items. Now, let's learn how to sort field items and show the top number of items for a given field.

AutoSort and AutoShow Items

The code examples in this section demonstrate how to sort items and show only the top number of items in a PivotTable field.

The following code example sorts items in a specific PivotTable field:

```
Sub AutoSortItems()

    ' Purpose:
    ' Sorts Salesperson field items in descending order
    ' based on data in the Sum of Transactions field.

    ' Assumes:
    ' 1. A worksheet named Sheet1 containing a PivotTable
    ' named HouseSalesPivotTable.
    ' 2. The PivotTable contains fields named Salesperson and
    ' Sum of Transactions.

    On Error GoTo AutoSortItems_Err

    Dim objPivotTable As PivotTable
    Dim objPivotField As PivotField

    Set objPivotTable = ActiveWorkbook.Worksheets. _
        Item(Index:="Sheet1").PivotTables. _
        Item(Index:="HouseSalesPivotTable")
    Set objPivotField = objPivotTable.PivotFields("Salesperson")

    With objPivotField
        .Orientation = xlRowField
        .AutoSort Order:=xlDescending, _
            Field:="Sum of Transactions"
    End With

AutoSortItems_End:

    Set objPivotField = Nothing
    Set objPivotTable = Nothing

    Exit Sub
```

```
AutoSortItems_Err:

    Select Case Err.Number
        Case 9
            MsgBox "Can't access worksheet. Check the worksheet " & _
                "name and try again."
        Case 1004
            MsgBox "Can't access PivotTable or field. Check " & _
                "the PivotTable or field name or field placement " & _
                "and try again."
        Case -2147024882
            MsgBox "Can't add data field. Remove existing data field or " & _
                "remove calculated items from existing fields " & _
                "and try again."
        Case Else
            MsgBox "Error " & Err.Number & ": " & Err.Description
    End Select

    Resume AutoSortItems_End

End Sub
```

In the preceding code, the PivotField object, representing the Salesperson
row field, has its AutoSort method called, specifying a descending sort order,
based on the Sum of Transactions field's data. The results of running this
code are shown in Figure 7-15. This figure assumes that you have already
run the code in the previous section.

	A	B
4	Sum of Transactions	
5	Salesperson ▼	Total
6	Crosby	193539
7	Johnson	128067
8	Lundgren	107338
9	Fisher	92279
10	McDonald	34001
11	Jones	23384
12	Smith	10357
13	Grand Total	588965

FIGURE 7-15

Sorting the Salesperson field's items in descending order based on the Sum of
Transactions field's data

The following code example shows the top item in a specific PivotTable field:

```
Sub AutoShowTopItems ()

    ' Purpose:
    ' Shows the top item in the Month field
    ' based on data in the Sum of Transactions field.

    ' Assumes:
    ' 1. A worksheet named Sheet1 containing a PivotTable
    ' named HouseSalesPivotTable.
    ' 2. The PivotTable contains fields named Month and
    ' Sum of Transactions.

    On Error GoTo AutoShowTopItems_Err

    Dim objPivotTable As PivotTable
    Dim objPivotField As PivotField

    Set objPivotTable = ActiveWorkbook.Worksheets. _
        Item(Index:="Sheet1").PivotTables. _
        Item(Index:="HouseSalesPivotTable")
    Set objPivotField = objPivotTable.PivotFields("Month")

    With objPivotField
        .Orientation = xlRowField
        .AutoShow Type:=xlAutomatic, Range:=xlTop, _
            Count:=1, Field:="Sum of Transactions"
    End With

AutoShowTopItems_End:

    Set objPivotField = Nothing
    Set objPivotTable = Nothing

    Exit Sub

AutoShowTopItems_Err:

    Select Case Err.Number
        Case 9
```

```
        MsgBox "Can't access worksheet. Check the worksheet " & _
            "name and try again."
    Case 1004
        MsgBox "Can't access PivotTable or field. Check " & _
            "the PivotTable or field name or field placement " & _
            "and try again."
    Case -2147024882
        MsgBox "Can't add data field. Remove existing data field or " & _
            "remove calculated items from existing fields " & _
            "and try again."
    Case Else
        MsgBox "Error " & Err.Number & ": " & Err.Description
End Select

Resume AutoShowTopItems_End

End Sub
```

The preceding code is very similar to the previous code, except that in this case the PivotField object's AutoShow method is called, specifying an automatic display of the top-most item in the Month field, based on the Sum of Transactions field's data. The results of running this code are shown in Figure 7-16. This figure assumes that you have already run the code in the previous section.

	A	B	C
4	Sum of Transactions		
5	Month ▼	Salesperson ▼	Total
6	July	Crosby	35274
7		Fisher	16542
8		Johnson	24264
9		Jones	4068
10		Lundgren	19674
11		McDonald	6354
12		Smith	1818
13	July Total		107994
14	Grand Total		107994

FIGURE 7-16

Showing the top-most item in the Month field based on the Sum of Transactions data

In this section, you've learned how to sort and show the top-most field items. Now, let's show you how to change a field's custom calculation.

Change a Field's Custom Calculation

The following code example changes the custom calculation for a specified field in a PivotTable:

```
Sub ShowDataFieldItemsAs ()

    ' Purpose:
    ' Changes the Sum of Transactions field's
    ' custom calculation to Running Total of the Salesperson field.

    ' Assumes:
    ' 1. A worksheet named Sheet1 containing a PivotTable
    ' named HouseSalesPivotTable.
    ' 2. The PivotTable contains fields named Salesperson and
    ' Sum of Transactions.

    On Error GoTo ShowDataFieldItemsAs_Err

    Dim objPivotTable As PivotTable
    Dim objPivotField As PivotField

    Set objPivotTable = ActiveWorkbook.Worksheets. _
        Item(Index:="Sheet1").PivotTables. _
        Item(Index:="HouseSalesPivotTable")
    Set objPivotField = _
        objPivotTable.PivotFields("Salesperson")

    objPivotField.Orientation = xlRowField

    With objPivotTable.PivotFields("Sum of Transactions")
        .Calculation = xlRunningTotal
        .BaseField = "Salesperson"
    End With

ShowDataFieldItemsAs_End:

    Set objPivotField = Nothing
    Set objPivotTable = Nothing

    Exit Sub
```

```
ShowDataFieldItemsAs_Err:

    Select Case Err.Number
        Case 9
            MsgBox "Can't access worksheet. Check the worksheet " & _
                "name and try again."
        Case 1004
            MsgBox "Can't access PivotTable or field or set field " & _
                "calculation type. Check " & _
                "the PivotTable name, field name, field placement, " & _
                "or calculation type and try again."
        Case -2147024882
            MsgBox "Can't add data field. Remove existing data field or " & _
                "remove calculated items from existing fields " & _
                "and try again."
        Case Else
            MsgBox "Error " & Err.Number & ": " & Err.Description
    End Select

    Resume ShowDataFieldItemsAs_End

End Sub
```

In the preceding code, the Sum of Transactions PivotField object's Calculation property is set to a running total, based on the Salesperson field's items. The results of running this code are shown in Figure 7-17. This figure assumes that you have already run the code in the previous section.

	A	B
4	Sum of Transactions	
5	Salesperson ▾	Total
6	Crosby	193539
7	Fisher	285818
8	Johnson	413885
9	Jones	437269
10	Lundgren	544607
11	McDonald	578608
12	Smith	588965
13	Grand Total	

FIGURE 7-17

Running total of transactions based on the Salesperson field's items

Now, let's end the chapter by showing you how to change a field's visual display format.

Change a Field's Display Format

The following code example changes the visual display format for all values of a specified PivotTable field:

```
Sub FormatDataFieldItems ()

    ' Purpose:
    ' Changes visual formatting for data items
    ' in the Sum of Transactions field.

    ' Assumes:
    ' 1. A worksheet named Sheet1 containing a PivotTable
    ' named HouseSalesPivotTable.
    ' 2. The PivotTable contains a field named
    ' Sum of Transactions.

    On Error GoTo FormatDataFieldItems_Err

    Dim objPivotTable As PivotTable
    Dim objPivotField As PivotField

    Set objPivotTable = ActiveWorkbook.Worksheets. _
        Item(Index:="Sheet1").PivotTables. _
        Item(Index:="HouseSalesPivotTable")
    Set objPivotField = _
        objPivotTable.PivotFields("Salesperson")

    objPivotField.Orientation = xlRowField
    objPivotTable.PivotFields("Sum of Transactions").NumberFormat = _
        "#,###;[Red](#,###)"

FormatDataFieldItems_End:

    Set objPivotField = Nothing
    Set objPivotTable = Nothing

    Exit Sub
```

```
FormatDataFieldItems_Err:

    Select Case Err.Number
        Case 9
            MsgBox "Can't access worksheet. Check the worksheet " & _
                "name and try again."
        Case 1004
            MsgBox "Can't access PivotTable or field. Check " & _
                "the PivotTable name or field name and try again."
        Case -2147024882
            MsgBox "Can't add data field. Remove existing data field or " & _
                "remove calculated items from existing fields " & _
                "and try again."
        Case Else
            MsgBox "Error " & Err.Number & ": " & Err.Description
    End Select

    Resume FormatDataFieldItems_End

End Sub
```

In the preceding code, the Sum of Transactions PivotField object's NumberFormat property is set to add a comma to the numbers as a thousands separator. Any negative numbers would also have their display set to red and be surrounded by parentheses. The results of running this code are shown in Figure 7-18. This figure assumes that you have already run the code in the previous section.

	A	B
4	Sum of Transactions	
5	Salesperson ▾	Total
6	Crosby	193,539
7	Fisher	92,279
8	Johnson	128,067
9	Jones	23,384
10	Lundgren	107,338
11	McDonald	34,001
12	Smith	10,357
13	Grand Total	588,965

FIGURE 7-18

Adding a thousands separator to values in the Sum of Transactions data field

Next Steps

Now that you've learned how to use code to programmatically create and format PivotTables and PivotCharts, you can begin to identify standard or repetitive tasks that can be automated using VBA, Visual Basic .NET, or C# code. Specifically, you learned how to create code that

- Creates PivotTables and PivotCharts based on existing data from a variety of sources

- Adds fields to the visual layout of PivotTables and PivotCharts and changes the fields' placement

- Sets and removes fields' item filters

- Creates calculated fields and calculated items

- Sorts and shows the most significant items for a field

- Changes the custom calculations and visual display formatting of PivotTable fields

Whenever you find yourself frequently selecting the same item filters in similar field sets again and again, changing the same sets of custom calculations over and over, laying out the same sets of fields in PivotTables or PivotCharts in a predictable sequence, or setting the same sort orders for fields' items repetitively, then consider automating these tasks with code.

Appendix

PivotTable Differences Between Excel 2000, 2002, and 2003

This appendix provides a list of the differences between Excel 2000, 2002, and 2003 concerning PivotTables and PivotCharts.

What's New for Excel 2000 for PivotTables and PivotCharts

Instead of making you build PivotTables completely within the PivotTable and PivotChart Wizard, you're now provided with a blank PivotTable layout, which displays your fields at the bottom of the PivotTable toolbar, and lets you drop fields from the PivotTable toolbar to the PivotTable's drop zones. (You can continue to design your PivotTable layouts using the PivotTable and PivotChart Wizard if you're more comfortable doing it as you did with Excel 97.)

You can create PivotCharts as well as PivotTables. You can change the field layouts for PivotCharts just like you do for PivotTables.

The GetPivotData worksheet function, introduced with Excel 97, allows you to work with PivotTable data outside of a PivotTable. For more information, see "GetPivotData" in Excel Help.

You can also create PivotTables based on multidimensional data sources.

What's New for Excel 2002 and 2003 for PivotTables and PivotCharts

The PivotTable Field List dialog box is easier to use than the field list that is attached to the bottom of the PivotTable toolbar in Excel 2000. For multidimensional data sources, the PivotTable Field List dialog box allows you to drill down and see the levels within each dimension.

When you drop a field in a PivotTable's row or column area, you will see its items immediately, instead of having to first drop a data field onto the PivotTable. This makes it easier to see how the PivotTable report will look.

There is also a new way to create a PivotTable other than by using the PivotTable and PivotChart Wizard. By clicking Data ➤ Import External Data ➤ Import Data, you can make PivotTables without using Microsoft Query or the Query wizard.

PivotTable commands have been gathered onto one menu to make it easier to figure out all of the features that PivotTables provide. The PivotTable right-click menu now represents the most commonly used PivotTable commands.

For PivotTables based on multidimensional data, you can select multiple page field items. Page fields allow you to display data for a single page field item or all of the page field items. You also can display member properties for multidimensional data sources, if they exist, in the PivotTable.

You can also create groupings in a PivotTable. Suppose you have a PivotTable with product sales by quarter grouped by state. After reviewing the data, you decide that you want to see the states grouped by region, such as East Coast, Midwest, Central, and West Coast. To do that, you just select the headings for the states that you want in a particular region (Washington, Oregon, and California for the West Coast region, for example), right-click, point to Group and Show Detail, and click Group. Excel creates a new heading called Group1. Just click on the Group1 heading and enter West Coast. Now you have a new grouping that didn't exist in the original data source.

Lastly, the GetPivotData worksheet function lets you reference a PivotTable item so that the reference is maintained, no matter how you change the PivotTable's visual layout. This allows you to create calculations on your PivotTable data that reference a particular cell without worrying where the cell moves. The cell references are provided for you automatically when you create a formula outside of the PivotTable.

Programmatic Changes for PivotTables and PivotCharts in Excel 2000

New objects and collections in Excel 2000 related to PivotTables and PivotCharts include

- The CubeField object and CubeFields collection, representing PivotTable fields based on multidimensional source data

- The PivotLayout object, representing field placement in a PivotChart

New methods and properties in Excel 2000 include

- The Chart object's

    HasPivotFields property

    PivotLayout property

- The PivotCache object's

    CommandText property

    CommandType property

    CreatePivotTable method

    LocalConnection property

    MaintainConnection property

    QueryType property

    Recordset property

    RefreshPeriod property

    ResetTimer method

    UseLocalConnection property

- The PivotCaches collection's Add method

- The PivotField object's

    Caption property

    CubeField property

    CurrentPageName property

    DragToData property

    DrilledDown property

    LayoutBlankLine property

    LayoutForm property

    LayoutPageBreak property

    LayoutSubtotalLocation property

    SubtotalName property

    Subtotals property

- The PivotItem object's

    Caption property

    DrilledDown property

- The PivotTable object's

    CubeFields property

    Format method

    GrandTotalName property

    PrintTitles property

    RepeatItemsOnEachPrintedPage property

    SmallGrid property

- The PivotTables collection's Add method

Programmatic Changes for PivotTables and PivotCharts in Excel 2002 and 2003

New objects and collections in Excel 2002 and 2003 related to PivotTables and PivotCharts include

- The PivotCell and PivotItemList objects, representing a cell in a PivotTable and a collection of a field's items in a PivotTable, respectively

- The CalculatedMember object and CalculatedMembers collection, representing both calculated fields and calculated items in a PivotTable

New methods and properties in Excel 2002 and Excel 2003 include

- The Application object's GenerateGetPivotData property

- The CalculatedMember object's

    IsValid property

    SolveOrder property

- The CubeField object's

    AddMemberPropertyField method

    EnableMultiplePageItems property

    HasMemberProperties property

    ShowInFieldList property

- The CubeFields collection's AddSet method

- The PivotCache object's

    ADOConnection property

    IsConnected property

    MakeConnection method

    MissingItemsLimit property

    OLAP property

    RobustConnect property

    SaveAsODC method

    SourceConnectionFile property

    SourceDataFile property

- The PivotCell object's

    ColumnItems property

    CustomSubtotalFunction property

    DataField property

    PivotCellType property

    RowItems property

- The PivotField object's

    AddPageItem method

    CurrentPageList property

    DatabaseSort property

    EnableItemSelection property

    HiddenItemsList property

    IsMemberProperty property

    PropertyOrder property

    PropertyParentField property

    StandardFormula property

- The PivotFormula object's StandardFormula property

- The PivotItem object's

    SourceNameStandard property

    StandardFormula property

- The PivotTable object's

    AddDataField method

    CalculatedMembers property

    CreateCubeFile method

    DataPivotField property

    DisplayEmptyColumn property

    DisplayEmptyRow property

    DisplayImmediateItems property

    EnableDataValueEditing property

    EnableFieldList property

    GetPivotData method

    MDX property

PivotSelectionStandard property

ShowCellBackgroundFromOLAP property

ShowPageMultipleItemLabel property

ViewCalculatedMembers property

VisualTotals property

- The Workbook object's

  PivotTableCloseConnection event

  PivotTableOpenConnection event

- The Worksheet object's PivotTableUpdate event

Index

Breinigsville, PA USA
28 October 2009
226606BV00004B/6/P